APOCALYPSE NERD ™

APOCALYPSE NERD™

by Peter Bagge

DARK HORSE BOOKS®

Publisher: Mike Richardson
Art Director: Lia Ribacchi
Designer: Josh Elliott
Editor: Dave Land

Published by
Dark Horse Books
A division of Dark Horse Comics, Inc.
10956 SE Main Street
Milwaukie, OR 97222

darkhorse.com

To find a comics shop in your area call the Comic Shop Locator Service toll-free at (888) 266-4226

First edition: March 2008
ISBN: 978-1-59307-902-4

10 9 8 7 6 5 4 3 2 1
PRINTED IN CANADA

APOCALYPSE NERD™

Introduction

Back in early 2003, when the leaders of the United States were doing everything in their power to start a war against Iraq, I heard a diplomat from that other member of the so-called "Axis of Evil," North Korea, brag on the radio that his country now had the capability to hit Seattle with a nuclear bomb.

This pronouncement got little to no play in the American media, let alone an official response from the US government, since it apparently was too much of a distraction from the impending fun we were about to have toppling Saddam Hussein. Nevertheless, I found this bit of news quite unnerving, not least because I happen to live in Seattle myself! And naturally I began to speculate on "what if . . . "

I'm sure that everyone has imagined what it would be like to be The Last Human on Earth, or one of the few survivors of some monumental disaster. For me, these imaginings can even take on the form of a fantasy, where I'd have enough food and resources to not only survive but thrive, as I putter about the planet unencumbered, picking at the remains of human civilization. Yet for this book, I forced myself to write a much more honest and realistic imagining of what things would be like for someone like me placed in such a situation, with little or no survival skills.

Needless to say, the protagonist would have to survive for some period of time or there'd be no story, but *how* would he survive? Would it be messy? Would moral compromises have to be made, if only out of sheer desperation? The answers to these questions were pretty inescapable, as you're about to find out.

I'd like to thank everyone at Dark Horse for allowing me to make this absurd project a reality, especially my editor, Dave Land, who's a great guy. I'd also like to thank my wife, Joanne, who helped me with the gray tones in this book, thus saving me a lot of tedious drudgery.

Enjoy!

Peter Bagge
Seattle, WA
December 2007

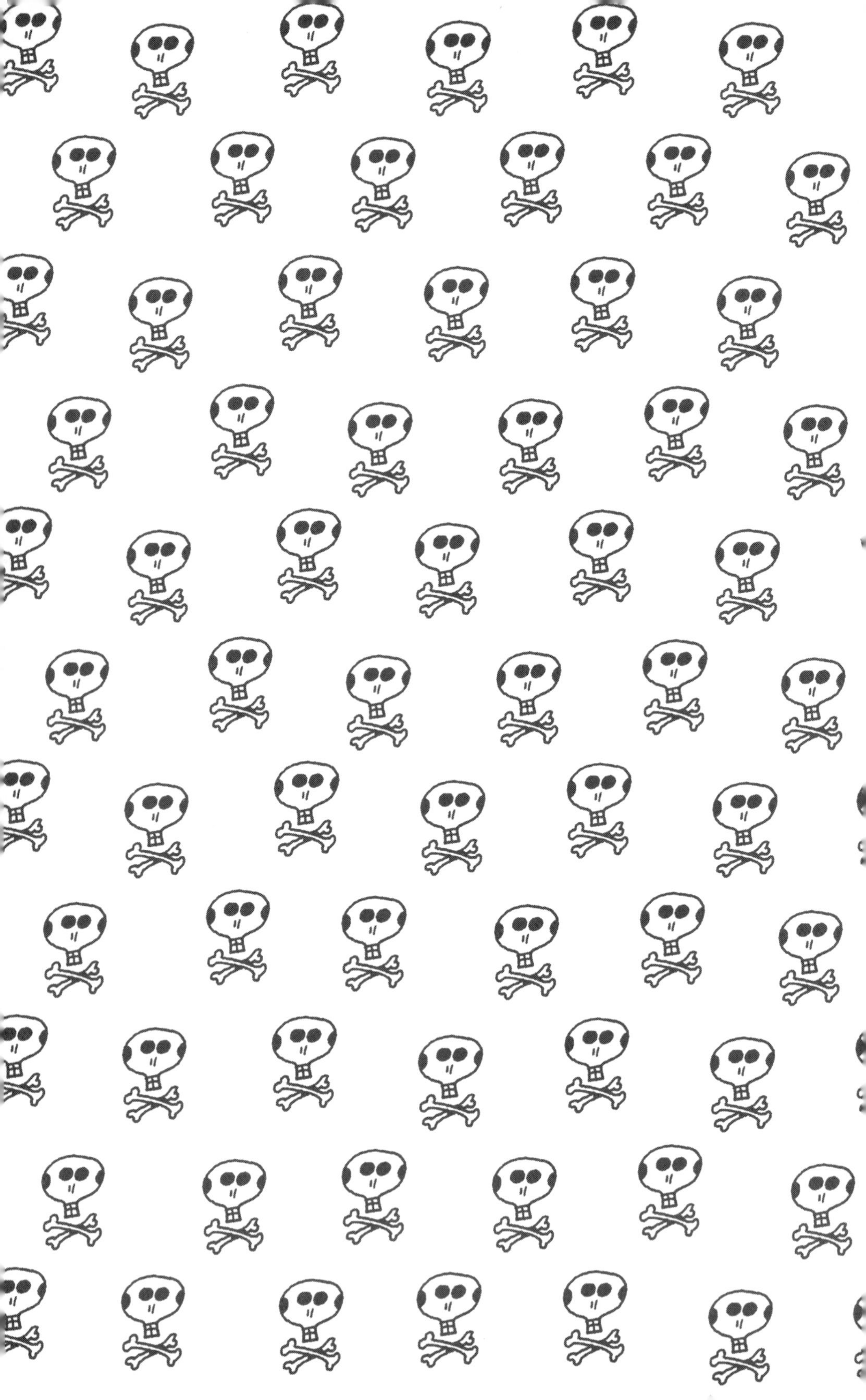

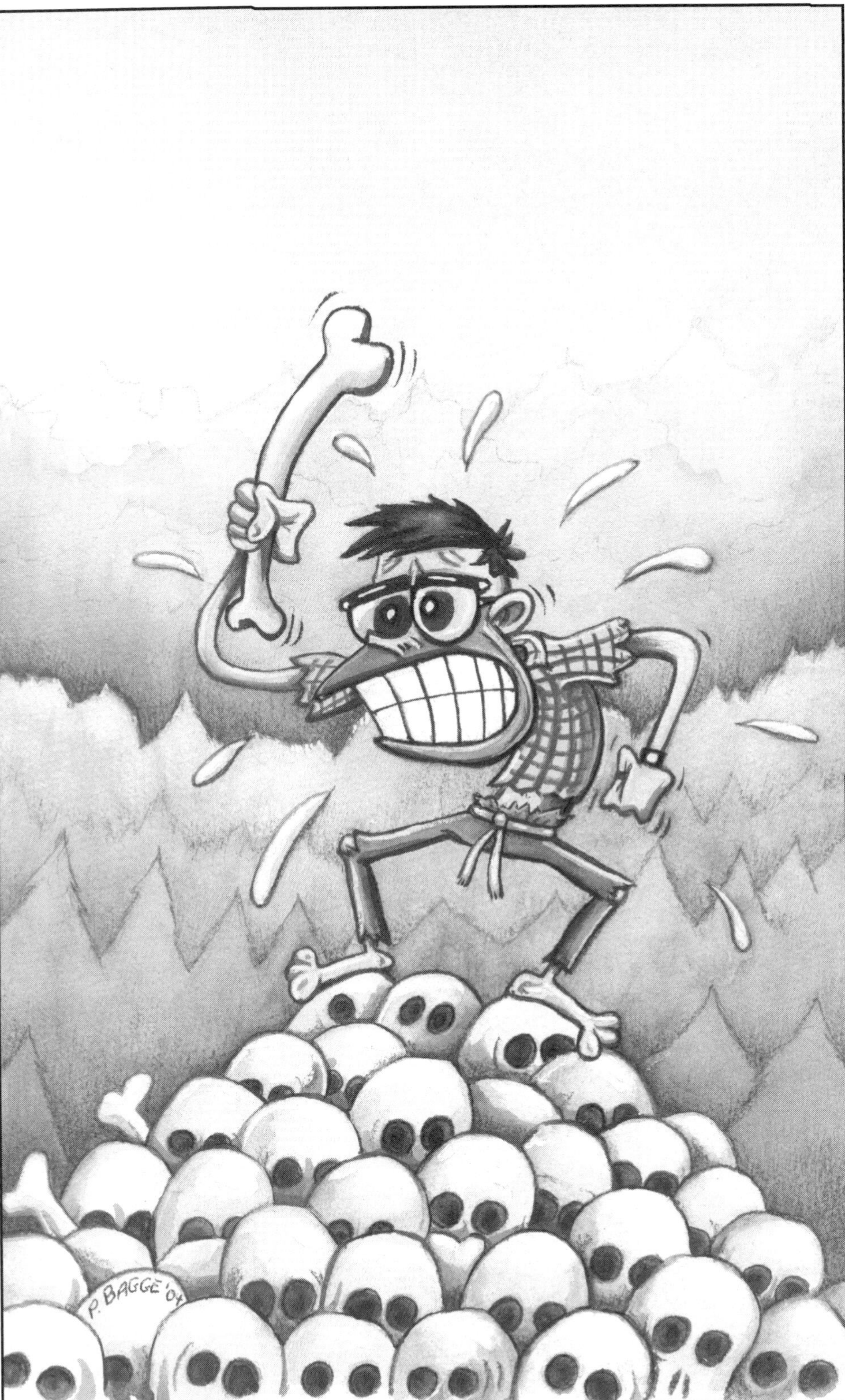
P. BAGGE '04

Chapter 1

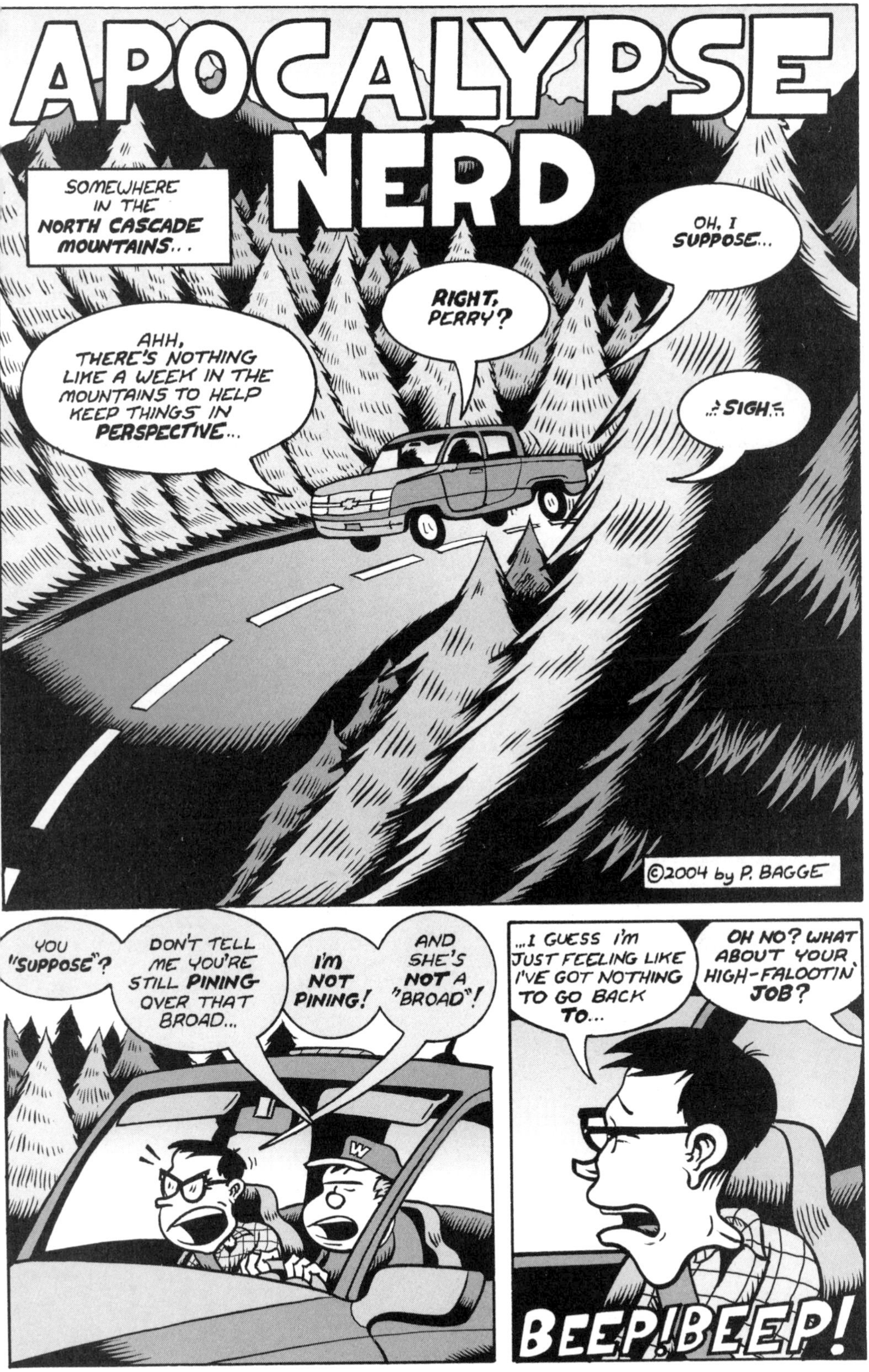
APOCALYPSE NERD
SOMEWHERE IN THE NORTH CASCADE MOUNTAINS...
AHH, THERE'S NOTHING LIKE A WEEK IN THE MOUNTAINS TO HELP KEEP THINGS IN PERSPECTIVE...
RIGHT, PERRY?
OH, I SUPPOSE...
SIGH
©2004 by P. BAGGE
YOU "SUPPOSE"?
DON'T TELL ME YOU'RE STILL PINING OVER THAT BROAD...
I'M NOT PINING!
AND SHE'S NOT A "BROAD"!
...I GUESS I'M JUST FEELING LIKE I'VE GOT NOTHING TO GO BACK TO...
OH NO? WHAT ABOUT YOUR HIGH-FALOOTIN' JOB?
BEEP! BEEP!

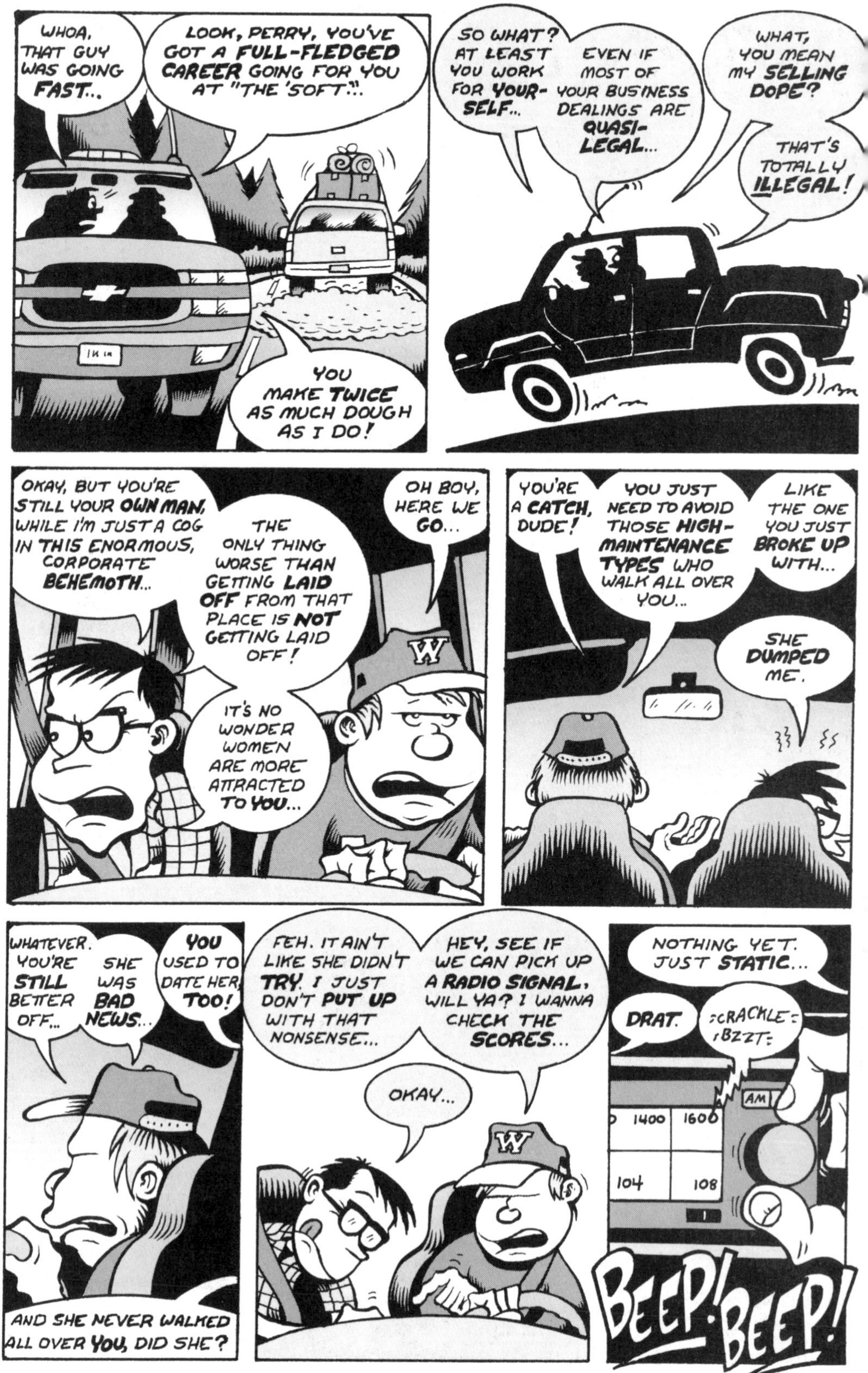
WHOA, THAT GUY WAS GOING FAST...
LOOK, PERRY, YOU'VE GOT A FULL-FLEDGED CAREER GOING FOR YOU AT "THE 'SOFT"...
YOU MAKE TWICE AS MUCH DOUGH AS I DO!
SO WHAT? AT LEAST YOU WORK FOR YOURSELF...
EVEN IF MOST OF YOUR BUSINESS DEALINGS ARE QUASI-LEGAL...
WHAT, YOU MEAN MY SELLING DOPE?
THAT'S TOTALLY ILLEGAL!
OKAY, BUT YOU'RE STILL YOUR OWN MAN, WHILE I'M JUST A COG IN THIS ENORMOUS, CORPORATE BEHEMOTH...
THE ONLY THING WORSE THAN GETTING LAID OFF FROM THAT PLACE IS NOT GETTING LAID OFF!
OH BOY, HERE WE GO...
IT'S NO WONDER WOMEN ARE MORE ATTRACTED TO YOU...
YOU'RE A CATCH, DUDE!
YOU JUST NEED TO AVOID THOSE HIGH-MAINTENANCE TYPES WHO WALK ALL OVER YOU...
LIKE THE ONE YOU JUST BROKE UP WITH...
SHE DUMPED ME.
WHATEVER. YOU'RE STILL BETTER OFF...
SHE WAS BAD NEWS...
YOU USED TO DATE HER, TOO!
AND SHE NEVER WALKED ALL OVER YOU, DID SHE?
FEH. IT AIN'T LIKE SHE DIDN'T TRY. I JUST DON'T PUT UP WITH THAT NONSENSE...
HEY, SEE IF WE CAN PICK UP A RADIO SIGNAL, WILL YA? I WANNA CHECK THE SCORES...
OKAY...
NOTHING YET. JUST STATIC...
DRAT.
CRACKLE BZZT
AM
1400 1600
104 108
BEEP! BEEP!

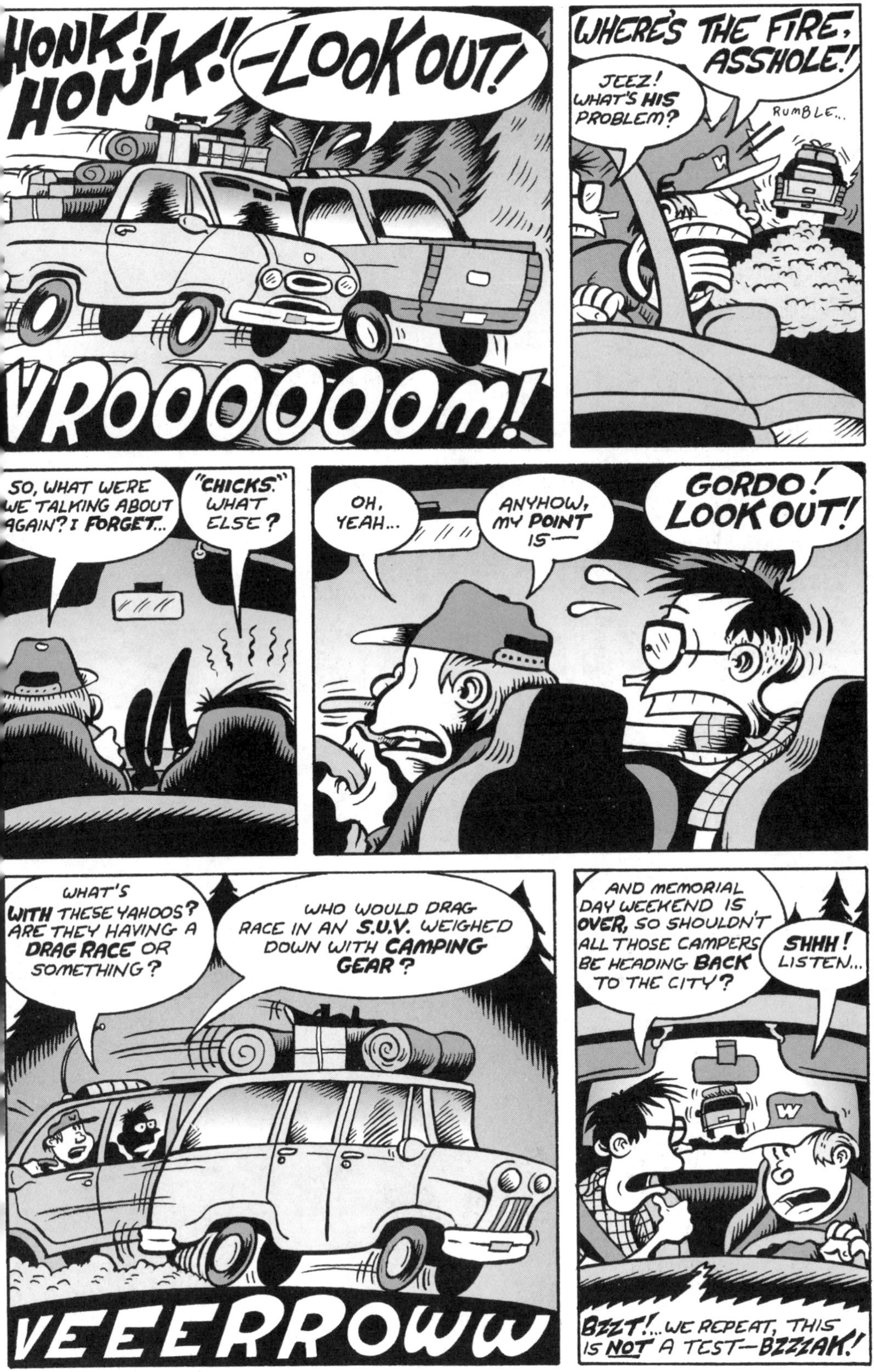
HONK! HONK!
-LOOK OUT!
VROOOOOOM!
WHERE'S THE FIRE, ASSHOLE!
JEEZ! WHAT'S HIS PROBLEM?
RUMBLE...
SO, WHAT WERE WE TALKING ABOUT AGAIN? I FORGET...
"CHICKS." WHAT ELSE?
OH, YEAH...
ANYHOW, MY POINT IS—
GORDO! LOOK OUT!
WHAT'S WITH THESE YAHOOS? ARE THEY HAVING A DRAG RACE OR SOMETHING?
WHO WOULD DRAG RACE IN AN S.U.V. WEIGHED DOWN WITH CAMPING GEAR?
VEEERROWW
AND MEMORIAL DAY WEEKEND IS OVER, SO SHOULDN'T ALL THOSE CAMPERS BE HEADING BACK TO THE CITY?
SHHH! LISTEN...
BZZT!... WE REPEAT, THIS IS NOT A TEST—BZZZAK!

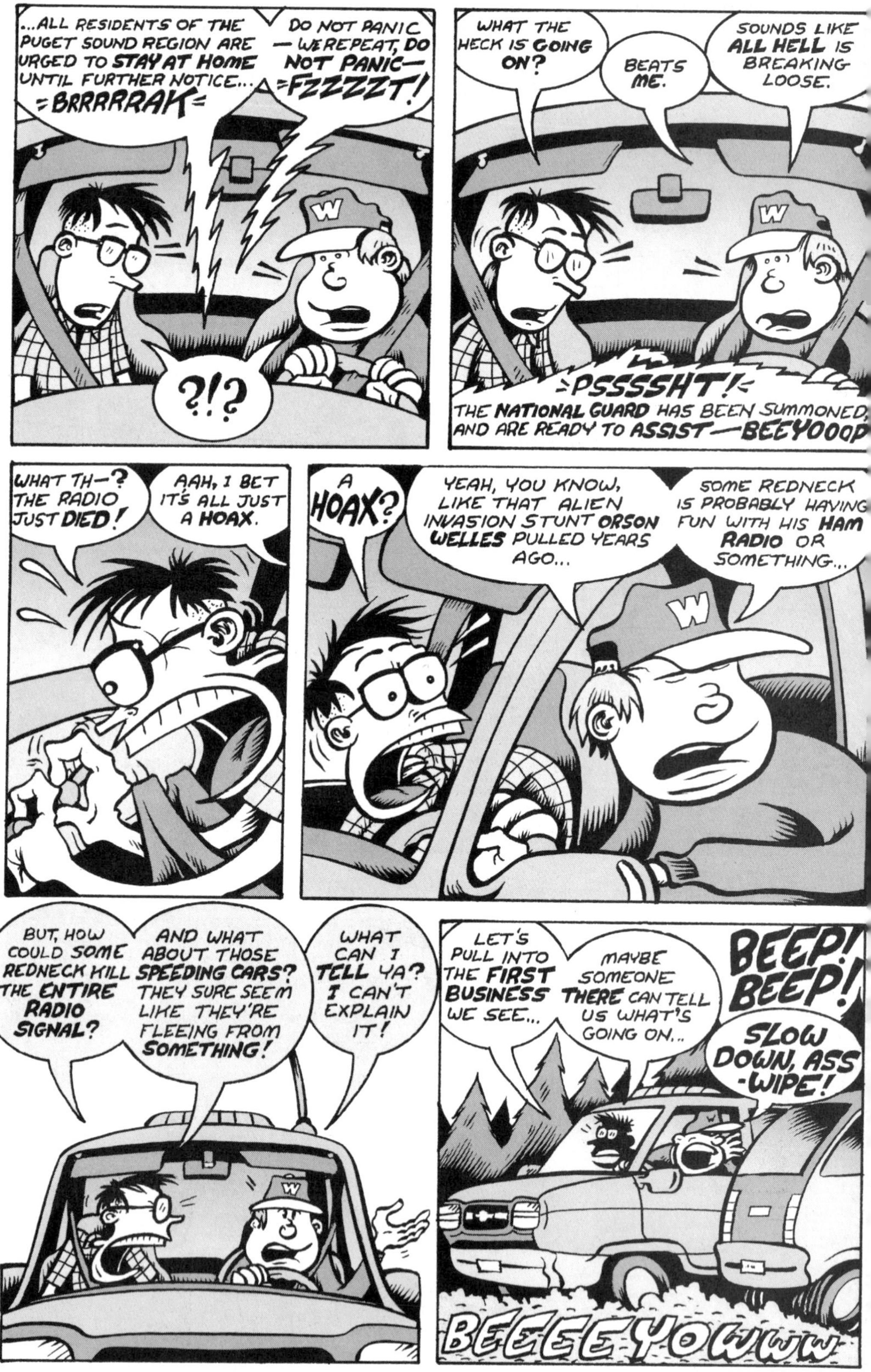
...ALL RESIDENTS OF THE PUGET SOUND REGION ARE URGED TO STAY AT HOME UNTIL FURTHER NOTICE... =BRRRRRAK=
DO NOT PANIC —WE REPEAT, DO NOT PANIC— =FZZZZT!
?!?
WHAT THE HECK IS GOING ON?
BEATS ME.
SOUNDS LIKE ALL HELL IS BREAKING LOOSE.
=PSSSSHT!=
THE NATIONAL GUARD HAS BEEN SUMMONED, AND ARE READY TO ASSIST—BEEYOOOP
WHAT TH—? THE RADIO JUST DIED!
AAH, I BET IT'S ALL JUST A HOAX.
A HOAX?
YEAH, YOU KNOW, LIKE THAT ALIEN INVASION STUNT ORSON WELLES PULLED YEARS AGO...
SOME REDNECK IS PROBABLY HAVING FUN WITH HIS HAM RADIO OR SOMETHING...
BUT, HOW COULD SOME REDNECK KILL THE ENTIRE RADIO SIGNAL?
AND WHAT ABOUT THOSE SPEEDING CARS? THEY SURE SEEM LIKE THEY'RE FLEEING FROM SOMETHING!
WHAT CAN I TELL YA? I CAN'T EXPLAIN IT!
LET'S PULL INTO THE FIRST BUSINESS WE SEE...
MAYBE SOMEONE THERE CAN TELL US WHAT'S GOING ON...
BEEP! BEEP!
SLOW DOWN, ASS-WIPE!
BEEEEYOWWW

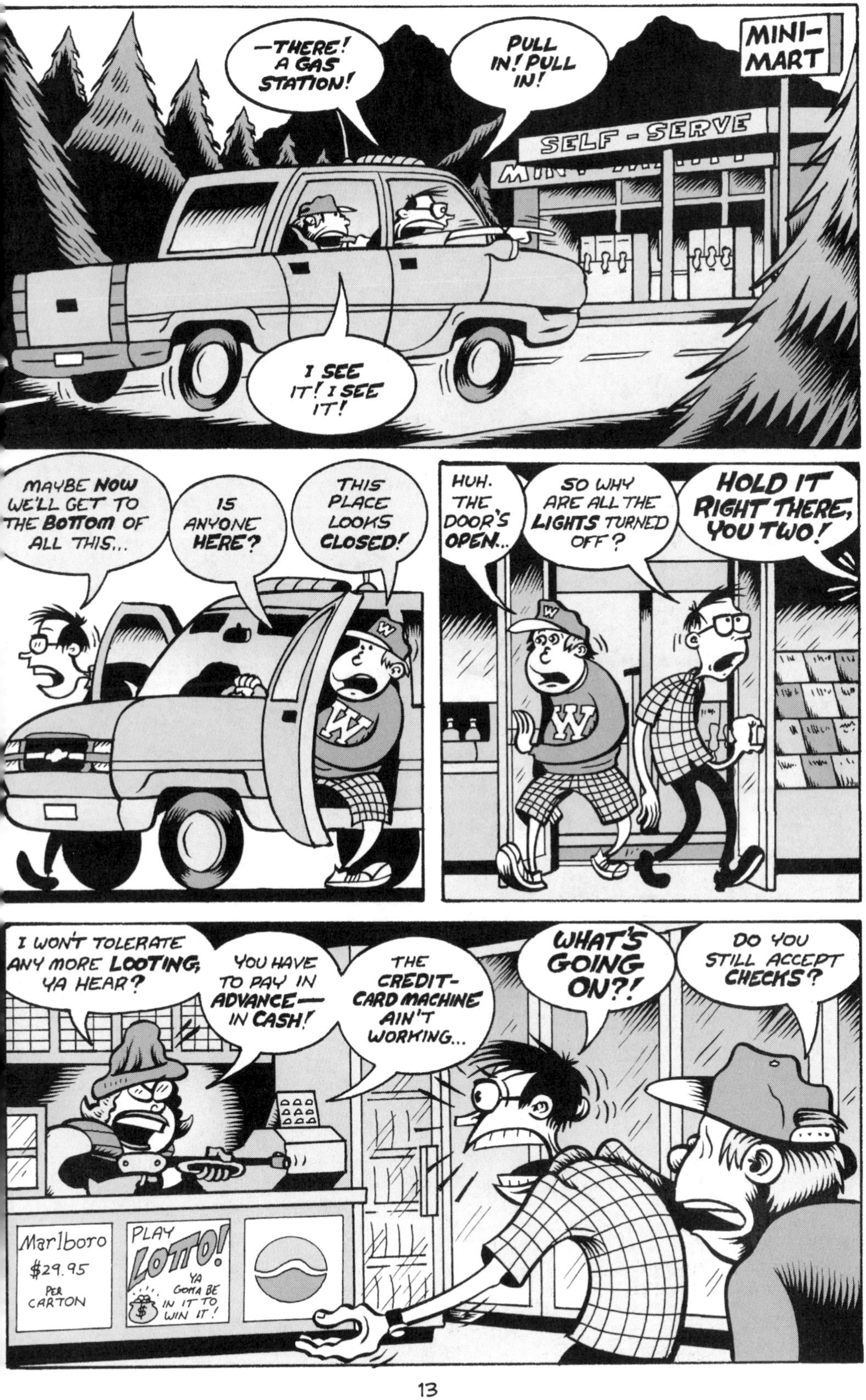
MINI-MART
—THERE! A GAS STATION!
PULL IN! PULL IN!
SELF - SERVE
I SEE IT! I SEE IT!
MAYBE NOW WE'LL GET TO THE BOTTOM OF ALL THIS...
IS ANYONE HERE?
THIS PLACE LOOKS CLOSED!
HUH. THE DOOR'S OPEN...
SO WHY ARE ALL THE LIGHTS TURNED OFF?
HOLD IT RIGHT THERE, YOU TWO!
I WON'T TOLERATE ANY MORE LOOTING, YA HEAR?
YOU HAVE TO PAY IN ADVANCE— IN CASH!
THE CREDIT-CARD MACHINE AIN'T WORKING...
WHAT'S GOING ON?!
DO YOU STILL ACCEPT CHECKS?
Marlboro $29.95 PER CARTON
PLAY LOTTO! YA GOTTA BE IN IT TO WIN IT!

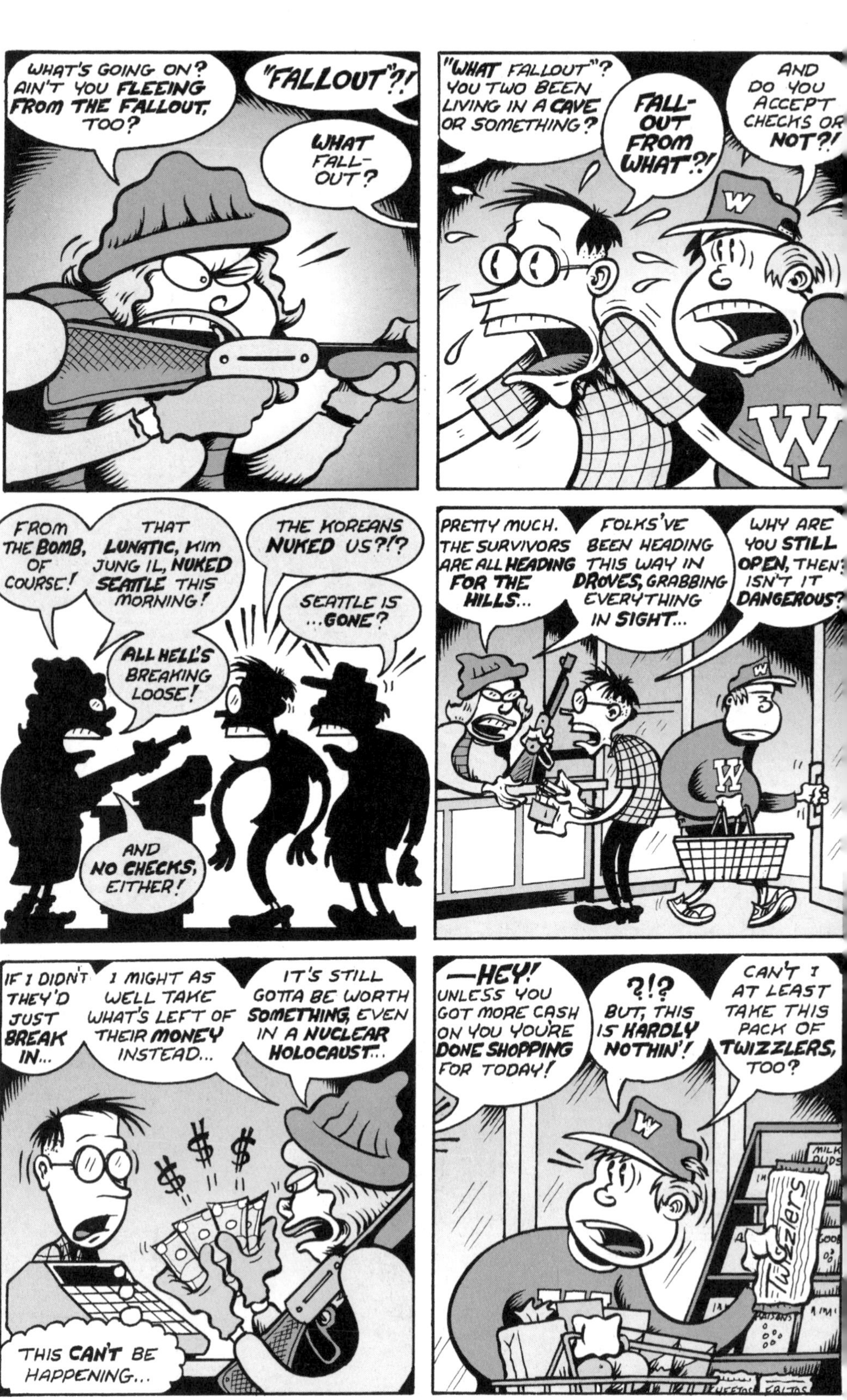
WHAT'S GOING ON? AIN'T YOU FLEEING FROM THE FALLOUT, TOO?
"FALLOUT"?!
WHAT FALL-OUT?
"WHAT FALLOUT"? YOU TWO BEEN LIVING IN A CAVE OR SOMETHING?
FALL-OUT FROM WHAT?!
AND DO YOU ACCEPT CHECKS OR NOT?!
FROM THE BOMB, OF COURSE!
THAT LUNATIC, KIM JUNG IL, NUKED SEATTLE THIS MORNING!
THE KOREANS NUKED US?!?
SEATTLE IS ...GONE?
ALL HELL'S BREAKING LOOSE!
AND NO CHECKS, EITHER!
PRETTY MUCH. THE SURVIVORS ARE ALL HEADING FOR THE HILLS...
FOLKS'VE BEEN HEADING THIS WAY IN DROVES, GRABBING EVERYTHING IN SIGHT...
WHY ARE YOU STILL OPEN, THEN? ISN'T IT DANGEROUS?
IF I DIDN'T THEY'D JUST BREAK IN...
I MIGHT AS WELL TAKE WHAT'S LEFT OF THEIR MONEY INSTEAD...
IT'S STILL GOTTA BE WORTH SOMETHING, EVEN IN A NUCLEAR HOLOCAUST...
THIS CAN'T BE HAPPENING...
—HEY! UNLESS YOU GOT MORE CASH ON YOU YOU'RE DONE SHOPPING FOR TODAY!
?!? BUT, THIS IS HARDLY NOTHIN'!
CAN'T I AT LEAST TAKE THIS PACK OF TWIZZLERS, TOO?
Twizzlers

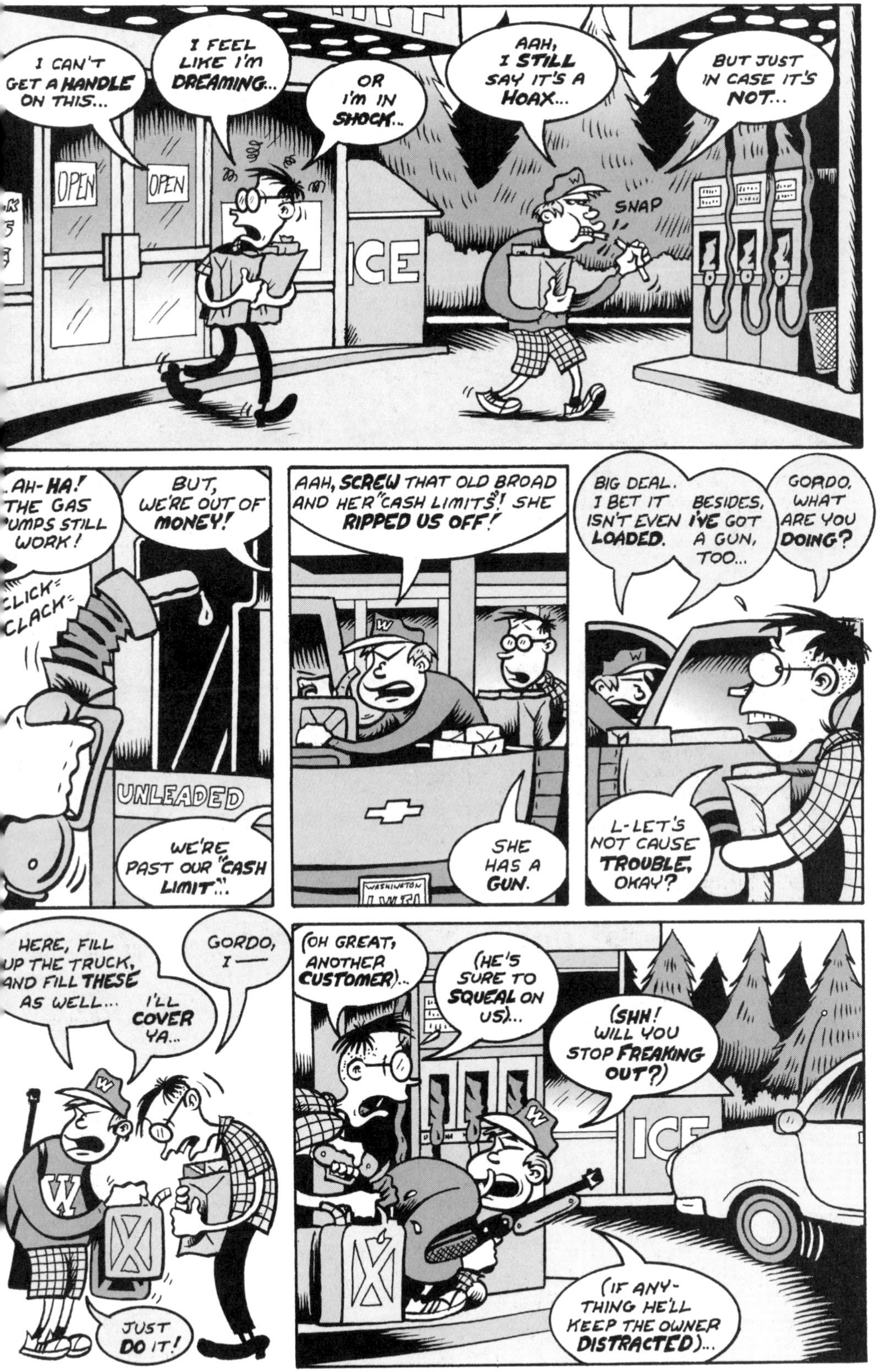
I CAN'T GET A HANDLE ON THIS...
I FEEL LIKE I'M DREAMING...
OR I'M IN SHOCK...
AAH, I STILL SAY IT'S A HOAX...
BUT JUST IN CASE IT'S NOT...
OPEN
OPEN
ICE
SNAP
AH-HA! THE GAS PUMPS STILL WORK!
BUT, WE'RE OUT OF MONEY!
CLICK CLACK
UNLEADED
WE'RE PAST OUR "CASH LIMIT"...
AAH, SCREW THAT OLD BROAD AND HER "CASH LIMITS"! SHE RIPPED US OFF!
SHE HAS A GUN.
BIG DEAL. I BET IT ISN'T EVEN LOADED.
BESIDES, I'VE GOT A GUN, TOO...
GORDO, WHAT ARE YOU DOING?
L-LET'S NOT CAUSE TROUBLE, OKAY?
HERE, FILL UP THE TRUCK, AND FILL THESE AS WELL...
I'LL COVER YA...
GORDO, I—
JUST DO IT!
(OH GREAT, ANOTHER CUSTOMER)...
(HE'S SURE TO SQUEAL ON US)...
(SHH! WILL YOU STOP FREAKING OUT?)
ICE
(IF ANYTHING HE'LL KEEP THE OWNER DISTRACTED)...

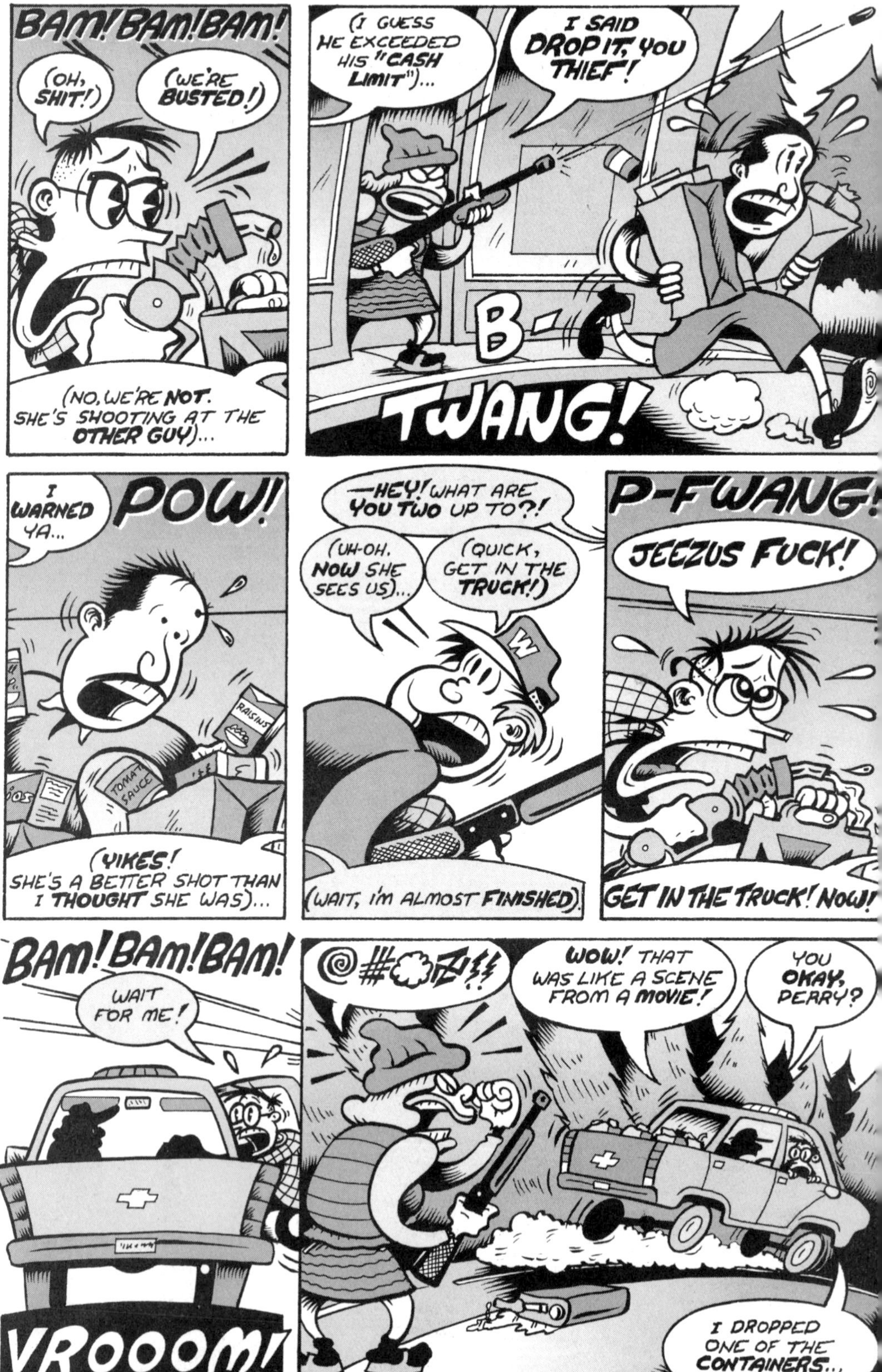
BAM! BAM! BAM!
(OH, SHIT!)
(WE'RE BUSTED!)
(NO, WE'RE NOT. SHE'S SHOOTING AT THE OTHER GUY)...
(I GUESS HE EXCEEDED HIS "CASH LIMIT")...
I SAID DROP IT, YOU THIEF!
B-
TWANG!
I WARNED YA...
POW!
RAISINS
TOMATO SAUCE
(YIKES! SHE'S A BETTER SHOT THAN I THOUGHT SHE WAS)...
—HEY! WHAT ARE YOU TWO UP TO?!
(UH-OH. NOW SHE SEES US)...
(QUICK, GET IN THE TRUCK!)
(WAIT, I'M ALMOST FINISHED)
P-FWANG!
JEEZUS FUCK!
GET IN THE TRUCK! NOW!
BAM! BAM! BAM!
WAIT FOR ME!
VROOOM!
WOW! THAT WAS LIKE A SCENE FROM A MOVIE!
YOU OKAY, PERRY?
I DROPPED ONE OF THE CONTAINERS...

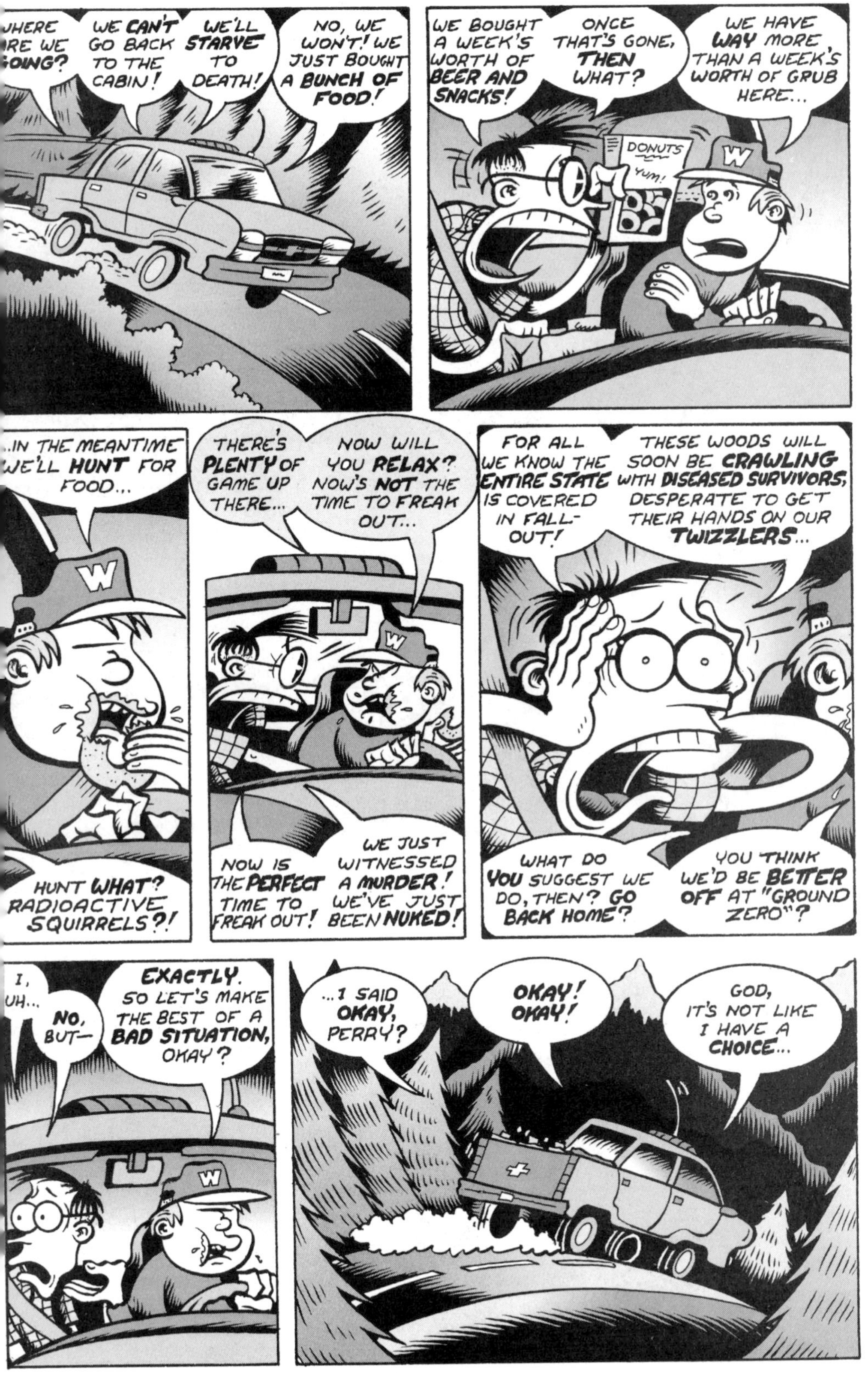

WHERE ARE WE GOING?
WE CAN'T GO BACK TO THE CABIN!
WE'LL STARVE TO DEATH!
NO, WE WON'T! WE JUST BOUGHT A BUNCH OF FOOD!
WE BOUGHT A WEEK'S WORTH OF BEER AND SNACKS!
ONCE THAT'S GONE, THEN WHAT?
WE HAVE WAY MORE THAN A WEEK'S WORTH OF GRUB HERE...
DONUTS
YUM!
...IN THE MEANTIME WE'LL HUNT FOR FOOD...
HUNT WHAT? RADIOACTIVE SQUIRRELS?!
THERE'S PLENTY OF GAME UP THERE...
NOW WILL YOU RELAX? NOW'S NOT THE TIME TO FREAK OUT...
NOW IS THE PERFECT TIME TO FREAK OUT!
WE JUST WITNESSED A MURDER! WE'VE JUST BEEN NUKED!
FOR ALL WE KNOW THE ENTIRE STATE IS COVERED IN FALL-OUT!
THESE WOODS WILL SOON BE CRAWLING WITH DISEASED SURVIVORS, DESPERATE TO GET THEIR HANDS ON OUR TWIZZLERS...
WHAT DO YOU SUGGEST WE DO, THEN? GO BACK HOME?
YOU THINK WE'D BE BETTER OFF AT "GROUND ZERO"?
I, UH...
NO, BUT—
EXACTLY. SO LET'S MAKE THE BEST OF A BAD SITUATION, OKAY?
...I SAID OKAY, PERRY?
OKAY! OKAY!
GOD, IT'S NOT LIKE I HAVE A CHOICE...

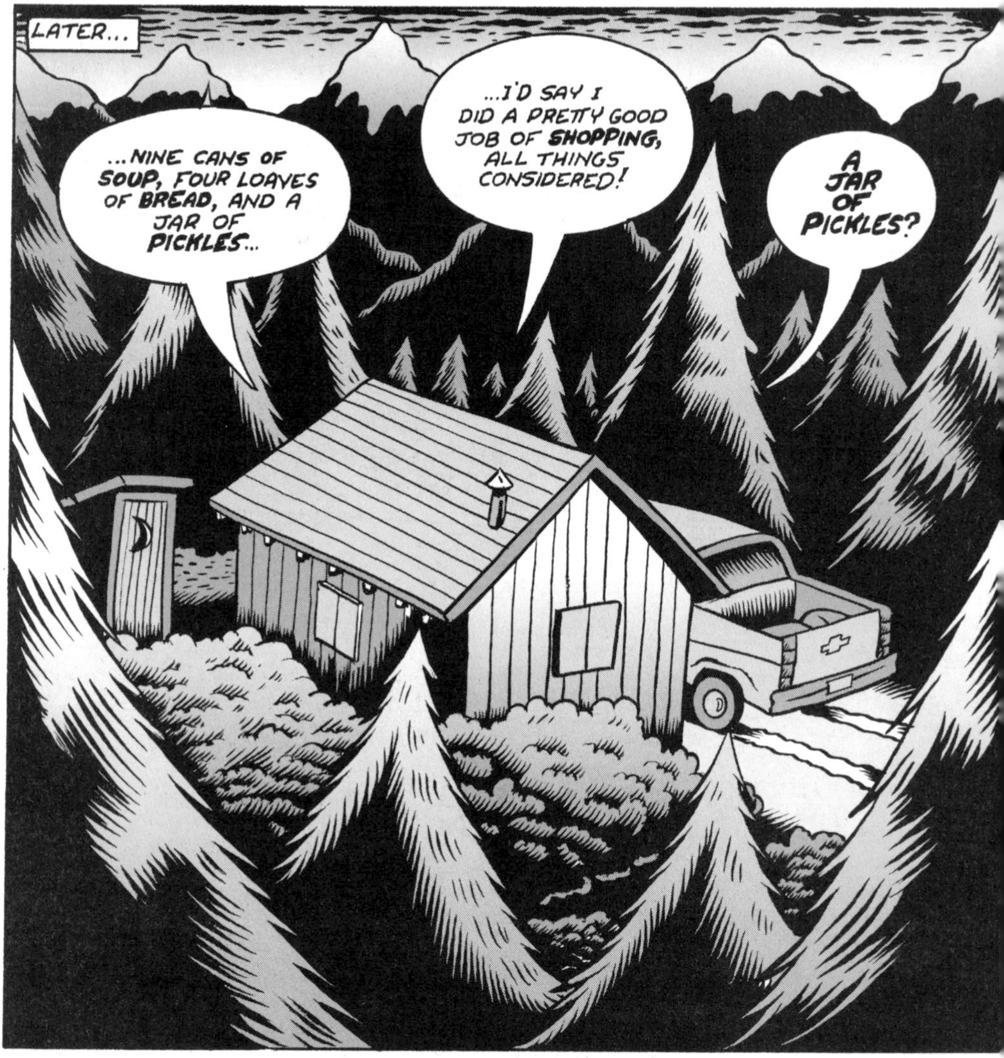
LATER...
...NINE CANS OF SOUP, FOUR LOAVES OF BREAD, AND A JAR OF PICKLES...
...I'D SAY I DID A PRETTY GOOD JOB OF SHOPPING, ALL THINGS CONSIDERED!
A JAR OF PICKLES?

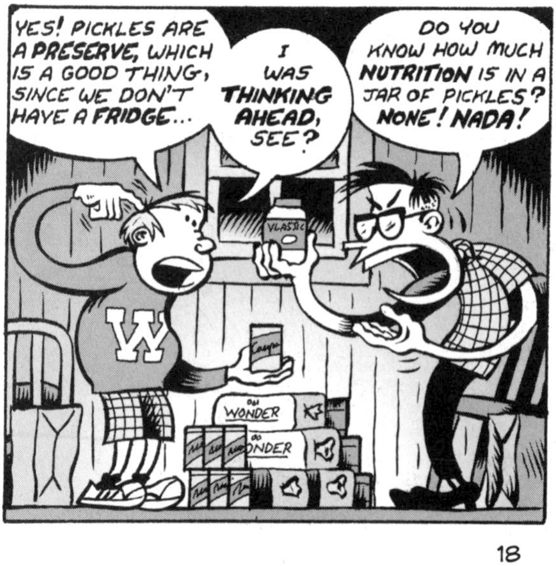
YES! PICKLES ARE A PRESERVE, WHICH IS A GOOD THING, SINCE WE DON'T HAVE A FRIDGE...
I WAS THINKING AHEAD, SEE?
DO YOU KNOW HOW MUCH NUTRITION IS IN A JAR OF PICKLES? NONE! NADA!
W
WONDER

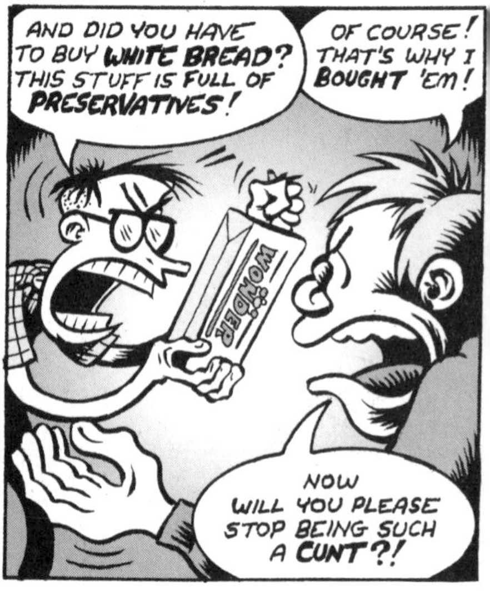
AND DID YOU HAVE TO BUY WHITE BREAD? THIS STUFF IS FULL OF PRESERVATIVES!
OF COURSE! THAT'S WHY I BOUGHT 'EM!
WONDER
NOW WILL YOU PLEASE STOP BEING SUCH A CUNT?!

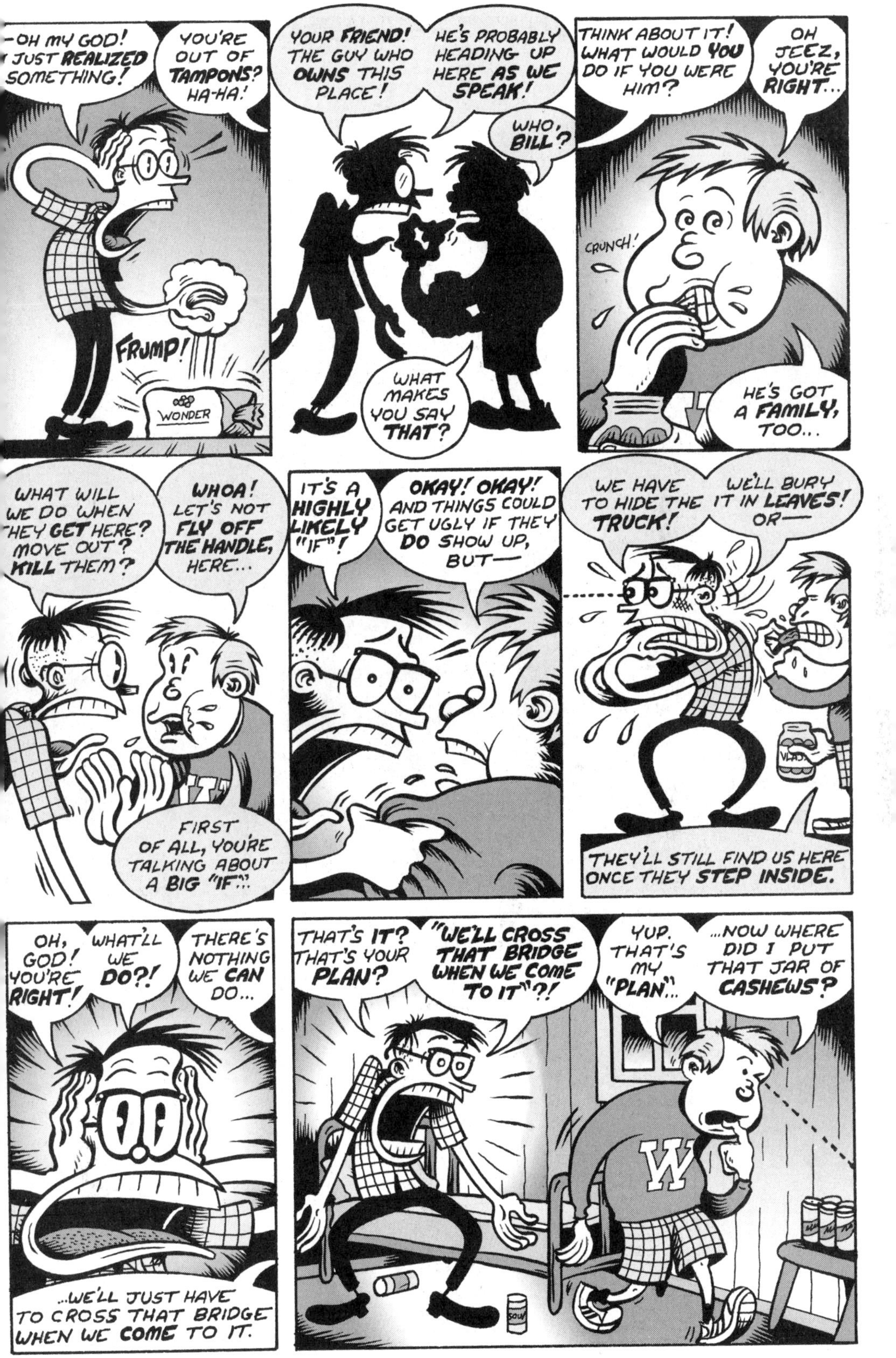

-OH MY GOD! I JUST REALIZED SOMETHING!
YOU'RE OUT OF TAMPONS? HA-HA!
FRUMP!
WONDER
YOUR FRIEND! THE GUY WHO OWNS THIS PLACE!
HE'S PROBABLY HEADING UP HERE AS WE SPEAK!
WHO, BILL?
WHAT MAKES YOU SAY THAT?
THINK ABOUT IT! WHAT WOULD YOU DO IF YOU WERE HIM?
OH JEEZ, YOU'RE RIGHT...
CRUNCH!
HE'S GOT A FAMILY, TOO...
WHAT WILL WE DO WHEN THEY GET HERE? MOVE OUT? KILL THEM?
WHOA! LET'S NOT FLY OFF THE HANDLE, HERE...
FIRST OF ALL, YOU'RE TALKING ABOUT A BIG "IF"...
IT'S A HIGHLY LIKELY "IF"!
OKAY! OKAY! AND THINGS COULD GET UGLY IF THEY DO SHOW UP, BUT—
WE HAVE TO HIDE THE TRUCK!
WE'LL BURY IT IN LEAVES! OR—
THEY'LL STILL FIND US HERE ONCE THEY STEP INSIDE.
OH, GOD! YOU'RE RIGHT!
WHAT'LL WE DO?!
THERE'S NOTHING WE CAN DO...
...WE'LL JUST HAVE TO CROSS THAT BRIDGE WHEN WE COME TO IT.
THAT'S IT? THAT'S YOUR PLAN?
"WE'LL CROSS THAT BRIDGE WHEN WE COME TO IT"?!
YUP. THAT'S MY "PLAN"...
...NOW WHERE DID I PUT THAT JAR OF CASHEWS?

THAT EVENING...

EASE UP ON THOSE **CASHEWS**, YOU.

WE AGREED TO **RATION** OUR FOOD FROM NOW ON, REMEMBER?

YOU ATE ALL THE **PICKLES!**

JUST A FEW MORE... I'm **STARVING!**

I CAN'T GET OVER HOW **CALM** YOU ARE, GORDO; **ALL THINGS CONSIDERED**, THAT IS...

AREN'T YOU AFRAID OF **DYING** OUT HERE?

PFFT. WHAT DIFFERENCE DOES IT MAKE **WHERE** YOU DIE?

TO BE HONEST, I LIKE OUR **CHANCES.** FOR ONE THING, THIS PLACE IS PRETTY **INACCESSIBLE**...

PLUS, WINTER IS A GOOD **SIX MONTHS** AWAY...

YEAH, BUT **THEN** WHAT? AND WHAT ABOUT **FOOD?**

I BET THAT MINI-MART'S BEEN **PICKED CLEAN** BY NOW...

I'M GONNA TRY MY LUCK AT **HUNTING** FIRST THING TOMORROW...

THINK YOU'LL **CATCH** ANYTHING?

SURE, WHY **NOT?** THESE WOODS ARE **LOUSY** WITH **DEER**...

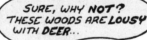

≈SIGH≈ SO MUCH FOR MY SHORT-LIVED ATTEMPT AT **VEGETARIAN-ISM**...

MY DAD AND UNC' USED TO TAKE ME HUNTING... AND

THEY TAUGHT ME HOW TO **SKIN** AND **CLEAN** A DEER, TOO...

AND HOW TO **COOK** IT WITHOUT IT TASTING **TOO GAMEY**...

YUM.

20

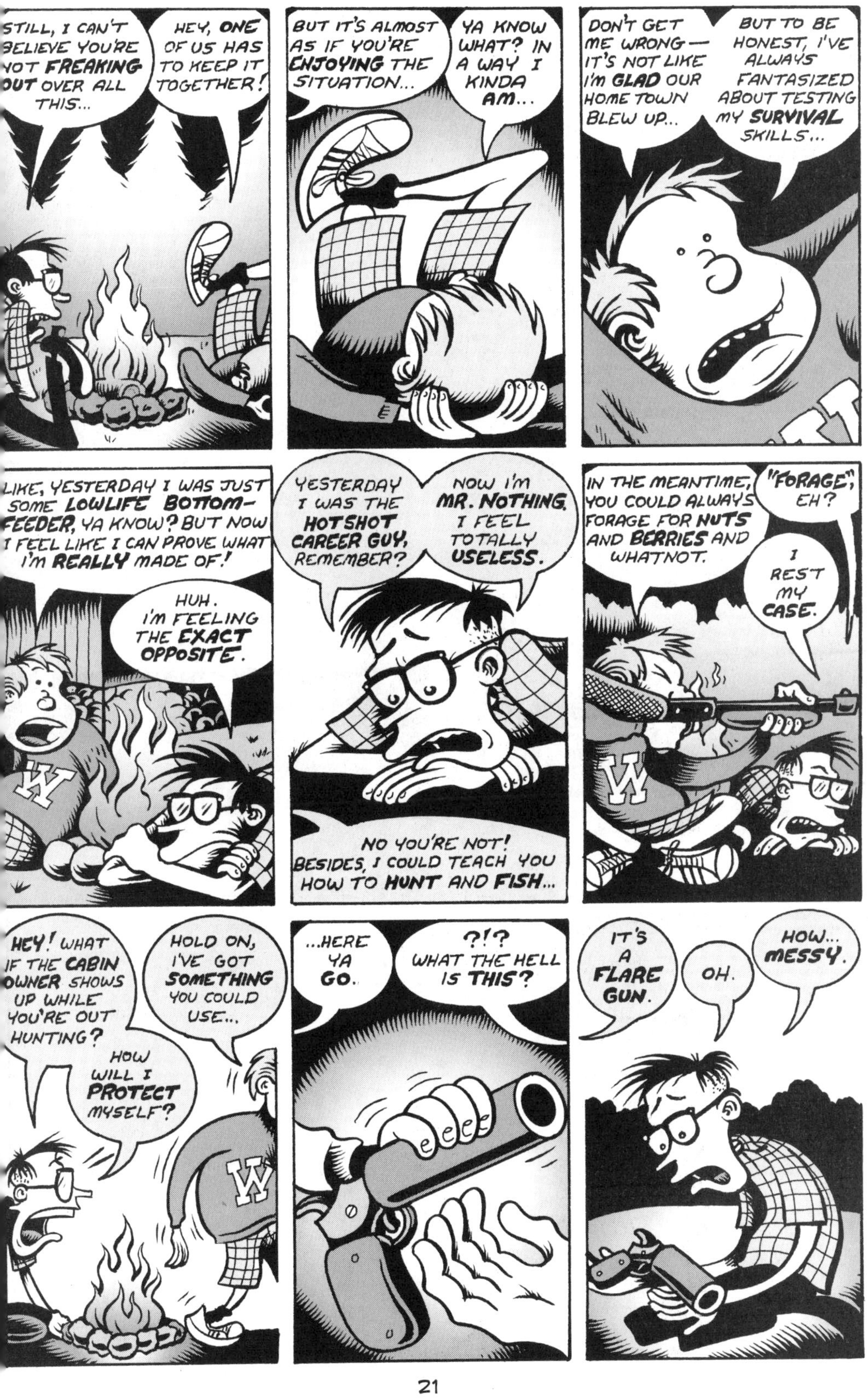
STILL, I CAN'T BELIEVE YOU'RE NOT FREAKING OUT OVER ALL THIS...
HEY, ONE OF US HAS TO KEEP IT TOGETHER!
BUT IT'S ALMOST AS IF YOU'RE ENJOYING THE SITUATION...
YA KNOW WHAT? IN A WAY I KINDA AM...
DON'T GET ME WRONG— IT'S NOT LIKE I'M GLAD OUR HOME TOWN BLEW UP...
BUT TO BE HONEST, I'VE ALWAYS FANTASIZED ABOUT TESTING MY SURVIVAL SKILLS...
LIKE, YESTERDAY I WAS JUST SOME LOWLIFE BOTTOM-FEEDER, YA KNOW? BUT NOW I FEEL LIKE I CAN PROVE WHAT I'M REALLY MADE OF!
HUH. I'M FEELING THE EXACT OPPOSITE.
YESTERDAY I WAS THE HOTSHOT CAREER GUY, REMEMBER?
NOW I'M MR. NOTHING. I FEEL TOTALLY USELESS.
NO YOU'RE NOT! BESIDES, I COULD TEACH YOU HOW TO HUNT AND FISH...
IN THE MEANTIME, YOU COULD ALWAYS FORAGE FOR NUTS AND BERRIES AND WHATNOT.
"FORAGE", EH?
I REST MY CASE.
HEY! WHAT IF THE CABIN OWNER SHOWS UP WHILE YOU'RE OUT HUNTING?
HOW WILL I PROTECT MYSELF?
HOLD ON, I'VE GOT SOMETHING YOU COULD USE...
...HERE YA GO.
?!? WHAT THE HELL IS THIS?
IT'S A FLARE GUN.
OH.
HOW... MESSY.

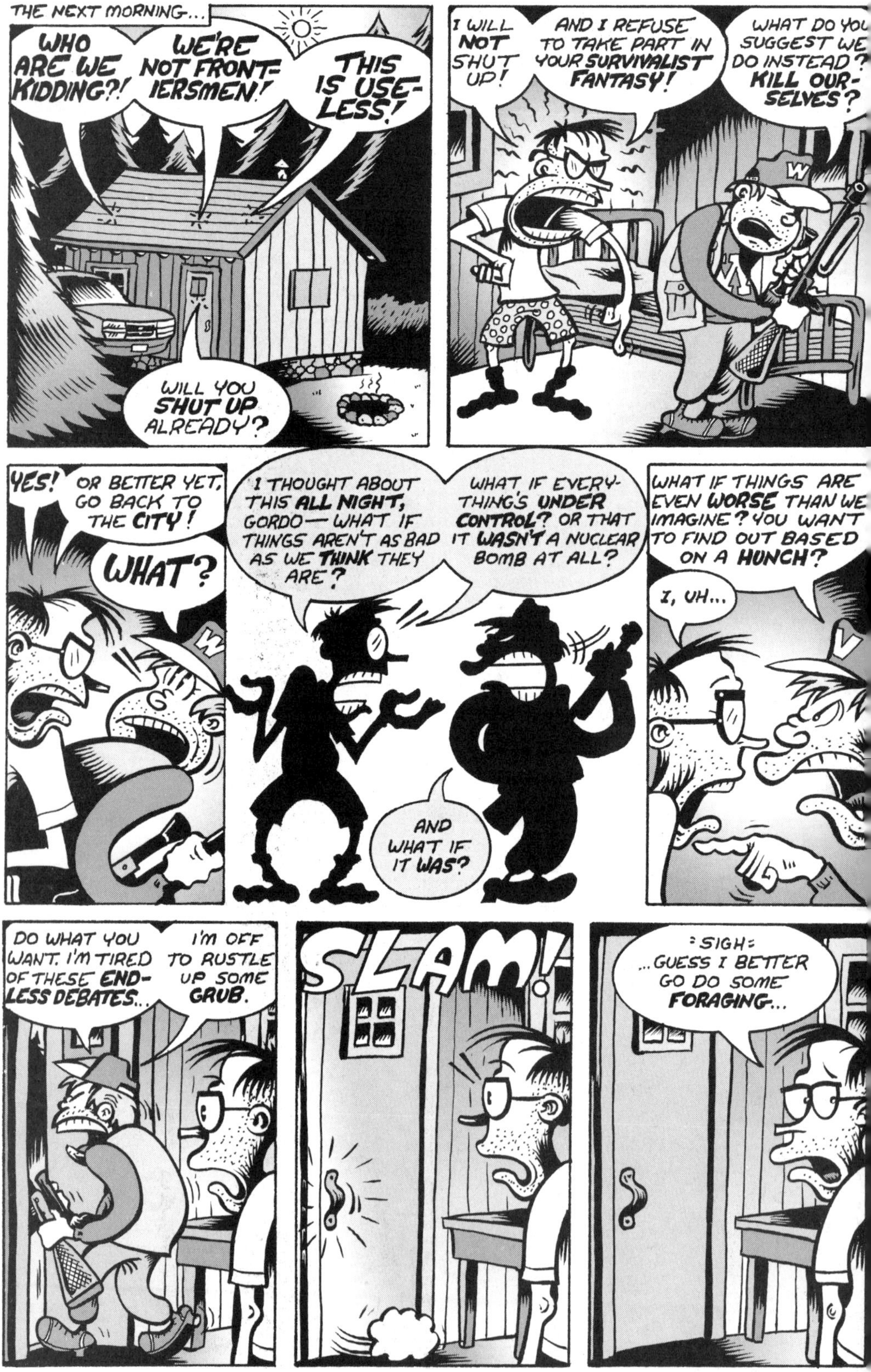
THE NEXT MORNING...
WHO ARE WE KIDDING?!
WE'RE NOT FRONTIERSMEN!
THIS IS USELESS!
WILL YOU SHUT UP ALREADY?
I WILL NOT SHUT UP!
AND I REFUSE TO TAKE PART IN YOUR SURVIVALIST FANTASY!
WHAT DO YOU SUGGEST WE DO INSTEAD? KILL OURSELVES?
YES!
OR BETTER YET, GO BACK TO THE CITY!
WHAT?
I THOUGHT ABOUT THIS ALL NIGHT, GORDO— WHAT IF THINGS AREN'T AS BAD AS WE THINK THEY ARE?
WHAT IF EVERYTHING'S UNDER CONTROL? OR THAT IT WASN'T A NUCLEAR BOMB AT ALL?
AND WHAT IF IT WAS?
WHAT IF THINGS ARE EVEN WORSE THAN WE IMAGINE? YOU WANT TO FIND OUT BASED ON A HUNCH?
I, UH...
DO WHAT YOU WANT. I'M TIRED OF THESE ENDLESS DEBATES...
I'M OFF TO RUSTLE UP SOME GRUB.
SLAM!
:SIGH:
...GUESS I BETTER GO DO SOME FORAGING...

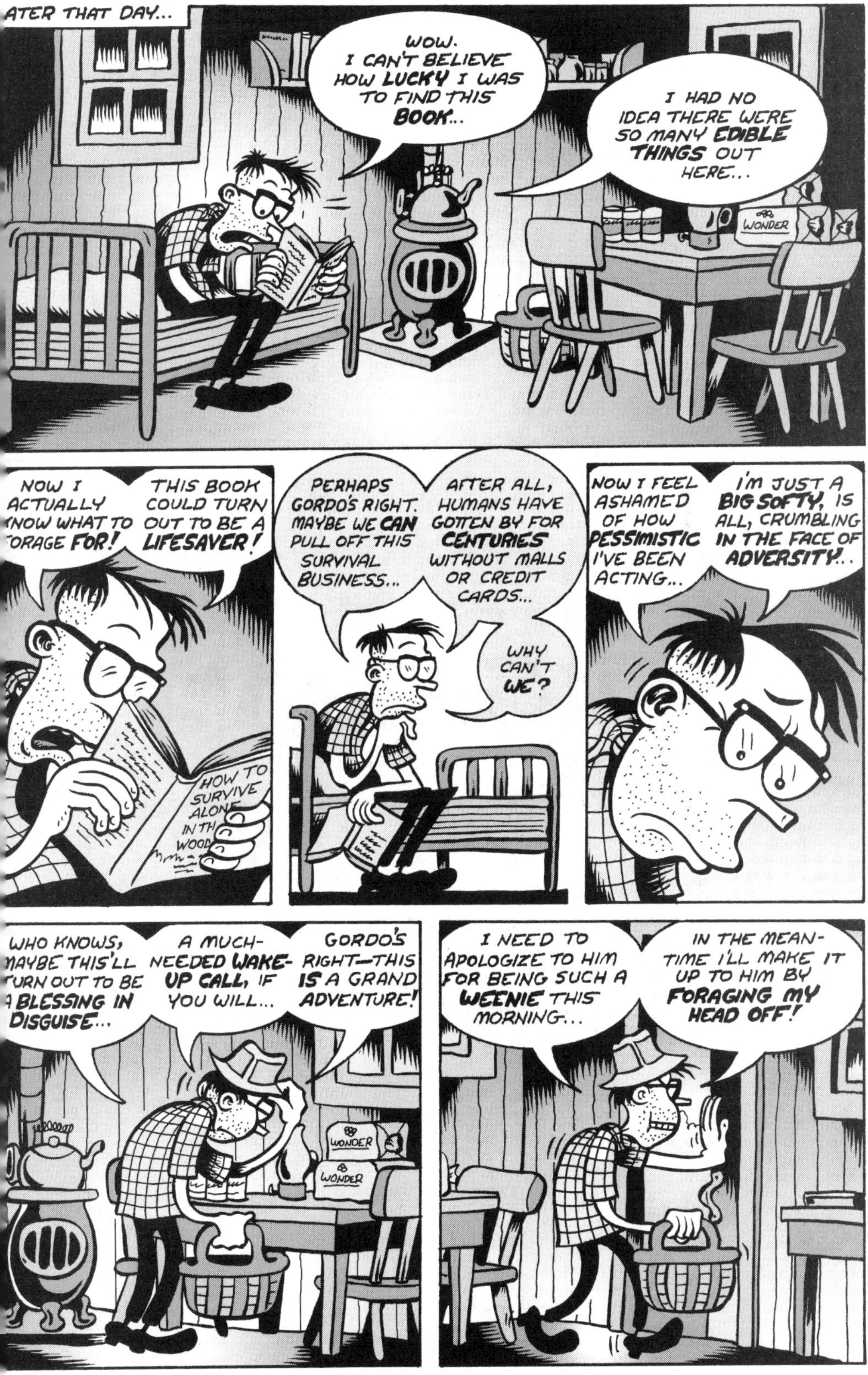
ATER THAT DAY...
WOW. I CAN'T BELIEVE HOW LUCKY I WAS TO FIND THIS BOOK...
I HAD NO IDEA THERE WERE SO MANY EDIBLE THINGS OUT HERE...
WONDER
NOW I ACTUALLY KNOW WHAT TO FORAGE FOR!
THIS BOOK COULD TURN OUT TO BE A LIFESAVER!
HOW TO SURVIVE ALONE IN TH WOOD
PERHAPS GORDO'S RIGHT. MAYBE WE CAN PULL OFF THIS SURVIVAL BUSINESS...
AFTER ALL, HUMANS HAVE GOTTEN BY FOR CENTURIES WITHOUT MALLS OR CREDIT CARDS...
WHY CAN'T WE?
NOW I FEEL ASHAMED OF HOW PESSIMISTIC I'VE BEEN ACTING...
I'M JUST A BIG SOFTY, IS ALL, CRUMBLING IN THE FACE OF ADVERSITY...
WHO KNOWS, MAYBE THIS'LL TURN OUT TO BE A BLESSING IN DISGUISE...
A MUCH-NEEDED WAKE-UP CALL, IF YOU WILL...
GORDO'S RIGHT—THIS IS A GRAND ADVENTURE!
WONDER
WONDER
I NEED TO APOLOGIZE TO HIM FOR BEING SUCH A WEENIE THIS MORNING...
IN THE MEAN-TIME I'LL MAKE IT UP TO HIM BY FORAGING MY HEAD OFF!

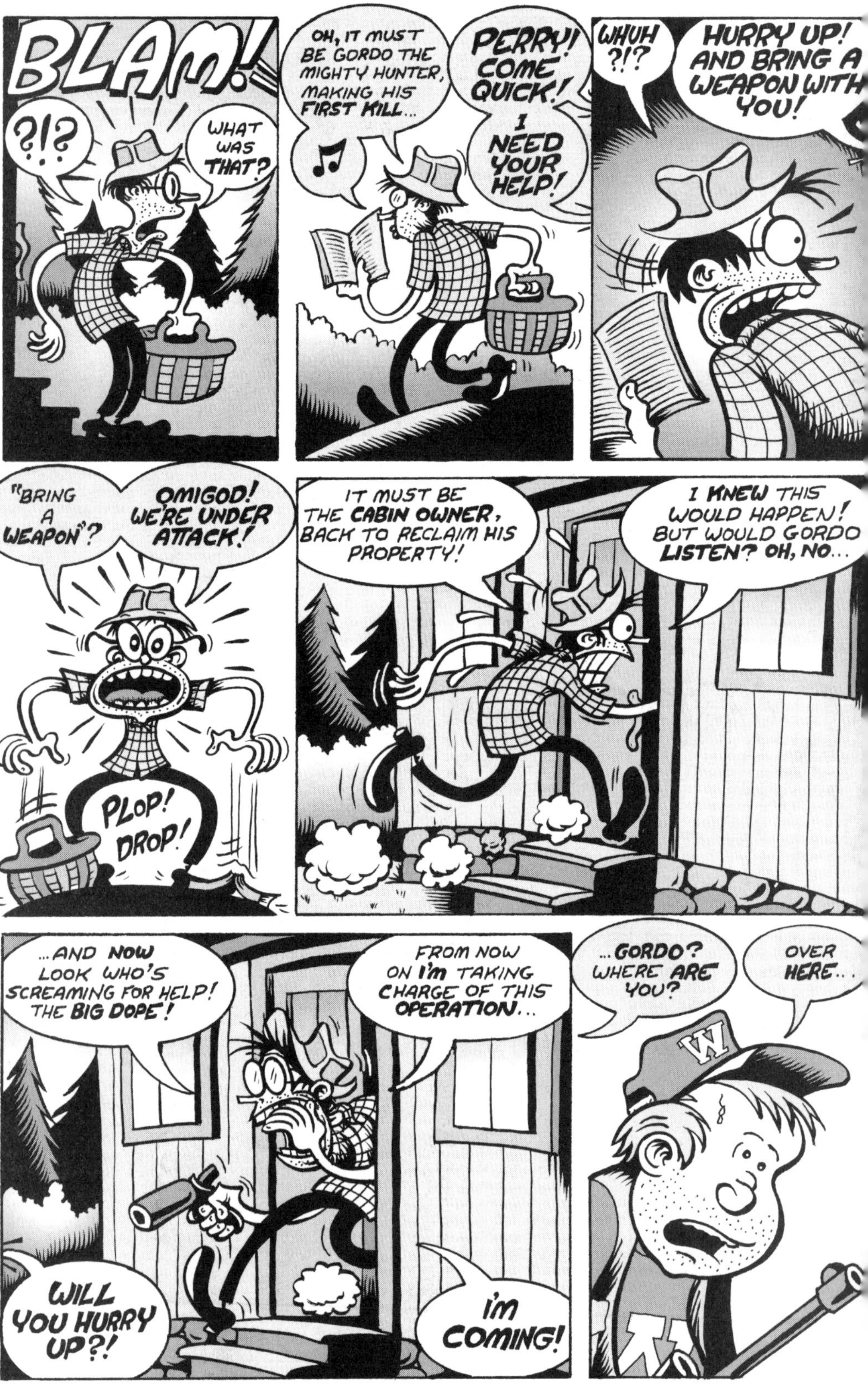
BLAM!
?!?
WHAT WAS THAT?
OH, IT MUST BE GORDO THE MIGHTY HUNTER, MAKING HIS FIRST KILL...
PERRY! COME QUICK!
I NEED YOUR HELP!
WHUH ?!?
HURRY UP! AND BRING A WEAPON WITH YOU!
"BRING A WEAPON"?
OMIGOD! WE'RE UNDER ATTACK!
PLOP! DROP!
IT MUST BE THE CABIN OWNER, BACK TO RECLAIM HIS PROPERTY!
I KNEW THIS WOULD HAPPEN! BUT WOULD GORDO LISTEN? OH, NO...
...AND NOW LOOK WHO'S SCREAMING FOR HELP! THE BIG DOPE!
FROM NOW ON I'M TAKING CHARGE OF THIS OPERATION...
WILL YOU HURRY UP?!
I'M COMING!
...GORDO? WHERE ARE YOU?
OVER HERE...

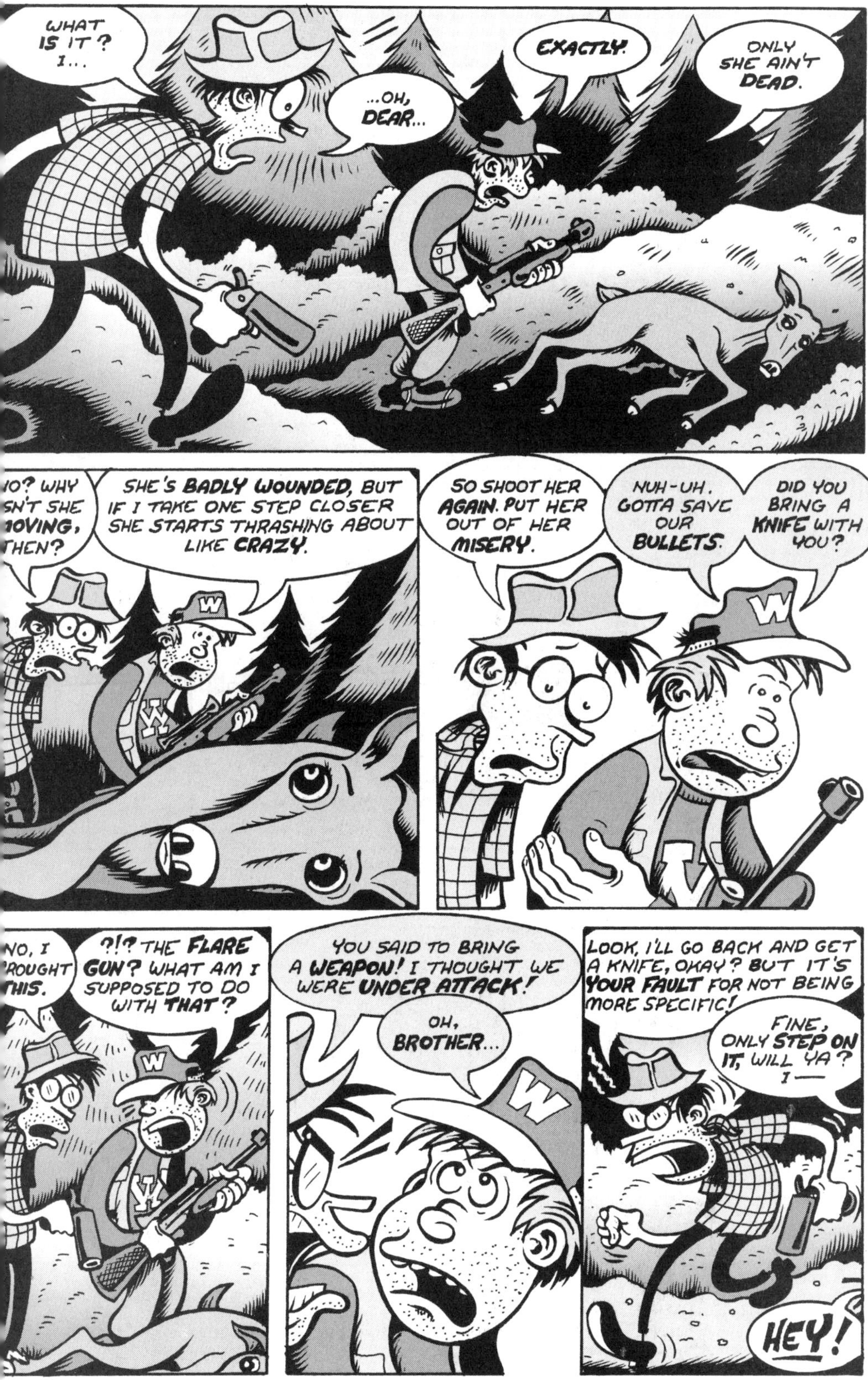
WHAT IS IT? I...
...OH, DEAR...
EXACTLY.
ONLY SHE AIN'T DEAD.
...HO? WHY ISN'T SHE MOVING, THEN?
SHE'S BADLY WOUNDED, BUT IF I TAKE ONE STEP CLOSER SHE STARTS THRASHING ABOUT LIKE CRAZY.
SO SHOOT HER AGAIN. PUT HER OUT OF HER MISERY.
NUH-UH. GOTTA SAVE OUR BULLETS.
DID YOU BRING A KNIFE WITH YOU?
NO, I ...ROUGHT THIS.
?!? THE FLARE GUN? WHAT AM I SUPPOSED TO DO WITH THAT?
YOU SAID TO BRING A WEAPON! I THOUGHT WE WERE UNDER ATTACK!
OH, BROTHER...
LOOK, I'LL GO BACK AND GET A KNIFE, OKAY? BUT IT'S YOUR FAULT FOR NOT BEING MORE SPECIFIC!
FINE, ONLY STEP ON IT, WILL YA? I—
HEY!

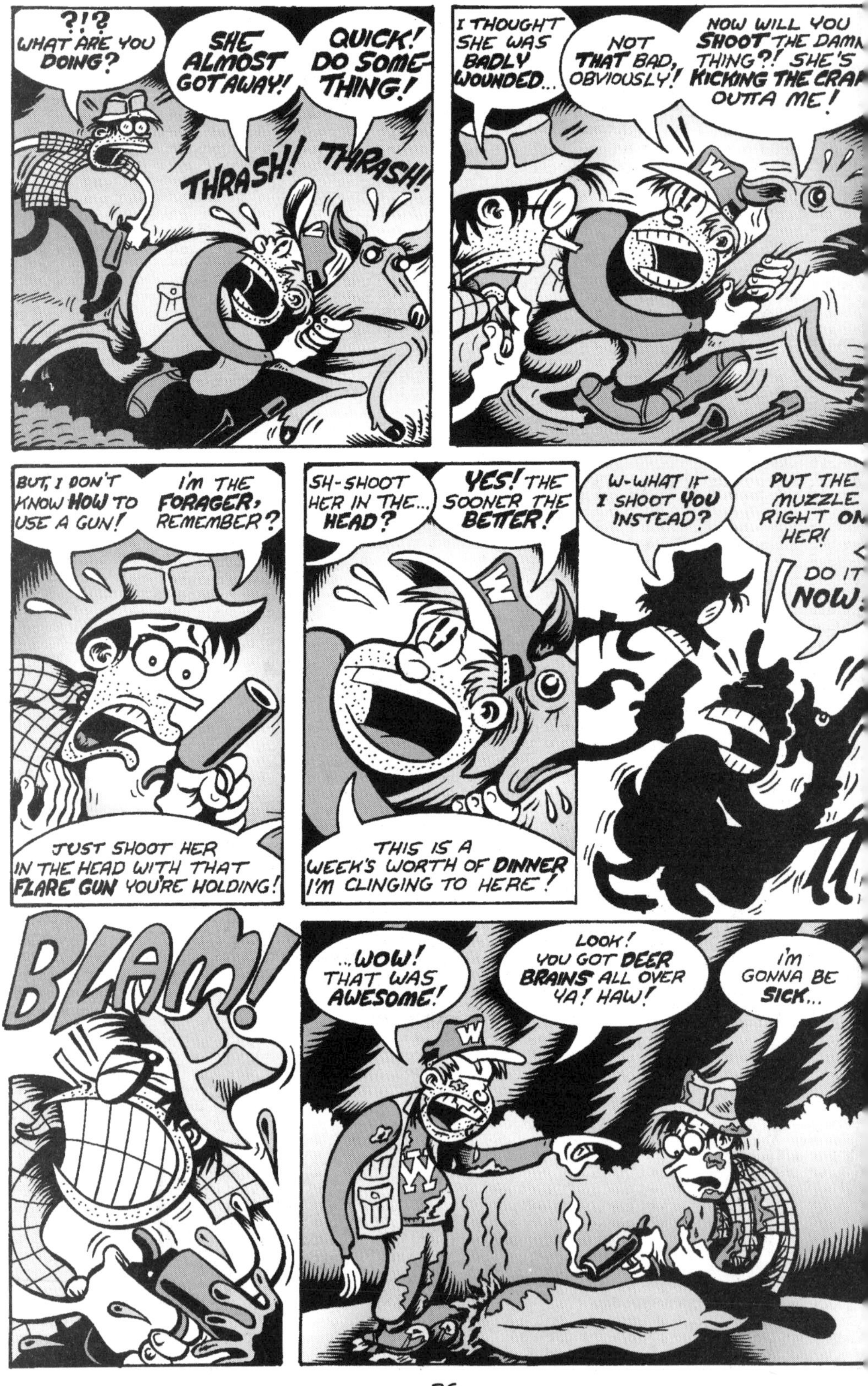
?!? WHAT ARE YOU DOING?
SHE ALMOST GOT AWAY!
QUICK! DO SOMETHING!
THRASH! THRASH!
I THOUGHT SHE WAS BADLY WOUNDED...
NOT THAT BAD, OBVIOUSLY!
NOW WILL YOU SHOOT THE DAMN THING?! SHE'S KICKING THE CRAP OUTTA ME!
BUT, I DON'T KNOW HOW TO USE A GUN!
I'M THE FORAGER, REMEMBER?
JUST SHOOT HER IN THE HEAD WITH THAT FLARE GUN YOU'RE HOLDING!
SH-SHOOT HER IN THE... HEAD?
YES! THE SOONER THE BETTER!
THIS IS A WEEK'S WORTH OF DINNER I'M CLINGING TO HERE!
W-WHAT IF I SHOOT YOU INSTEAD?
PUT THE MUZZLE RIGHT ON HER!
DO IT NOW!
BLAM!
...WOW! THAT WAS AWESOME!
LOOK! YOU GOT DEER BRAINS ALL OVER YA! HAW!
I'M GONNA BE SICK...

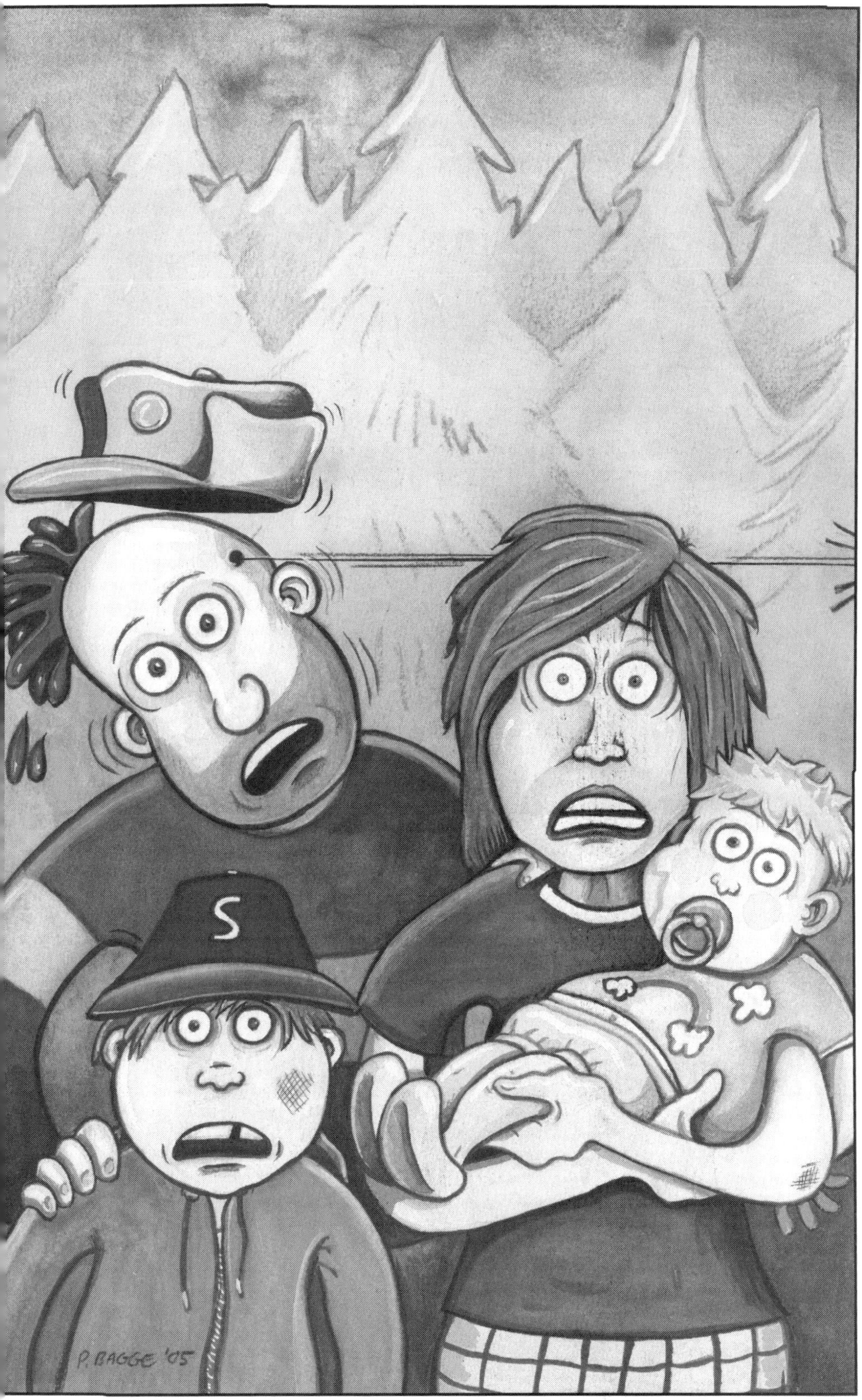
S
P. BAGGE '05

Chapter 2

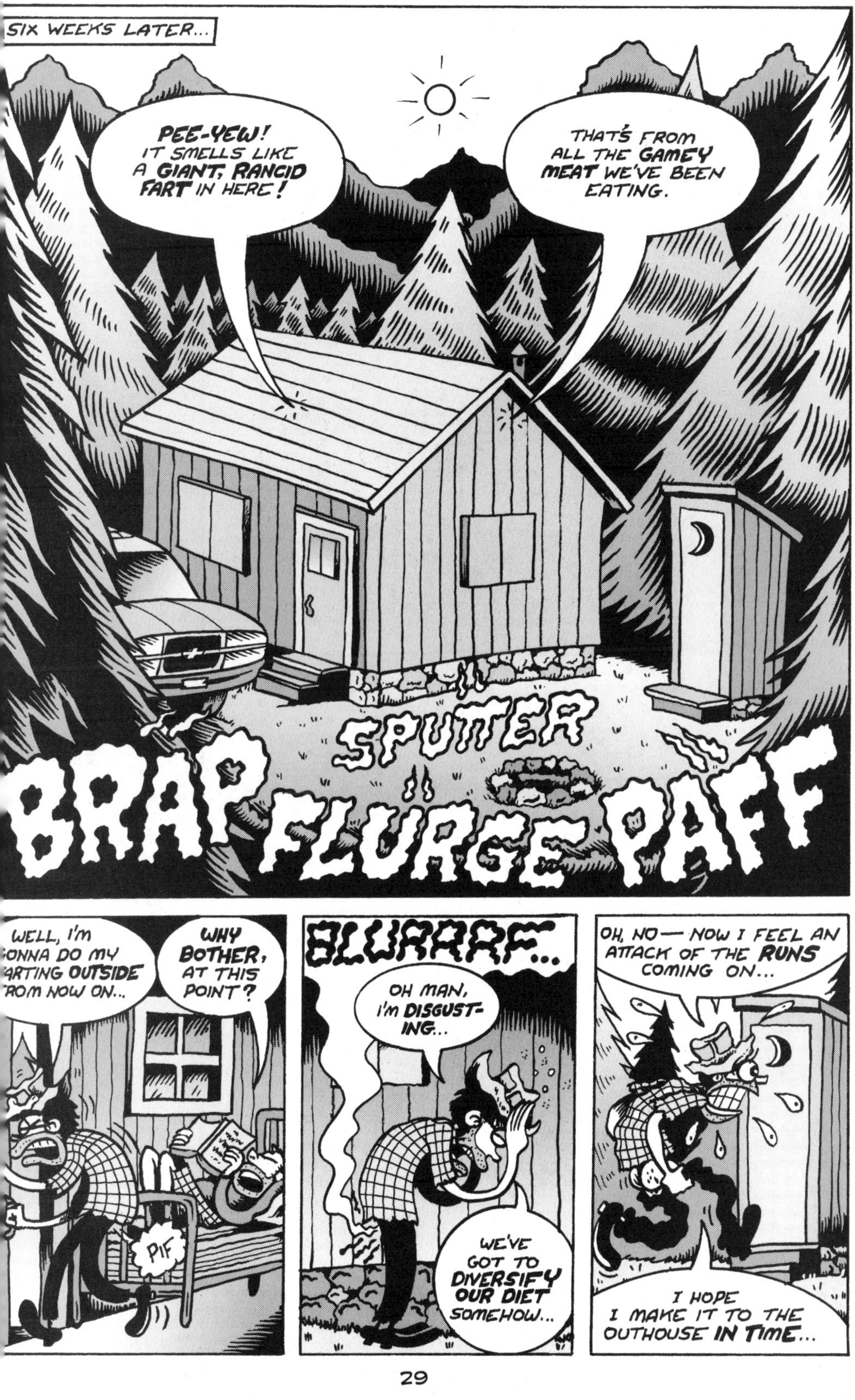
SIX WEEKS LATER...
PEE-YEW! IT SMELLS LIKE A GIANT, RANCID FART IN HERE!
THAT'S FROM ALL THE GAMEY MEAT WE'VE BEEN EATING.
SPUTTER
BRAP
FLURGE
PAFF
WELL, I'M GONNA DO MY FARTING OUTSIDE FROM NOW ON...
WHY BOTHER, AT THIS POINT?
PIF
BLURRRF...
OH MAN, I'M DISGUST-ING...
WE'VE GOT TO DIVERSIFY OUR DIET SOMEHOW...
OH, NO— NOW I FEEL AN ATTACK OF THE RUNS COMING ON...
I HOPE I MAKE IT TO THE OUTHOUSE IN TIME...

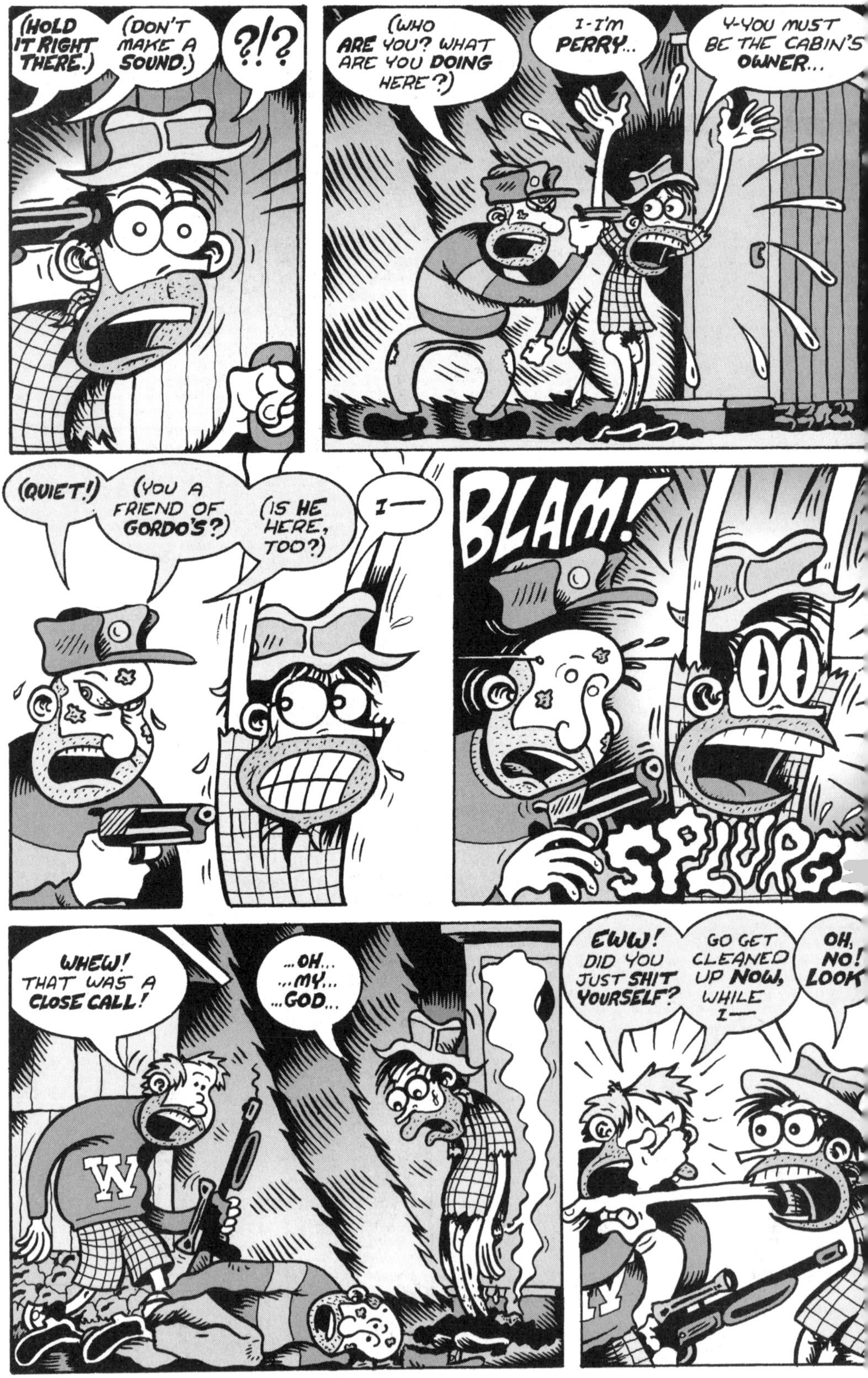
(HOLD IT RIGHT THERE.)
(DON'T MAKE A SOUND.)
?!?
(WHO ARE YOU? WHAT ARE YOU DOING HERE?)
I-I'M PERRY...
Y-YOU MUST BE THE CABIN'S OWNER...
(QUIET!)
(YOU A FRIEND OF GORDO'S?)
(IS HE HERE, TOO?)
I—
BLAM!
SPLURGE
WHEW! THAT WAS A CLOSE CALL!
...OH... ...MY... ...GOD...
EWW! DID YOU JUST SHIT YOURSELF?
GO GET CLEANED UP NOW, WHILE I—
OH, NO! LOOK

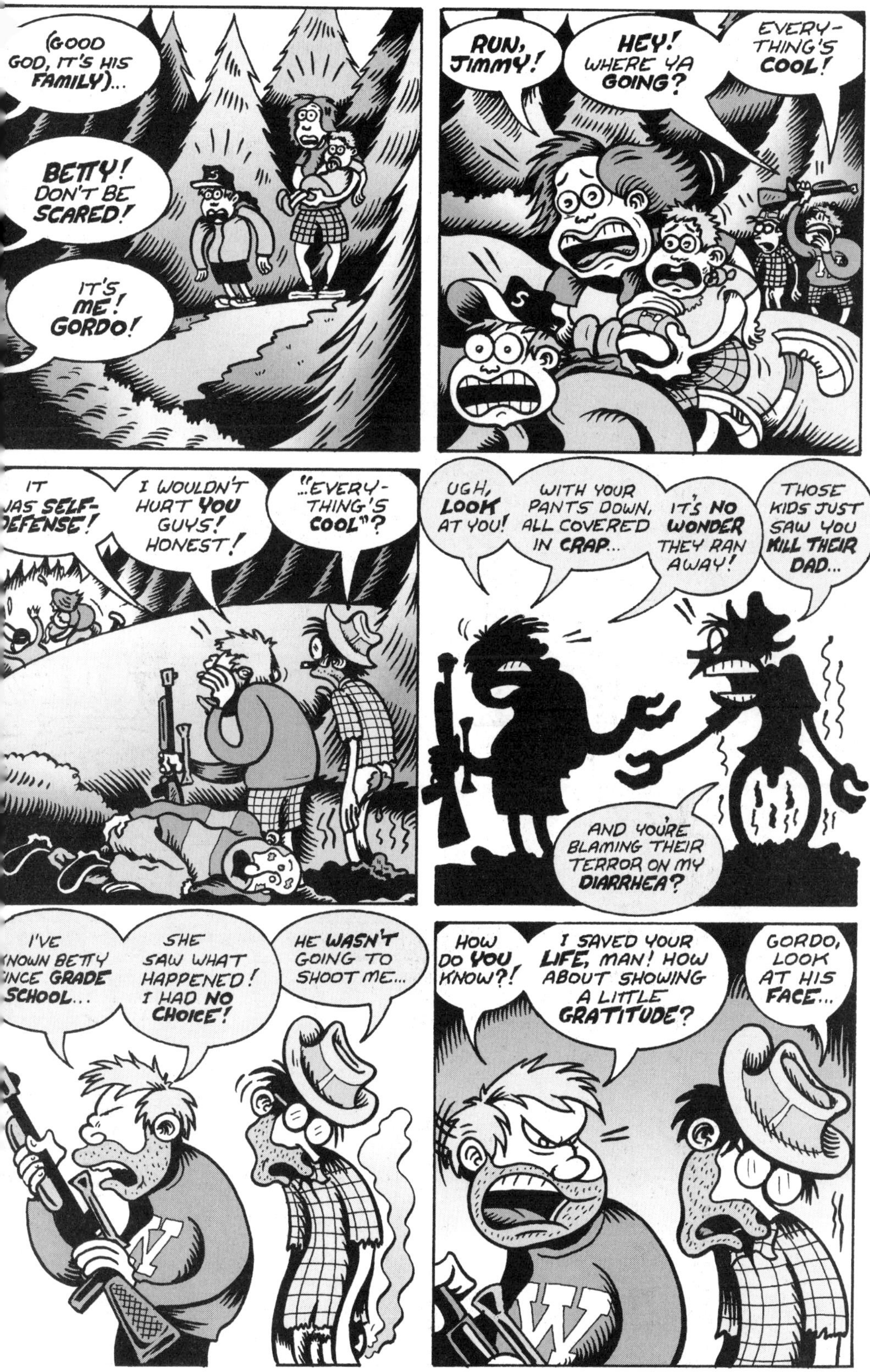
(GOOD GOD, IT'S HIS FAMILY)...
BETTY! DON'T BE SCARED!
IT'S ME! GORDO!
RUN, JIMMY!
HEY! WHERE YA GOING?
EVERY-THING'S COOL!
IT WAS SELF-DEFENSE!
I WOULDN'T HURT YOU GUYS! HONEST!
..."EVERY-THING'S COOL"?
UGH, LOOK AT YOU!
WITH YOUR PANTS DOWN, ALL COVERED IN CRAP...
IT'S NO WONDER THEY RAN AWAY!
THOSE KIDS JUST SAW YOU KILL THEIR DAD...
AND YOU'RE BLAMING THEIR TERROR ON MY DIARRHEA?
I'VE KNOWN BETTY SINCE GRADE SCHOOL...
SHE SAW WHAT HAPPENED! I HAD NO CHOICE!
HE WASN'T GOING TO SHOOT ME...
HOW DO YOU KNOW?!
I SAVED YOUR LIFE, MAN! HOW ABOUT SHOWING A LITTLE GRATITUDE?
GORDO, LOOK AT HIS FACE...

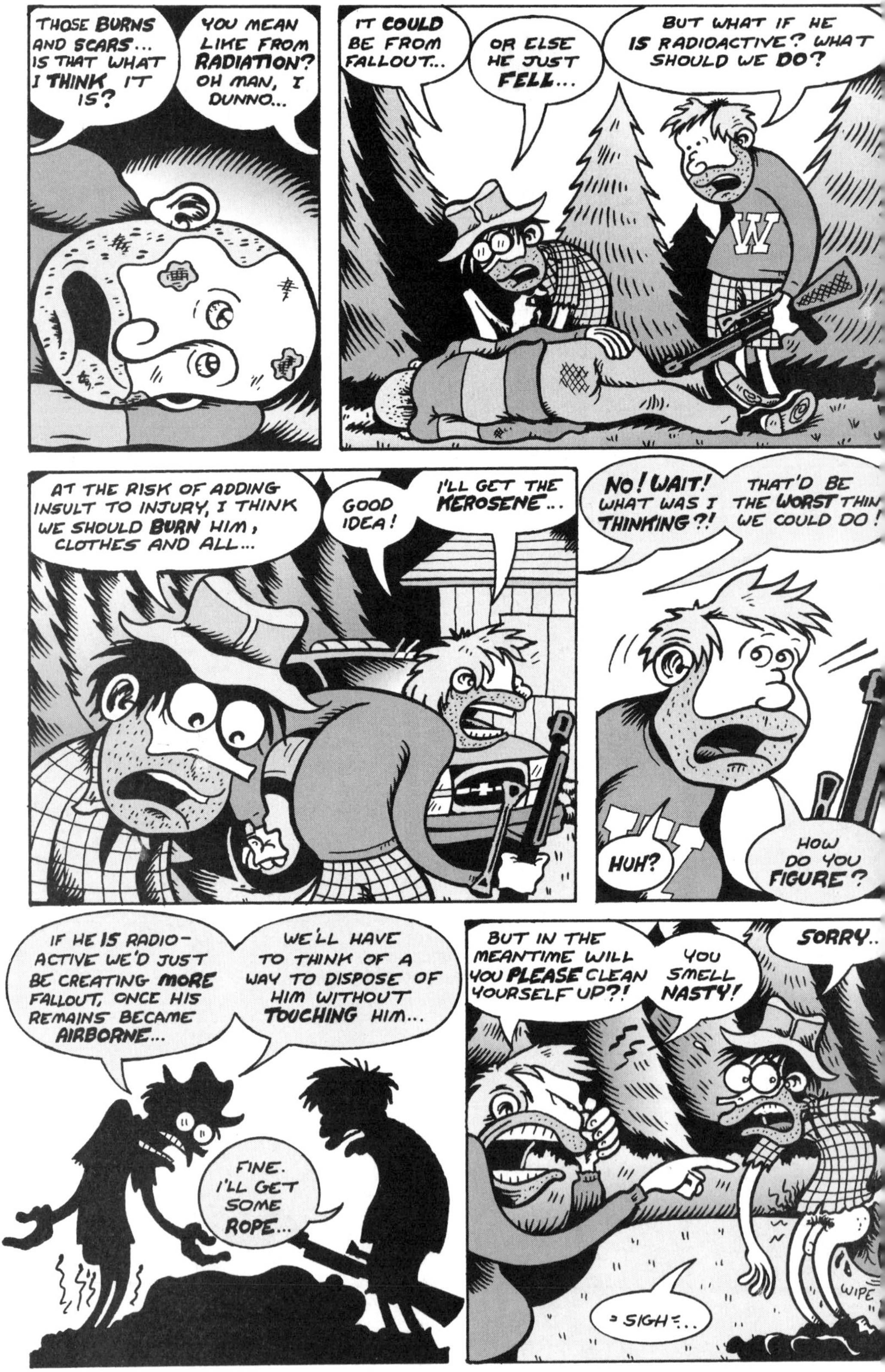
THOSE BURNS AND SCARS... IS THAT WHAT I THINK IT IS?
YOU MEAN LIKE FROM RADIATION? OH MAN, I DUNNO...
IT COULD BE FROM FALLOUT...
OR ELSE HE JUST FELL...
BUT WHAT IF HE IS RADIOACTIVE? WHAT SHOULD WE DO?
AT THE RISK OF ADDING INSULT TO INJURY, I THINK WE SHOULD BURN HIM, CLOTHES AND ALL...
GOOD IDEA!
I'LL GET THE KEROSENE...
NO! WAIT! WHAT WAS I THINKING?!
THAT'D BE THE WORST THIN WE COULD DO!
HUH?
HOW DO YOU FIGURE?
IF HE IS RADIO-ACTIVE WE'D JUST BE CREATING MORE FALLOUT, ONCE HIS REMAINS BECAME AIRBORNE...
WE'LL HAVE TO THINK OF A WAY TO DISPOSE OF HIM WITHOUT TOUCHING HIM...
FINE. I'LL GET SOME ROPE...
BUT IN THE MEANTIME WILL YOU PLEASE CLEAN YOURSELF UP?!
YOU SMELL NASTY!
SORRY...
= SIGH =...
WIPE

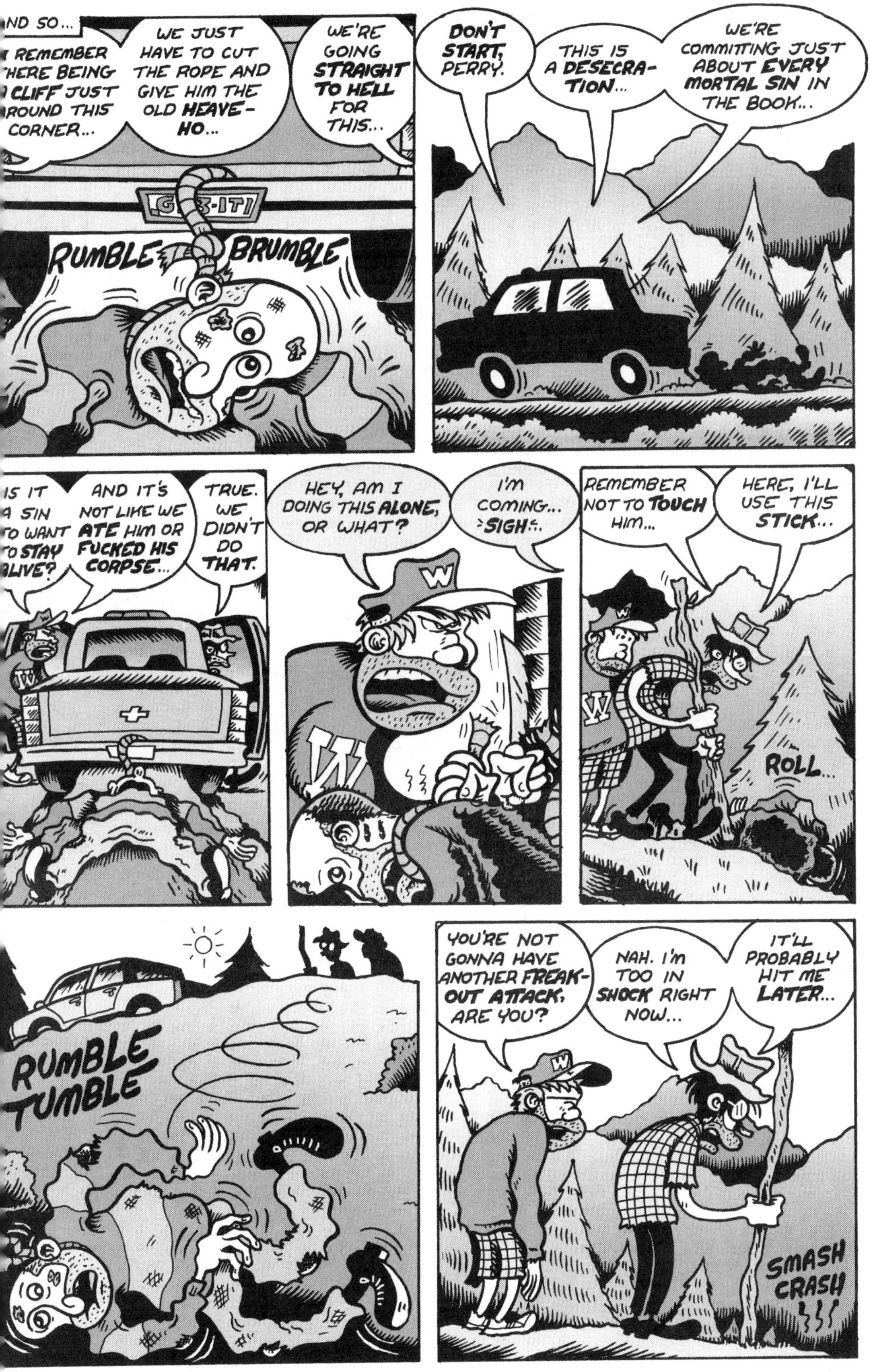

ND SO...
REMEMBER HERE BEING CLIFF JUST ROUND THIS CORNER...
WE JUST HAVE TO CUT THE ROPE AND GIVE HIM THE OLD HEAVE-HO...
WE'RE GOING STRAIGHT TO HELL FOR THIS...
RUMBLE BRUMBLE
DON'T START, PERRY.
THIS IS A DESECRATION...
WE'RE COMMITTING JUST ABOUT EVERY MORTAL SIN IN THE BOOK...
IS IT A SIN TO WANT TO STAY ALIVE?
AND IT'S NOT LIKE WE ATE HIM OR FUCKED HIS CORPSE...
TRUE. WE DIDN'T DO THAT.
HEY, AM I DOING THIS ALONE, OR WHAT?
I'M COMING... SIGH.
REMEMBER NOT TO TOUCH HIM...
HERE, I'LL USE THIS STICK...
ROLL...
RUMBLE TUMBLE
YOU'RE NOT GONNA HAVE ANOTHER FREAK-OUT ATTACK, ARE YOU?
NAH. I'M TOO IN SHOCK RIGHT NOW...
IT'LL PROBABLY HIT ME LATER...
SMASH CRASH

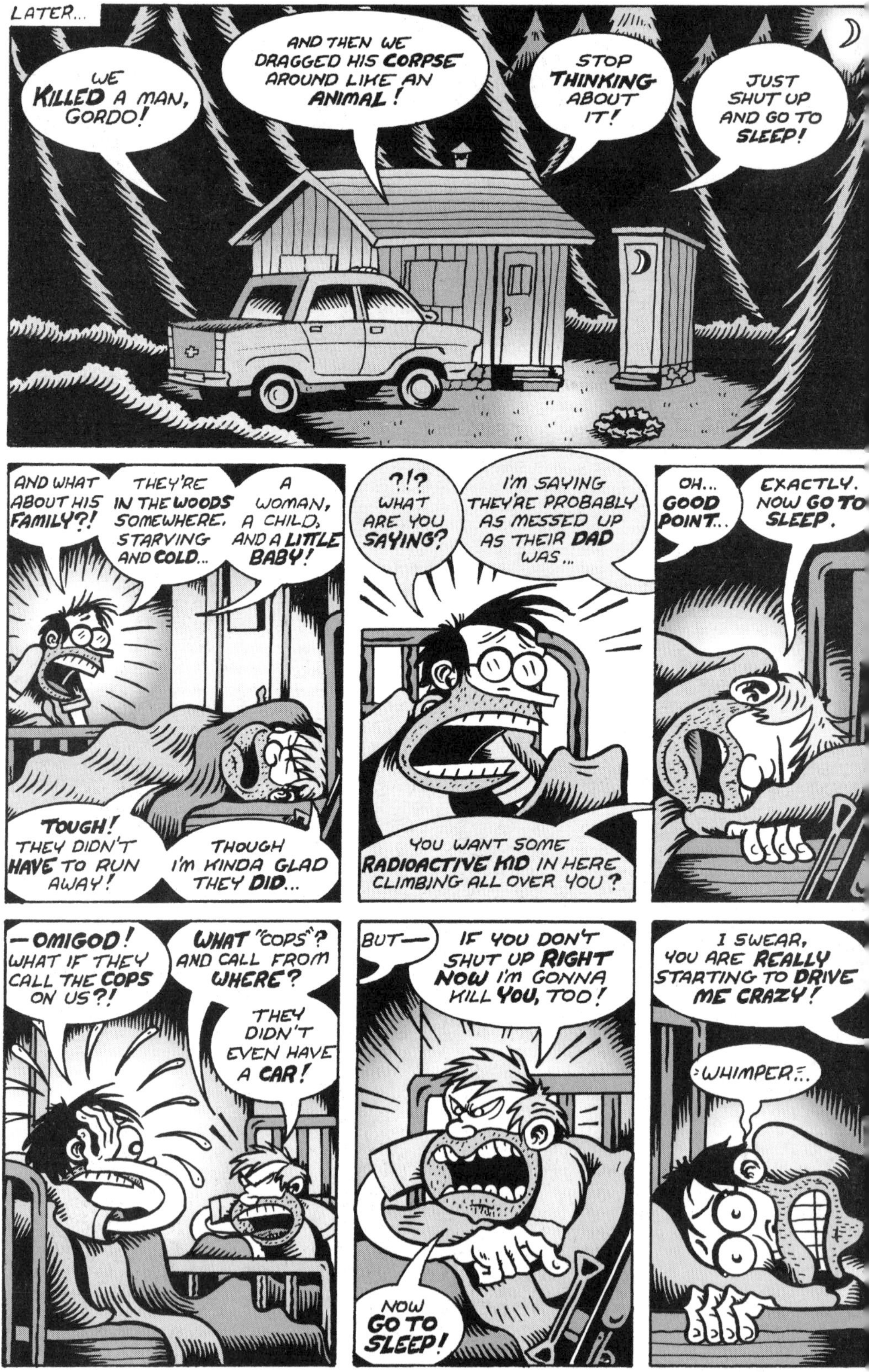
LATER...
WE KILLED A MAN, GORDO!
AND THEN WE DRAGGED HIS CORPSE AROUND LIKE AN ANIMAL!
STOP THINKING ABOUT IT!
JUST SHUT UP AND GO TO SLEEP!
AND WHAT ABOUT HIS FAMILY?!
THEY'RE IN THE WOODS SOMEWHERE, STARVING AND COLD...
A WOMAN, A CHILD, AND A LITTLE BABY!
TOUGH! THEY DIDN'T HAVE TO RUN AWAY!
THOUGH I'M KINDA GLAD THEY DID...
?!? WHAT ARE YOU SAYING?
I'M SAYING THEY'RE PROBABLY AS MESSED UP AS THEIR DAD WAS...
YOU WANT SOME RADIOACTIVE KID IN HERE CLIMBING ALL OVER YOU?
OH... GOOD POINT...
EXACTLY. NOW GO TO SLEEP.
—OMIGOD! WHAT IF THEY CALL THE COPS ON US?!
WHAT "COPS"? AND CALL FROM WHERE?
THEY DIDN'T EVEN HAVE A CAR!
BUT—
IF YOU DON'T SHUT UP RIGHT NOW I'M GONNA KILL YOU, TOO!
NOW GO TO SLEEP!
I SWEAR, YOU ARE REALLY STARTING TO DRIVE ME CRAZY!
WHIMPER...

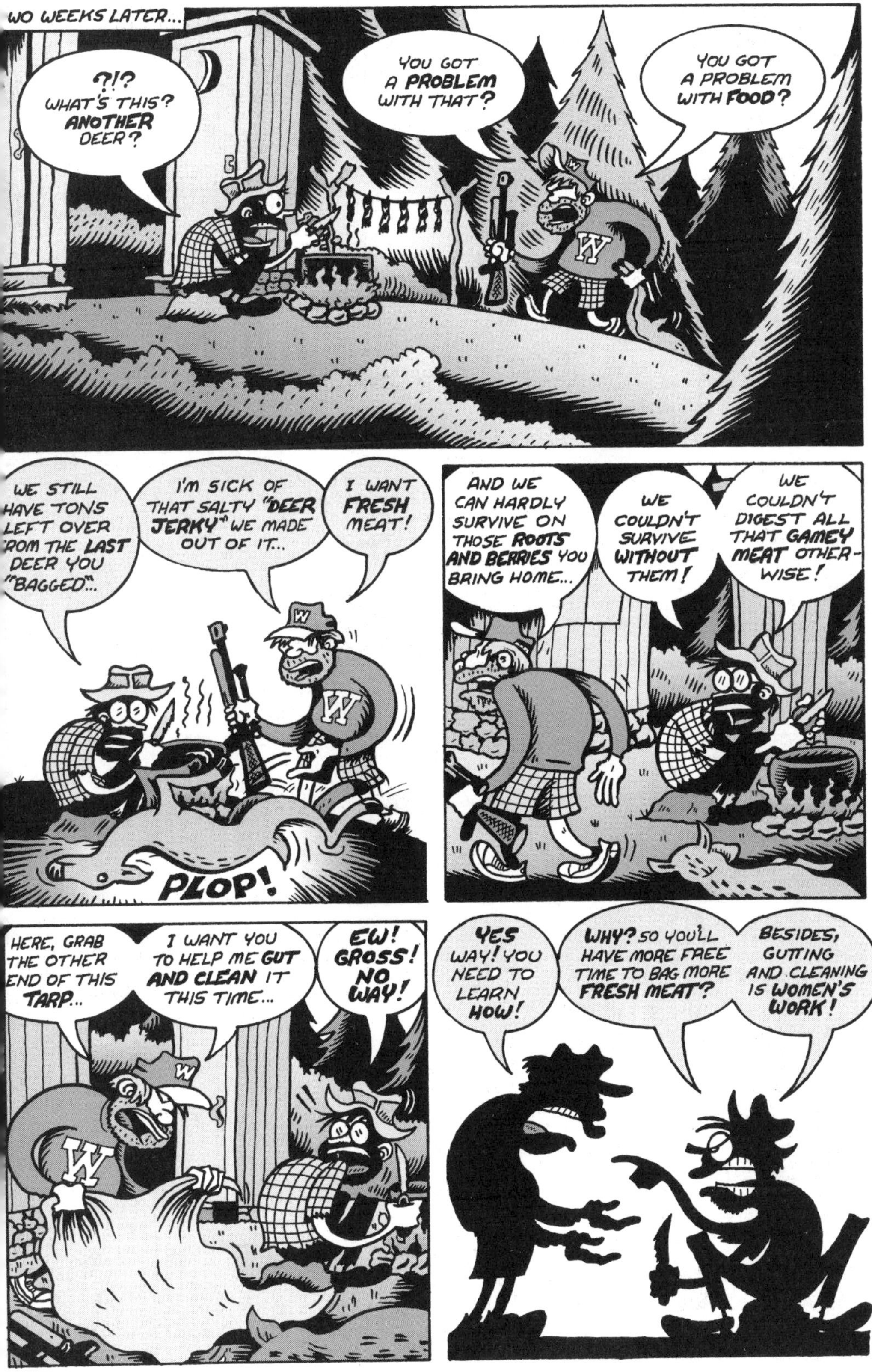
WO WEEKS LATER...
?!? WHAT'S THIS? ANOTHER DEER?
YOU GOT A PROBLEM WITH THAT?
YOU GOT A PROBLEM WITH FOOD?
WE STILL HAVE TONS LEFT OVER ROM THE LAST DEER YOU "BAGGED"...
I'M SICK OF THAT SALTY "DEER JERKY" WE MADE OUT OF IT...
I WANT FRESH MEAT!
PLOP!
AND WE CAN HARDLY SURVIVE ON THOSE ROOTS AND BERRIES YOU BRING HOME...
WE COULDN'T SURVIVE WITHOUT THEM!
WE COULDN'T DIGEST ALL THAT GAMEY MEAT OTHER-WISE!
HERE, GRAB THE OTHER END OF THIS TARP...
I WANT YOU TO HELP ME GUT AND CLEAN IT THIS TIME...
EW! GROSS! NO WAY!
YES WAY! YOU NEED TO LEARN HOW!
WHY? SO YOU'LL HAVE MORE FREE TIME TO BAG MORE FRESH MEAT?
BESIDES, GUTTING AND CLEANING IS WOMEN'S WORK!

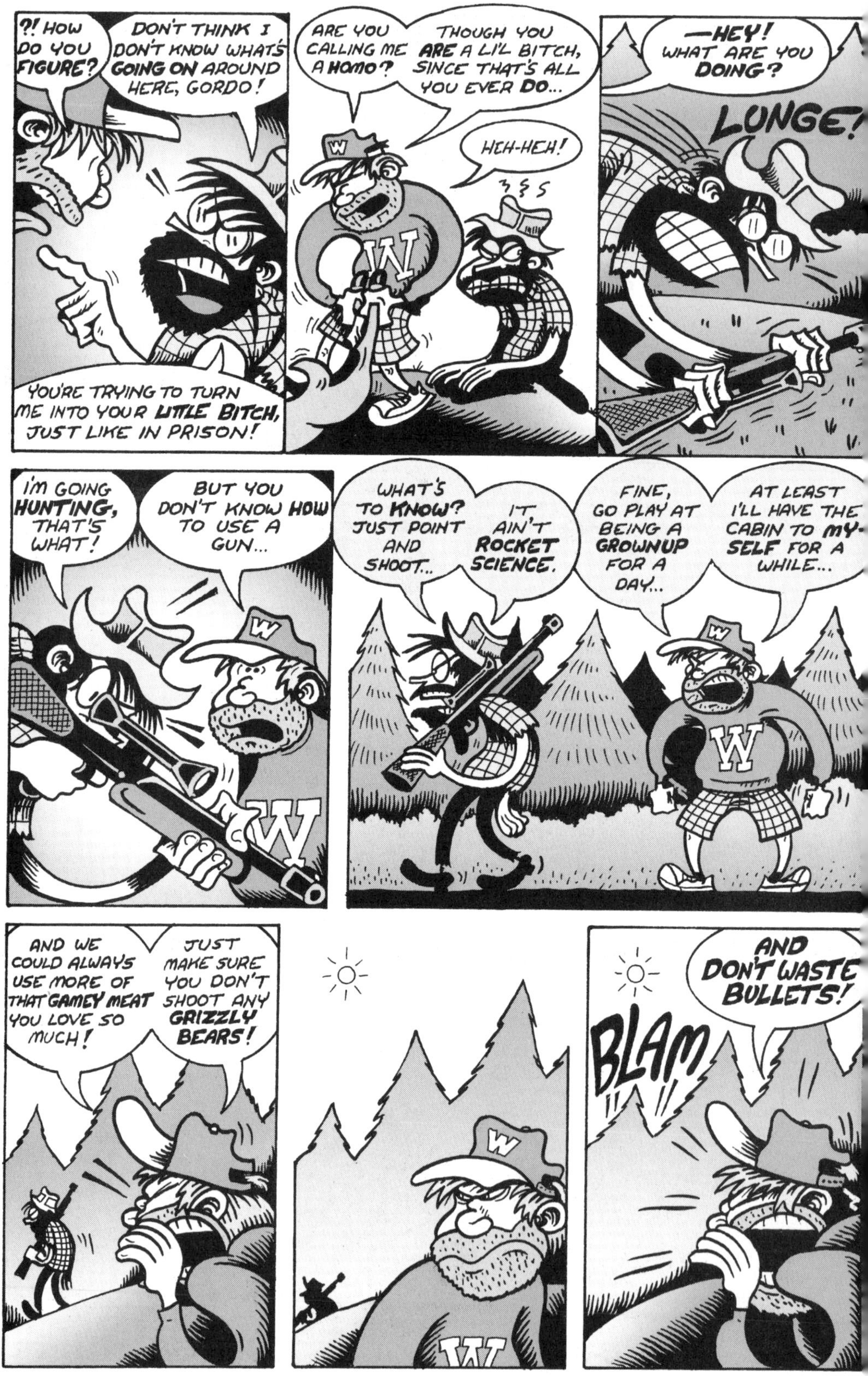

?! HOW DO YOU FIGURE?
DON'T THINK I DON'T KNOW WHAT'S GOING ON AROUND HERE, GORDO!
YOU'RE TRYING TO TURN ME INTO YOUR LITTLE BITCH, JUST LIKE IN PRISON!
ARE YOU CALLING ME A HOMO?
THOUGH YOU ARE A LI'L BITCH, SINCE THAT'S ALL YOU EVER DO...
HEH-HEH!
—HEY! WHAT ARE YOU DOING?
LUNGE!
I'M GOING HUNTING, THAT'S WHAT!
BUT YOU DON'T KNOW HOW TO USE A GUN...
WHAT'S TO KNOW? JUST POINT AND SHOOT...
IT AIN'T ROCKET SCIENCE.
FINE, GO PLAY AT BEING A GROWNUP FOR A DAY...
AT LEAST I'LL HAVE THE CABIN TO MY-SELF FOR A WHILE...
AND WE COULD ALWAYS USE MORE OF THAT GAMEY MEAT YOU LOVE SO MUCH!
JUST MAKE SURE YOU DON'T SHOOT ANY GRIZZLY BEARS!
BLAM
AND DON'T WASTE BULLETS!

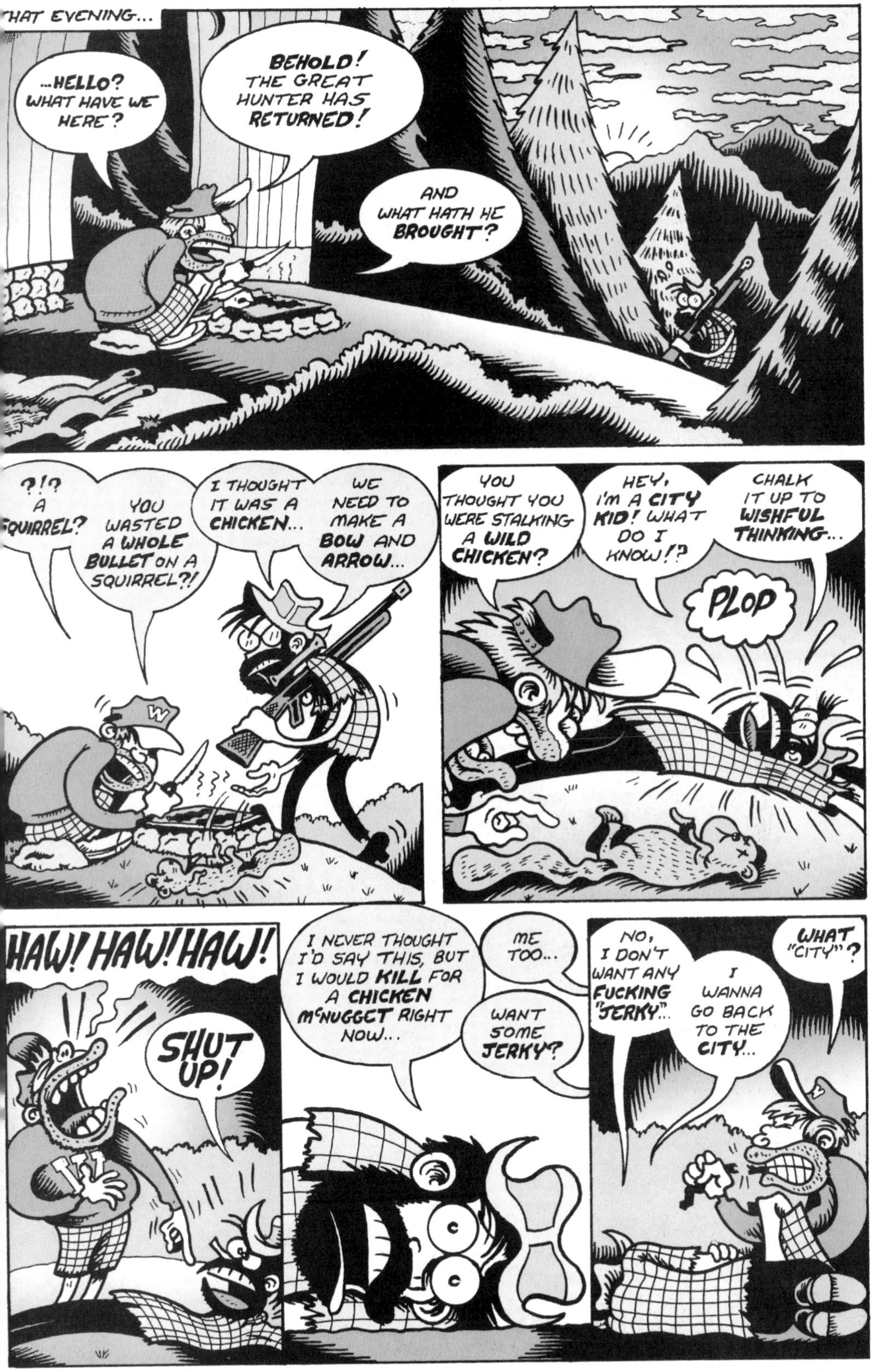
THAT EVENING...
...HELLO? WHAT HAVE WE HERE?
BEHOLD! THE GREAT HUNTER HAS RETURNED!
AND WHAT HATH HE BROUGHT?
?!? A SQUIRREL?
YOU WASTED A WHOLE BULLET ON A SQUIRREL?!
I THOUGHT IT WAS A CHICKEN...
WE NEED TO MAKE A BOW AND ARROW...
YOU THOUGHT YOU WERE STALKING A WILD CHICKEN?
HEY, I'M A CITY KID! WHAT DO I KNOW!?
CHALK IT UP TO WISHFUL THINKING...
PLOP
HAW! HAW! HAW!
SHUT UP!
I NEVER THOUGHT I'D SAY THIS, BUT I WOULD KILL FOR A CHICKEN McNUGGET RIGHT NOW...
ME TOO...
WANT SOME JERKY?
NO, I DON'T WANT ANY FUCKING "JERKY"...
I WANNA GO BACK TO THE CITY...
WHAT "CITY"?

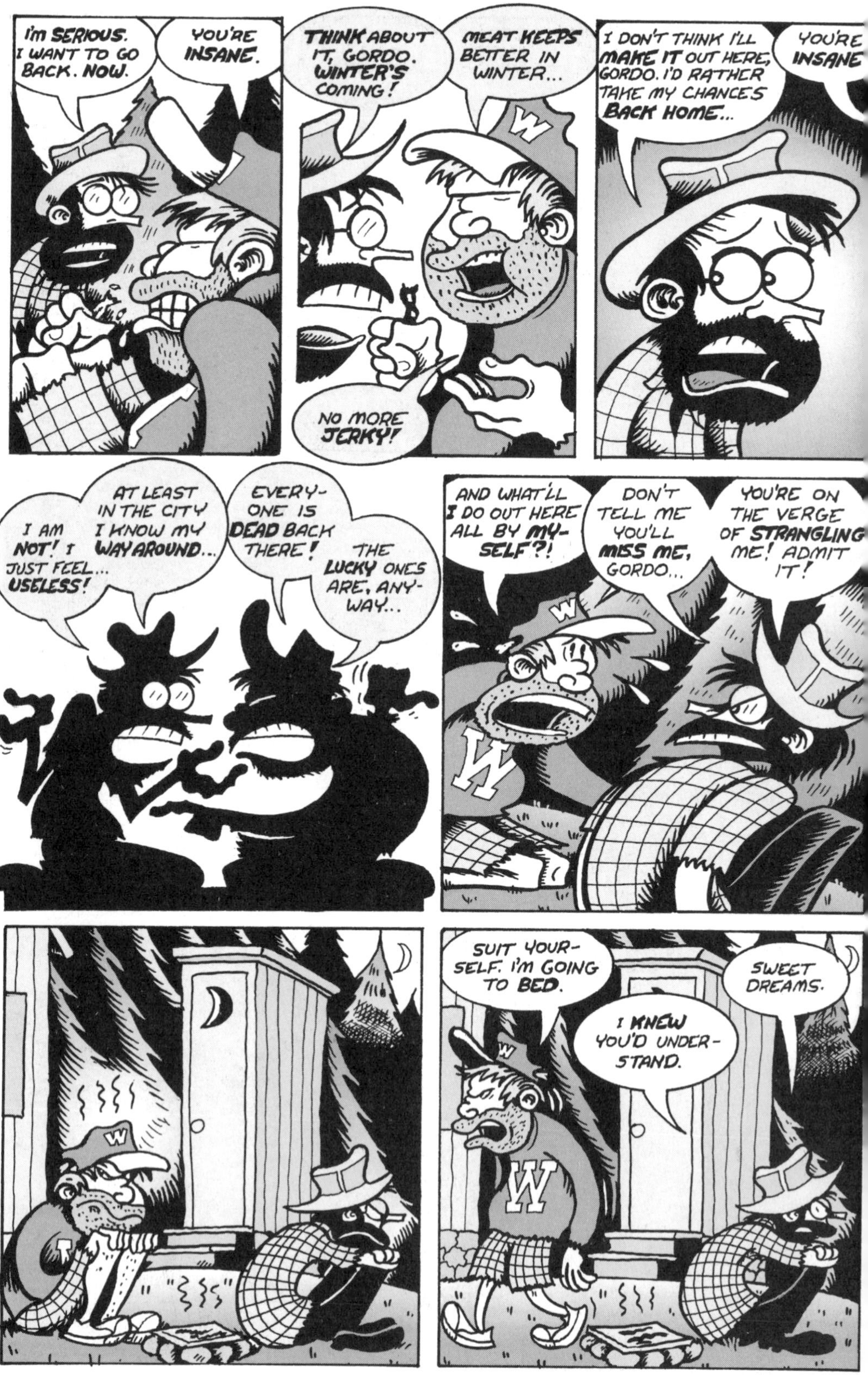
I'M SERIOUS. I WANT TO GO BACK. NOW.
YOU'RE INSANE.
THINK ABOUT IT, GORDO. WINTER'S COMING!
MEAT KEEPS BETTER IN WINTER...
NO MORE JERKY!
I DON'T THINK I'LL MAKE IT OUT HERE, GORDO. I'D RATHER TAKE MY CHANCES BACK HOME...
YOU'RE INSANE
I AM NOT! I JUST FEEL... USELESS!
AT LEAST IN THE CITY I KNOW MY WAY AROUND...
EVERY-ONE IS DEAD BACK THERE!
THE LUCKY ONES ARE, ANY-WAY...
AND WHAT'LL I DO OUT HERE ALL BY MY-SELF?!
DON'T TELL ME YOU'LL MISS ME, GORDO...
YOU'RE ON THE VERGE OF STRANGLING ME! ADMIT IT!
SUIT YOUR-SELF. I'M GOING TO BED.
I KNEW YOU'D UNDER-STAND.
SWEET DREAMS.

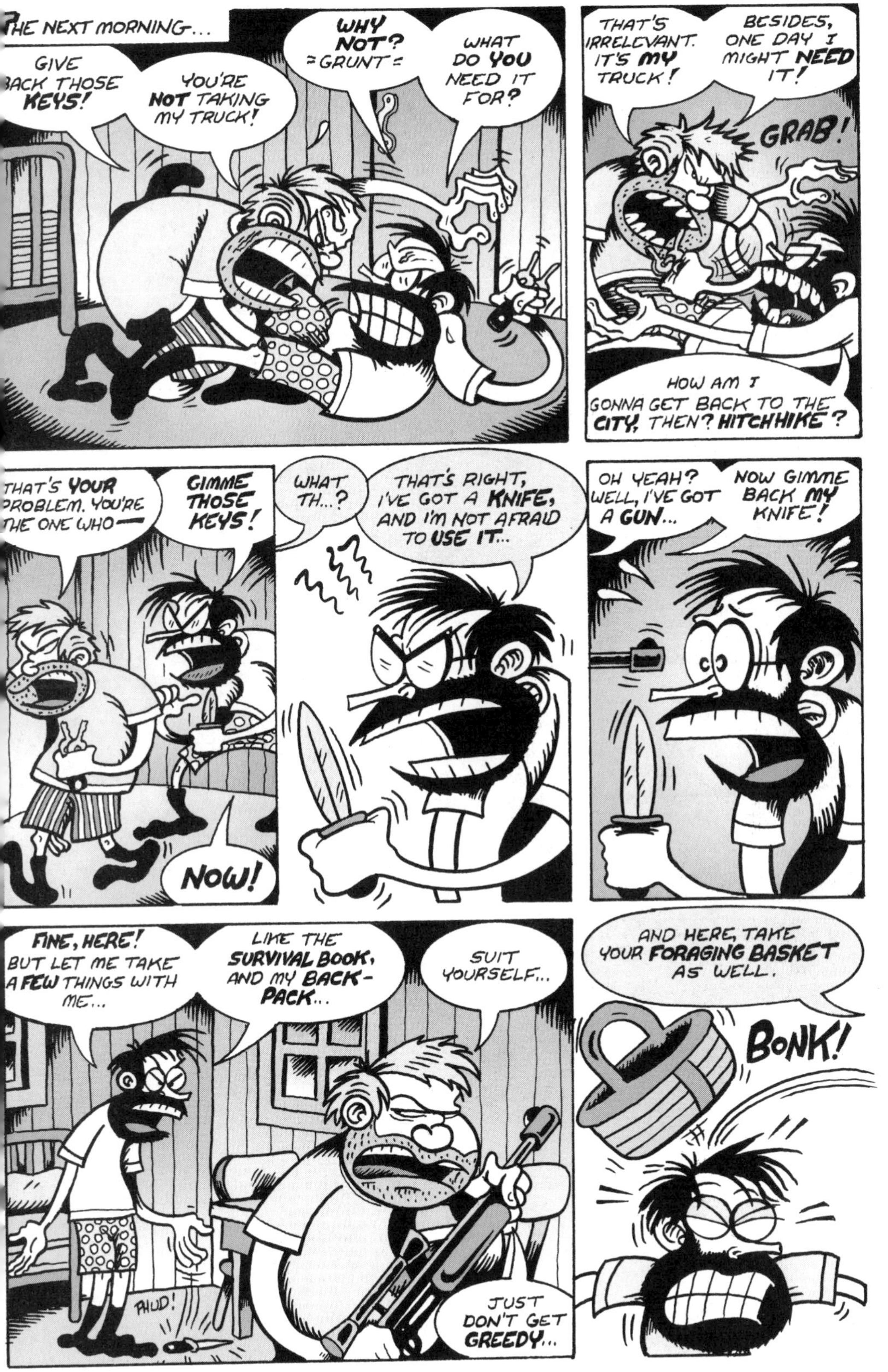

THE NEXT MORNING...
GIVE BACK THOSE KEYS!
YOU'RE NOT TAKING MY TRUCK!
WHY NOT? =GRUNT=
WHAT DO YOU NEED IT FOR?
THAT'S IRRELEVANT. IT'S MY TRUCK!
BESIDES, ONE DAY I MIGHT NEED IT!
GRAB!
HOW AM I GONNA GET BACK TO THE CITY, THEN? HITCHHIKE?
THAT'S YOUR PROBLEM. YOU'RE THE ONE WHO—
GIMME THOSE KEYS!
NOW!
WHAT TH...?
THAT'S RIGHT, I'VE GOT A KNIFE, AND I'M NOT AFRAID TO USE IT...
OH YEAH? WELL, I'VE GOT A GUN...
NOW GIMME BACK MY KNIFE!
FINE, HERE! BUT LET ME TAKE A FEW THINGS WITH ME...
LIKE THE SURVIVAL BOOK, AND MY BACK-PACK...
SUIT YOURSELF...
THUD!
JUST DON'T GET GREEDY...
AND HERE, TAKE YOUR FORAGING BASKET AS WELL.
BONK!

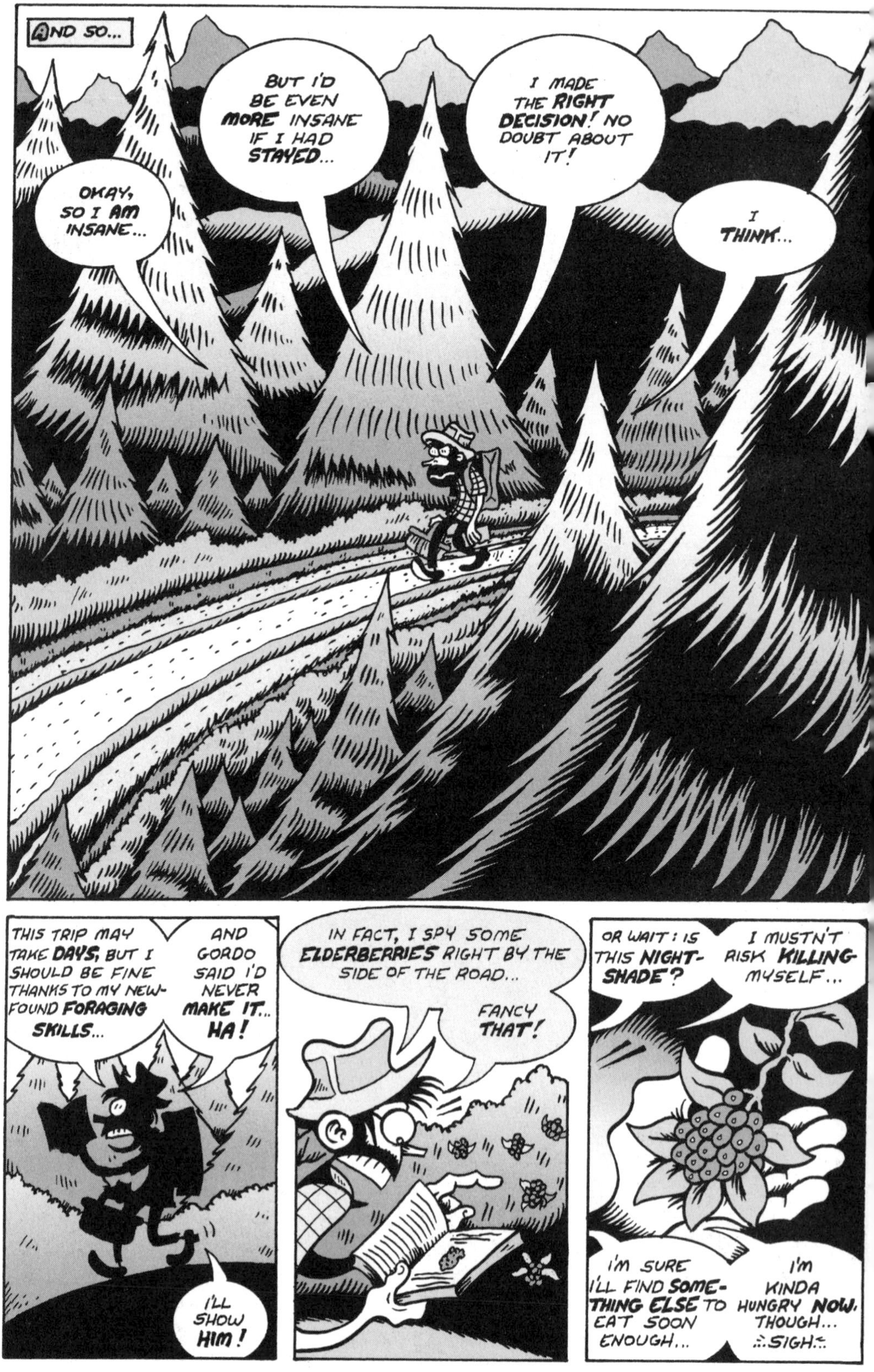
AND SO...
OKAY, SO I AM INSANE...
BUT I'D BE EVEN MORE INSANE IF I HAD STAYED...
I MADE THE RIGHT DECISION! NO DOUBT ABOUT IT!
I THINK...
THIS TRIP MAY TAKE DAYS, BUT I SHOULD BE FINE THANKS TO MY NEW-FOUND FORAGING SKILLS...
AND GORDO SAID I'D NEVER MAKE IT... HA!
I'LL SHOW HIM!
IN FACT, I SPY SOME ELDERBERRIES RIGHT BY THE SIDE OF THE ROAD...
FANCY THAT!
OR WAIT: IS THIS NIGHT-SHADE?
I MUSTN'T RISK KILLING MYSELF...
I'M SURE I'LL FIND SOME-THING ELSE TO EAT SOON ENOUGH...
I'M KINDA HUNGRY NOW, THOUGH... ∴SIGH∴

...WHAAAAAAAAAAAAH!!

MY FEET ARE **KILLING ME!** AND I'M **STILL** NOWHERE NEAR "CIVILIZATION"...

OH GOD, WHAT WAS I THINKING...

THIS WAS A TOTAL **PANIC MOVE** ON MY PART...

IF I HAD A GUN I'D JUST **BLOW MY BRAINS OUT** AND GET IT OVER WITH...

OR GO FIND A SHARP STICK AND **FALL** ON IT...

I'M **EXHAUSTED!**

AND **FAMISHED!**

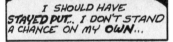

I SHOULD HAVE **STAYED PUT**... I DON'T STAND A CHANCE ON MY **OWN**...

RUMMBLE...

?!? WHAT'S **THAT**? SOUNDS LIKE A **TRUCK!**

THAT GIVES ME AN **IDEA**...

SPROING!

RUMBLE...

I'LL USE MY BODY TO **BLOCK THE ROAD**...

THAT WAY THEY'LL **HAVE** TO STOP AND GIVE ME A RIDE...

OR THEY'LL RUN OVER ME AND **KILL ME**...

EITHER WAY I COME OUT **AHEAD**...

...BURRUMBBLE...

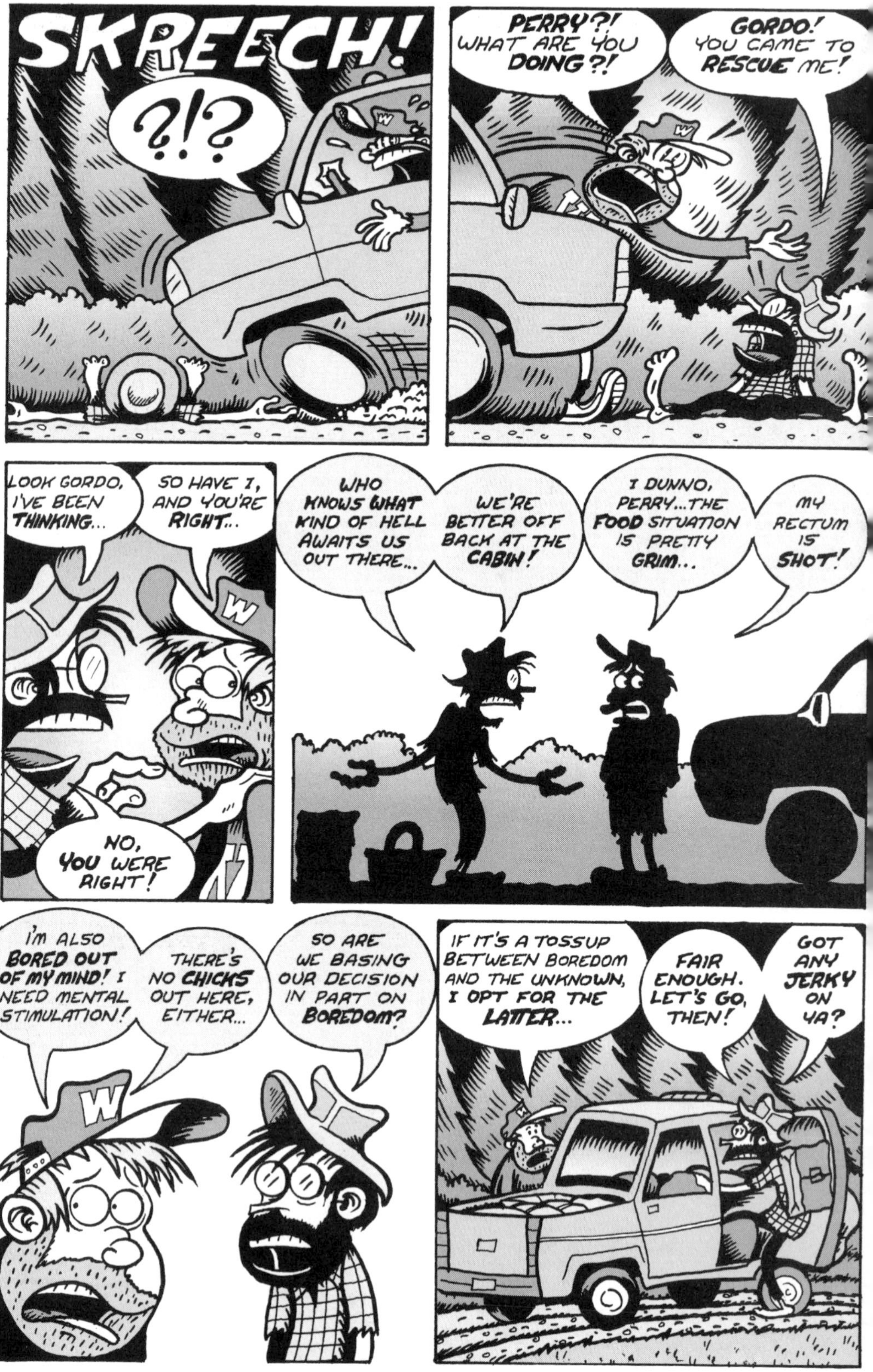
SKREECH!
?!?
PERRY?! WHAT ARE YOU DOING?!
GORDO! YOU CAME TO RESCUE ME!
LOOK GORDO, I'VE BEEN THINKING...
SO HAVE I, AND YOU'RE RIGHT...
NO, YOU WERE RIGHT!
WHO KNOWS WHAT KIND OF HELL AWAITS US OUT THERE...
WE'RE BETTER OFF BACK AT THE CABIN!
I DUNNO, PERRY...THE FOOD SITUATION IS PRETTY GRIM...
MY RECTUM IS SHOT!
I'M ALSO BORED OUT OF MY MIND! I NEED MENTAL STIMULATION!
THERE'S NO CHICKS OUT HERE, EITHER...
SO ARE WE BASING OUR DECISION IN PART ON BOREDOM?
IF IT'S A TOSSUP BETWEEN BOREDOM AND THE UNKNOWN, I OPT FOR THE LATTER...
FAIR ENOUGH. LET'S GO, THEN!
GOT ANY JERKY ON YA?

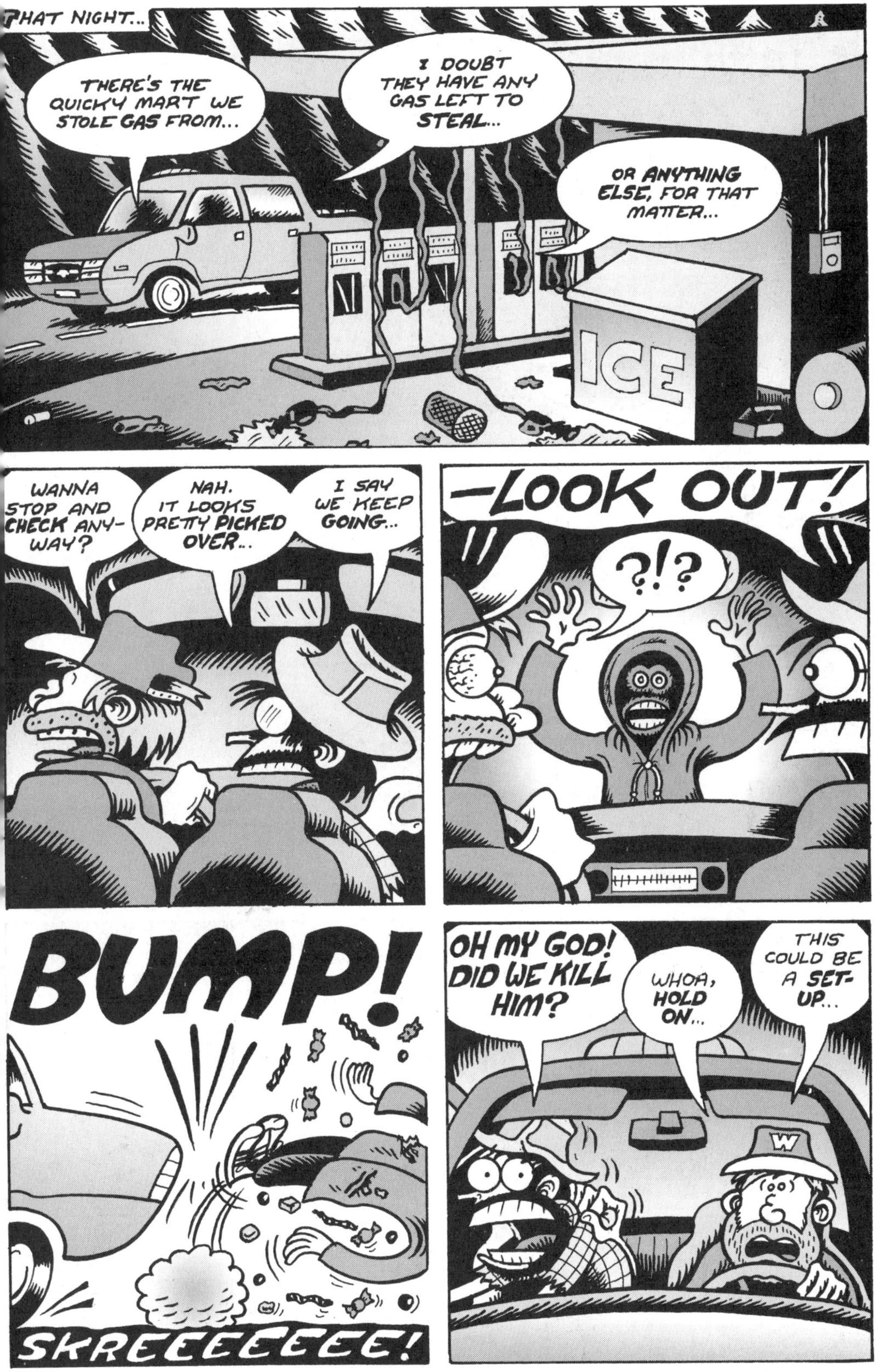
THAT NIGHT...
THERE'S THE QUICKY MART WE STOLE GAS FROM...
I DOUBT THEY HAVE ANY GAS LEFT TO STEAL...
OR ANYTHING ELSE, FOR THAT MATTER...
ICE
WANNA STOP AND CHECK ANY-WAY?
NAH. IT LOOKS PRETTY PICKED OVER...
I SAY WE KEEP GOING...
—LOOK OUT!
?!?
BUMP!
SKREEEEEEEE!
OH MY GOD! DID WE KILL HIM?
WHOA, HOLD ON...
THIS COULD BE A SET-UP...
W

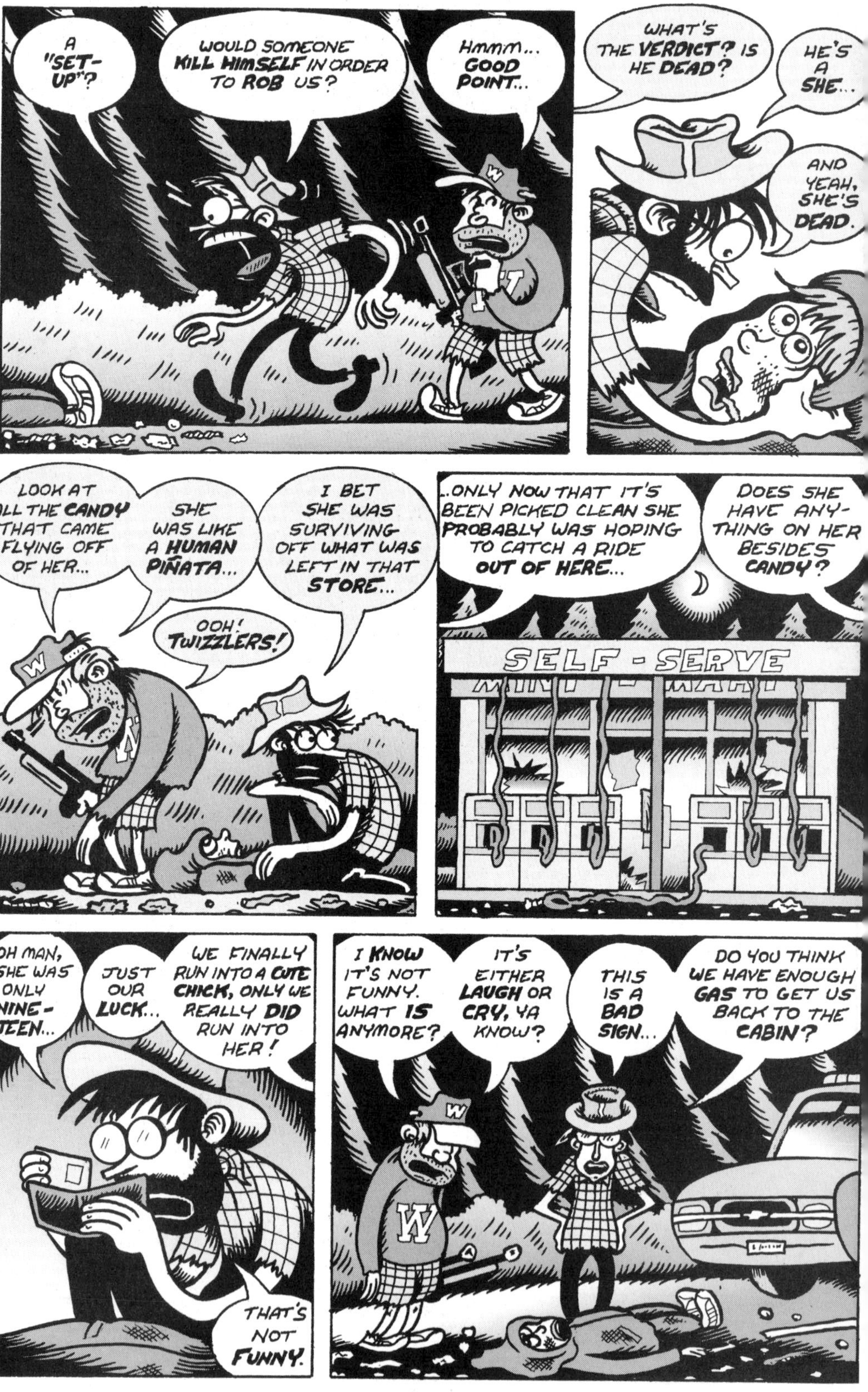
A "SET-UP"?
WOULD SOMEONE KILL HIMSELF IN ORDER TO ROB US?
Hmmm... GOOD POINT...
WHAT'S THE VERDICT? IS HE DEAD?
HE'S A SHE...
AND YEAH, SHE'S DEAD.
LOOK AT ALL THE CANDY THAT CAME FLYING OFF OF HER...
SHE WAS LIKE A HUMAN PIÑATA...
I BET SHE WAS SURVIVING OFF WHAT WAS LEFT IN THAT STORE...
OOH! TWIZZLERS!
..ONLY NOW THAT IT'S BEEN PICKED CLEAN SHE PROBABLY WAS HOPING TO CATCH A RIDE OUT OF HERE...
DOES SHE HAVE ANYTHING ON HER BESIDES CANDY?
SELF - SERVE
OH MAN, SHE WAS ONLY NINETEEN...
JUST OUR LUCK...
WE FINALLY RUN INTO A CUTE CHICK, ONLY WE REALLY DID RUN INTO HER!
THAT'S NOT FUNNY.
I KNOW IT'S NOT FUNNY. WHAT IS ANYMORE?
IT'S EITHER LAUGH OR CRY, YA KNOW?
THIS IS A BAD SIGN...
DO YOU THINK WE HAVE ENOUGH GAS TO GET US BACK TO THE CABIN?

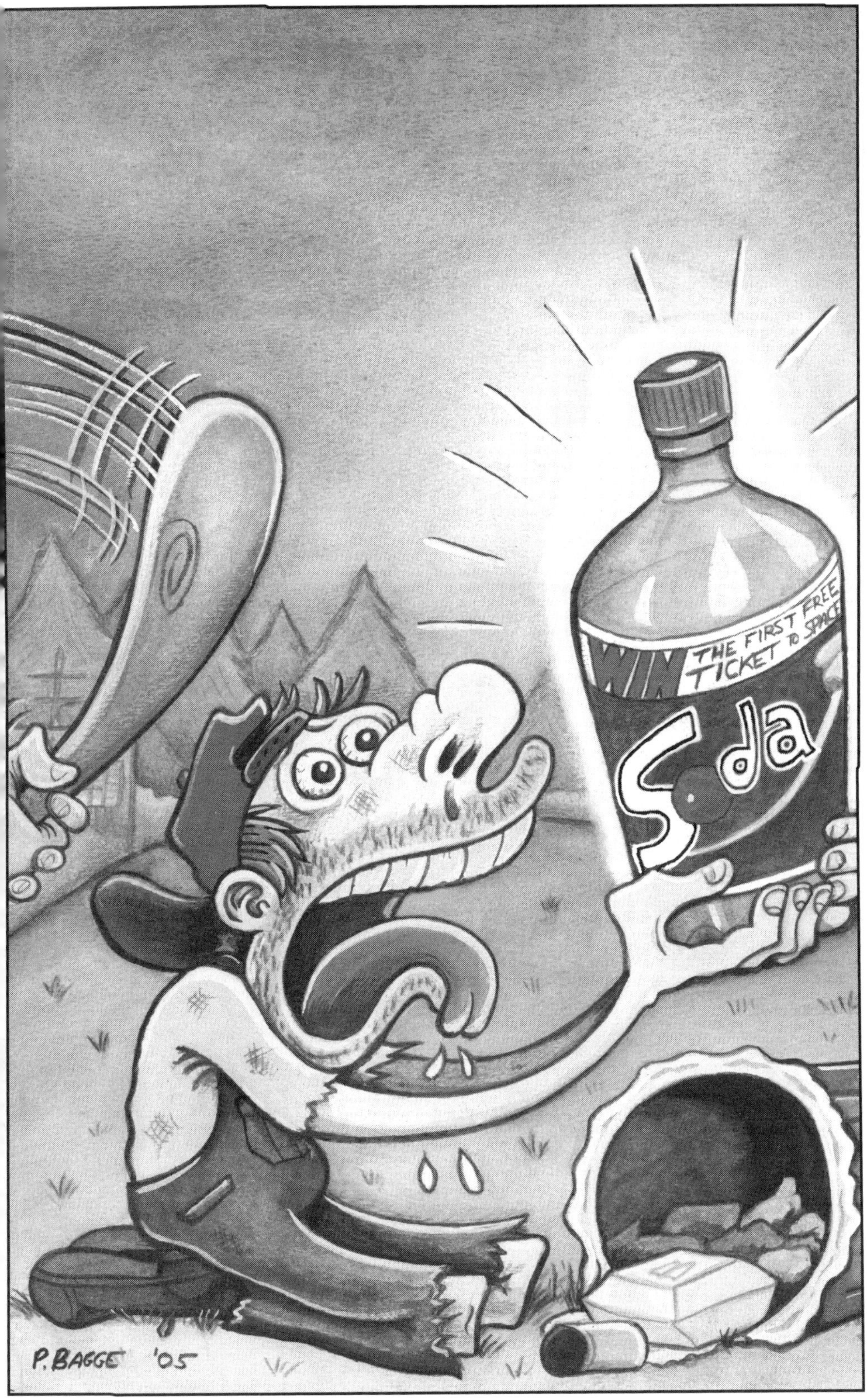
WIN
THE FIRST FREE TICKET TO SPACE
Soda
P. BAGGE '05

Chapter 3

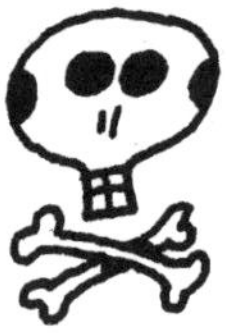

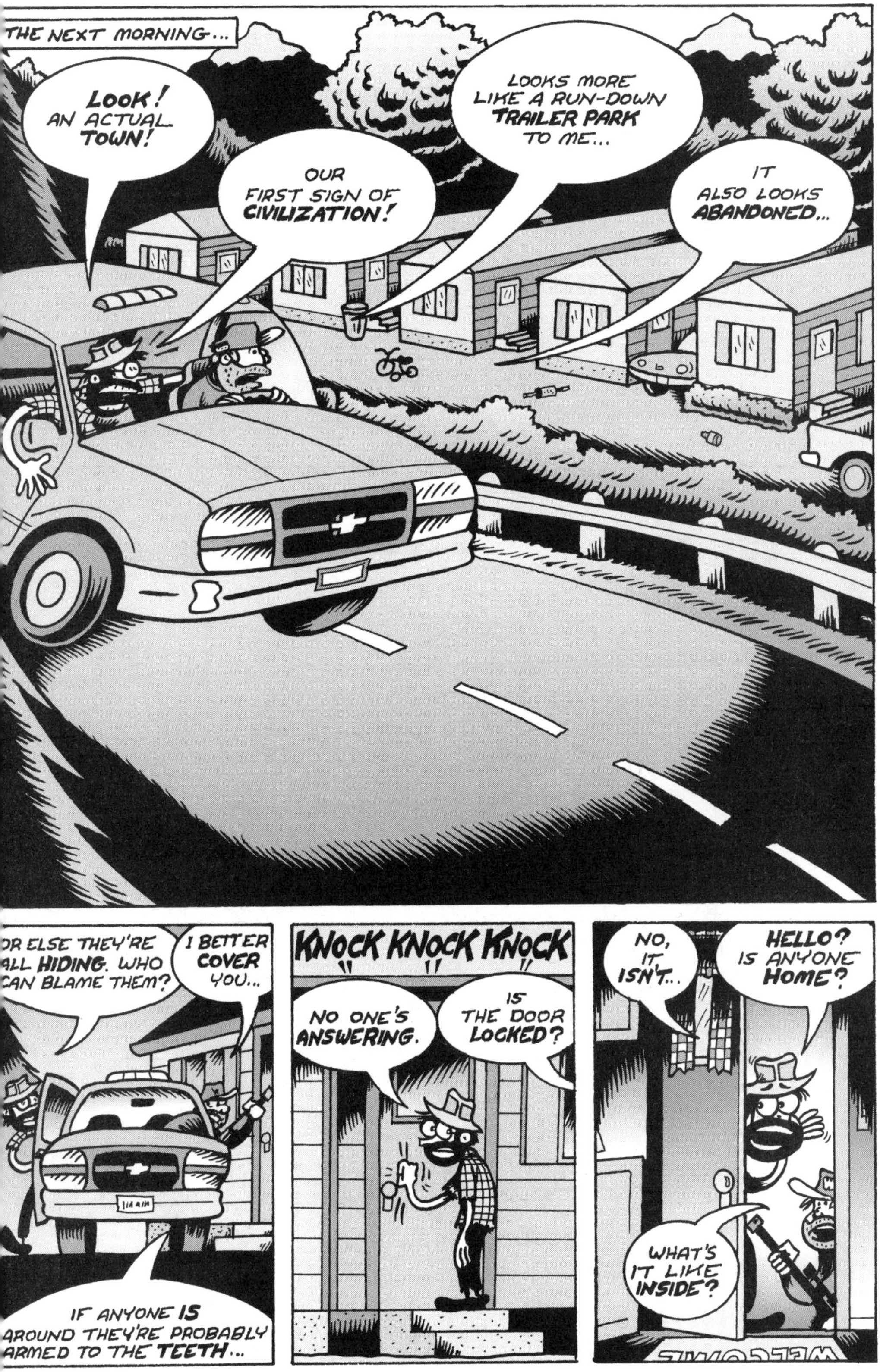
THE NEXT MORNING...
LOOK! AN ACTUAL TOWN!
OUR FIRST SIGN OF CIVILIZATION!
LOOKS MORE LIKE A RUN-DOWN TRAILER PARK TO ME...
IT ALSO LOOKS ABANDONED...
OR ELSE THEY'RE ALL HIDING. WHO CAN BLAME THEM?
I BETTER COVER YOU...
IF ANYONE IS AROUND THEY'RE PROBABLY ARMED TO THE TEETH...
KNOCK KNOCK KNOCK
NO ONE'S ANSWERING.
IS THE DOOR LOCKED?
NO, IT ISN'T...
HELLO? IS ANYONE HOME?
WHAT'S IT LIKE INSIDE?

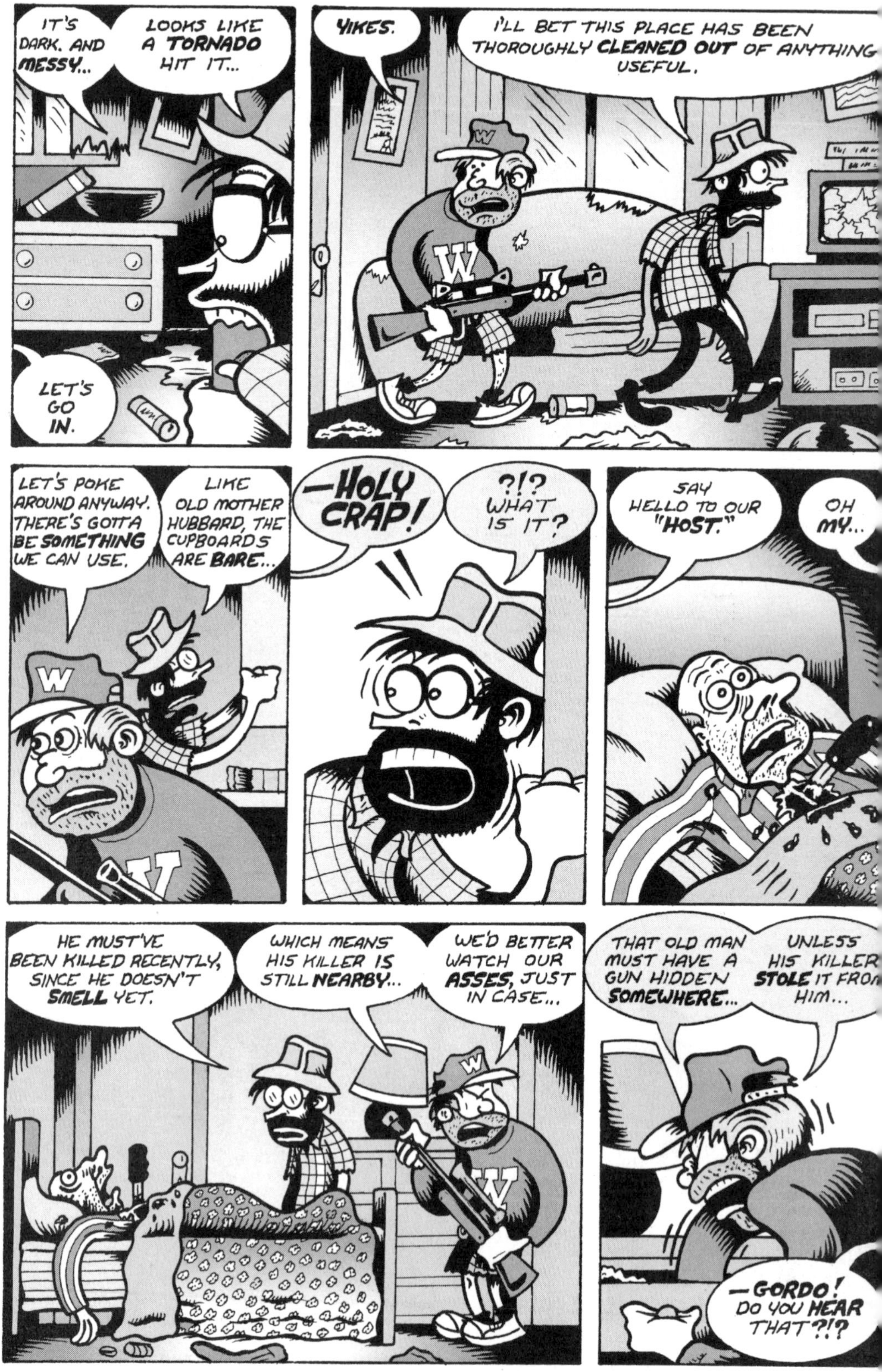
IT'S DARK. AND MESSY...
LOOKS LIKE A TORNADO HIT IT...
LET'S GO IN.
YIKES.
I'LL BET THIS PLACE HAS BEEN THOROUGHLY CLEANED OUT OF ANYTHING USEFUL.
LET'S POKE AROUND ANYWAY. THERE'S GOTTA BE SOMETHING WE CAN USE.
LIKE OLD MOTHER HUBBARD, THE CUPBOARDS ARE BARE...
—HOLY CRAP!
?!? WHAT IS IT?
SAY HELLO TO OUR "HOST."
OH MY...
HE MUST'VE BEEN KILLED RECENTLY, SINCE HE DOESN'T SMELL YET.
WHICH MEANS HIS KILLER IS STILL NEARBY...
WE'D BETTER WATCH OUR ASSES, JUST IN CASE...
THAT OLD MAN MUST HAVE A GUN HIDDEN SOMEWHERE...
UNLESS HIS KILLER STOLE IT FROM HIM...
—GORDO! DO YOU HEAR THAT?!?

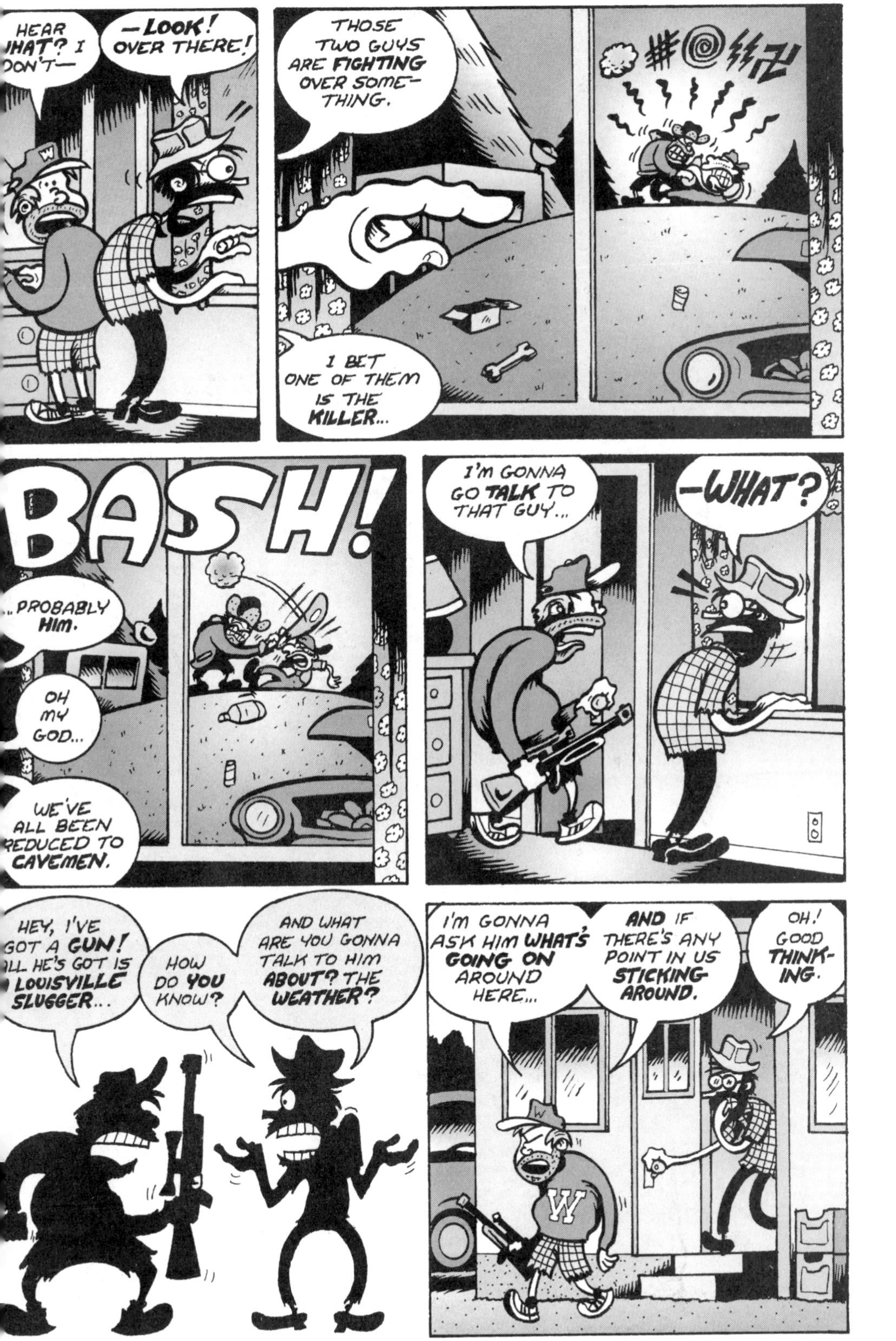
HEAR WHAT? I DON'T—
—LOOK! OVER THERE!
THOSE TWO GUYS ARE FIGHTING OVER SOMETHING.
I BET ONE OF THEM IS THE KILLER...
BASH!
...PROBABLY HIM.
OH MY GOD...
WE'VE ALL BEEN REDUCED TO CAVEMEN.
I'M GONNA GO TALK TO THAT GUY...
—WHAT?
HEY, I'VE GOT A GUN! ALL HE'S GOT IS LOUISVILLE SLUGGER...
HOW DO YOU KNOW?
AND WHAT ARE YOU GONNA TALK TO HIM ABOUT? THE WEATHER?
I'M GONNA ASK HIM WHAT'S GOING ON AROUND HERE...
AND IF THERE'S ANY POINT IN US STICKING AROUND.
OH! GOOD THINKING.

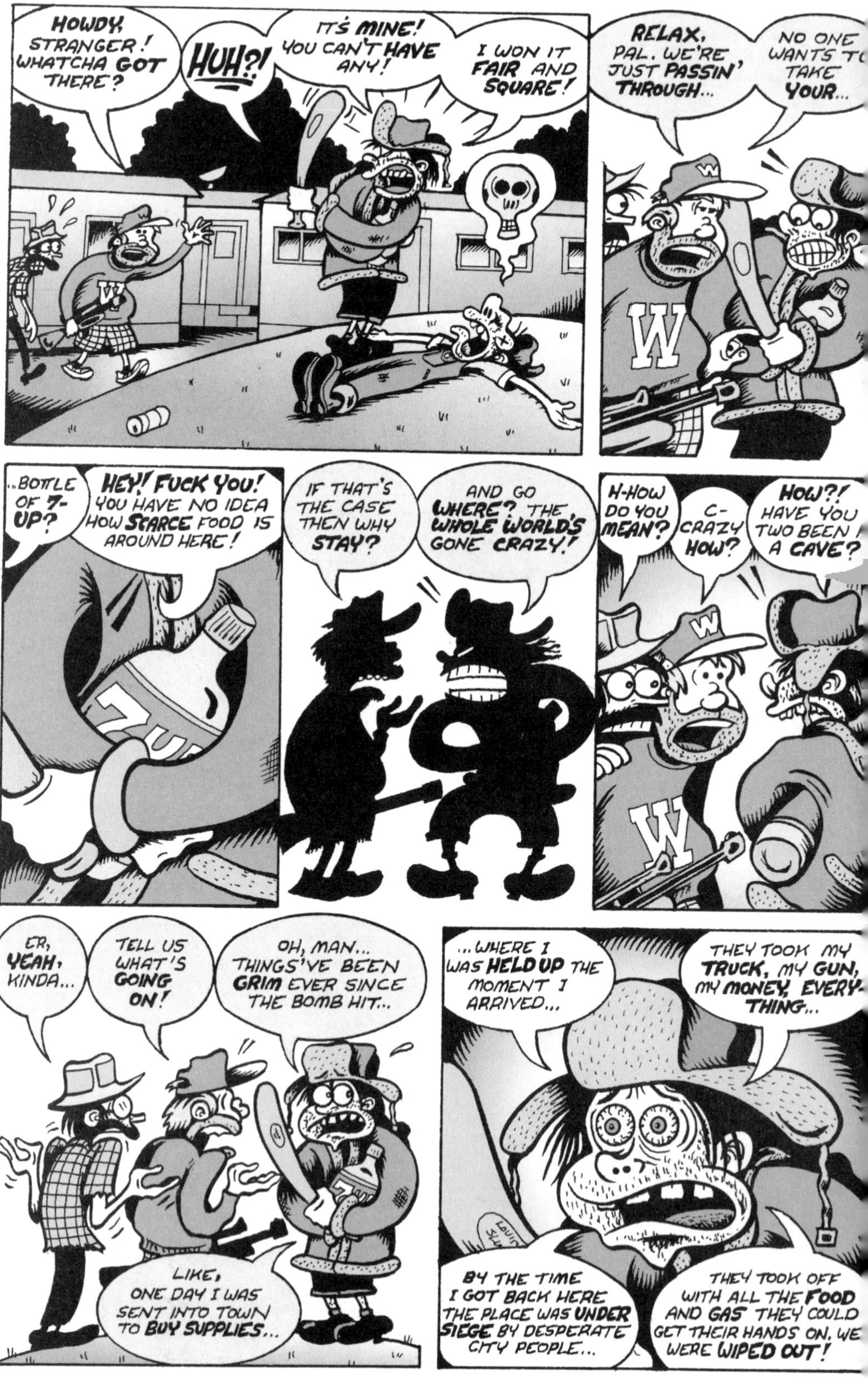

HOWDY, STRANGER! WHATCHA GOT THERE?
HUH?!
IT'S MINE! YOU CAN'T HAVE ANY!
I WON IT FAIR AND SQUARE!
RELAX, PAL. WE'RE JUST PASSIN' THROUGH...
NO ONE WANTS TO TAKE YOUR...
...BOTTLE OF 7-UP?
HEY! FUCK YOU! YOU HAVE NO IDEA HOW SCARCE FOOD IS AROUND HERE!
IF THAT'S THE CASE THEN WHY STAY?
AND GO WHERE? THE WHOLE WORLD'S GONE CRAZY!
H-HOW DO YOU MEAN?
C-CRAZY HOW?
HOW?! HAVE YOU TWO BEEN IN A CAVE?
ER, YEAH, KINDA...
TELL US WHAT'S GOING ON!
OH, MAN... THINGS'VE BEEN GRIM EVER SINCE THE BOMB HIT...
LIKE, ONE DAY I WAS SENT INTO TOWN TO BUY SUPPLIES...
...WHERE I WAS HELD UP THE MOMENT I ARRIVED...
THEY TOOK MY TRUCK, MY GUN, MY MONEY, EVERY-THING...
BY THE TIME I GOT BACK HERE THE PLACE WAS UNDER SIEGE BY DESPERATE CITY PEOPLE...
THEY TOOK OFF WITH ALL THE FOOD AND GAS THEY COULD GET THEIR HANDS ON. WE WERE WIPED OUT!

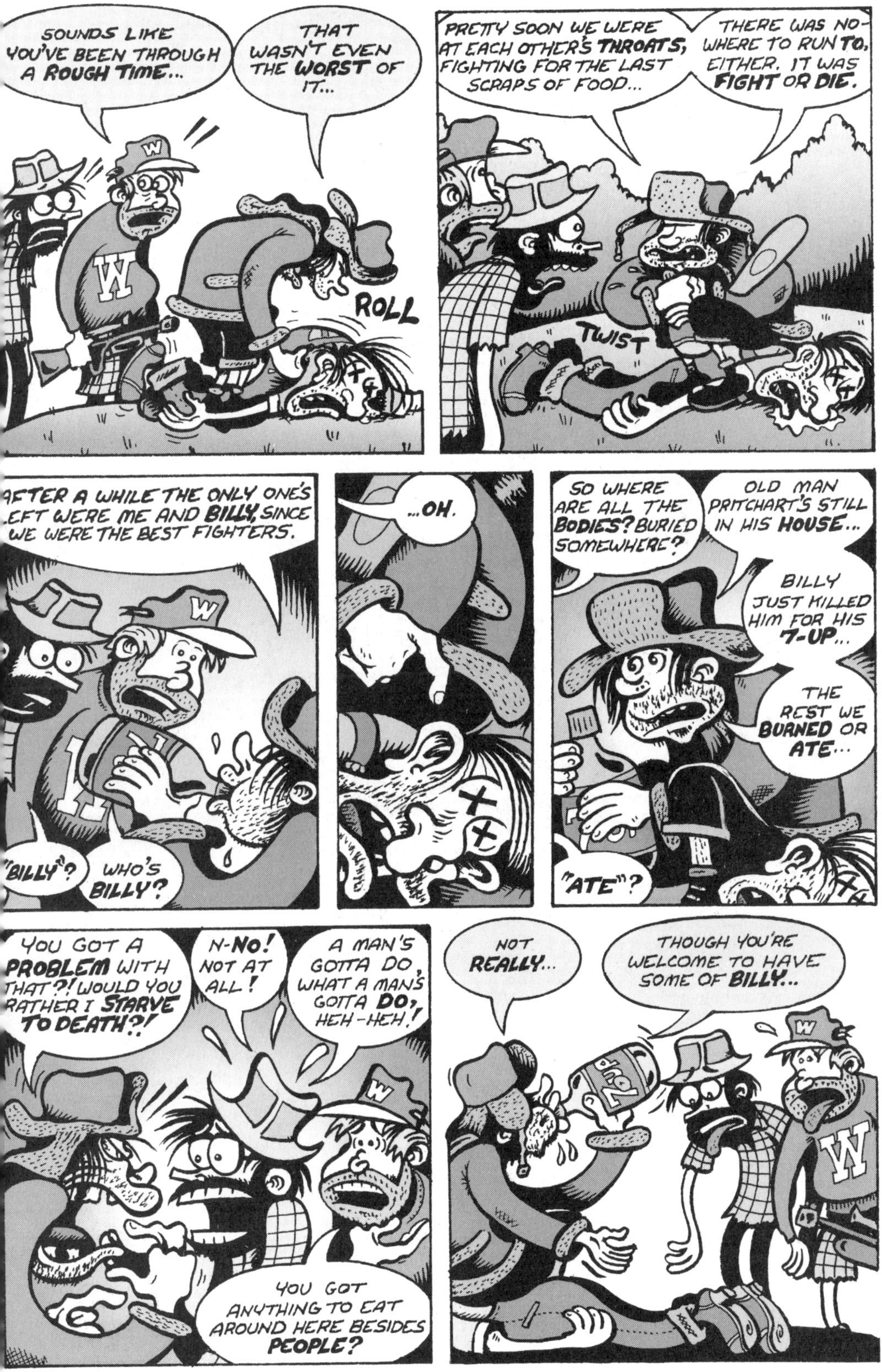
SOUNDS LIKE YOU'VE BEEN THROUGH A ROUGH TIME...
THAT WASN'T EVEN THE WORST OF IT...
ROLL
PRETTY SOON WE WERE AT EACH OTHER'S THROATS, FIGHTING FOR THE LAST SCRAPS OF FOOD...
THERE WAS NO-WHERE TO RUN TO, EITHER. IT WAS FIGHT OR DIE.
TWIST
AFTER A WHILE THE ONLY ONE'S LEFT WERE ME AND BILLY, SINCE WE WERE THE BEST FIGHTERS.
"BILLY"?
WHO'S BILLY?
...OH.
SO WHERE ARE ALL THE BODIES? BURIED SOMEWHERE?
OLD MAN PRITCHART'S STILL IN HIS HOUSE...
BILLY JUST KILLED HIM FOR HIS 7-UP...
THE REST WE BURNED OR ATE...
"ATE"?
YOU GOT A PROBLEM WITH THAT?! WOULD YOU RATHER I STARVE TO DEATH?!
N-NO! NOT AT ALL!
A MAN'S GOTTA DO, WHAT A MAN'S GOTTA DO, HEH-HEH!
YOU GOT ANYTHING TO EAT AROUND HERE BESIDES PEOPLE?
NOT REALLY...
THOUGH YOU'RE WELCOME TO HAVE SOME OF BILLY...

THAT NIGHT...

WELP, HERE WE ARE...

CAMPING OUT IN AN **ABANDONED TRAILER PARK**...

WITH **HANNIBAL THE CANNIBAL** LURKING OUTSIDE...

THESE BEDS ARE **PRETTY COMFY**, THOUGH, YA GOTTA ADMIT.

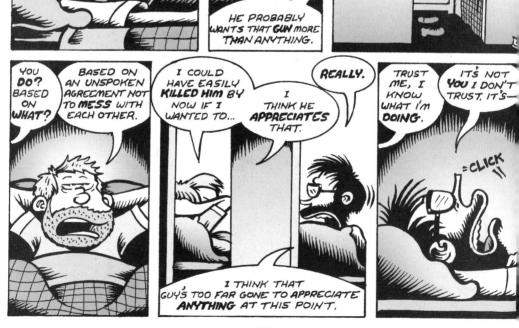

AREN'T YOU THE LEAST BIT WORRIED THAT HE'S GONNA TRY TO **KILL** US?

NAH. WHY **WOULD** HE? HE'S GOT **BILLY** TO TIDE HIM OVER FOR NOW...

BESIDES, HE WON'T MESS WITH US AS LONG AS WE GOT **OL' BETSY** HERE.

HE PROBABLY WANTS THAT **GUN** MORE THAN ANYTHING.

ALL THE MORE REASON FOR HIM TO SNEAK IN HERE WHILE WE'RE ASLEEP AND **BASH OUR BRAINS IN** WITH HIS BAT.

OH, STOP. HE AND I HAVE AN **UNDER-STANDING**.

YOU **DO?** BASED ON **WHAT?**

BASED ON AN UNSPOKEN AGREEMENT NOT TO **MESS** WITH EACH OTHER.

I COULD HAVE EASILY **KILLED HIM BY** NOW IF I WANTED TO...

I THINK HE **APPRECIATES** THAT.

REALLY.

I THINK THAT GUY'S TOO FAR GONE TO APPRECIATE **ANYTHING** AT THIS POINT.

TRUST ME, I KNOW WHAT I'M **DOING**.

IT'S NOT **YOU** I DON'T TRUST, IT'S—

=CLICK

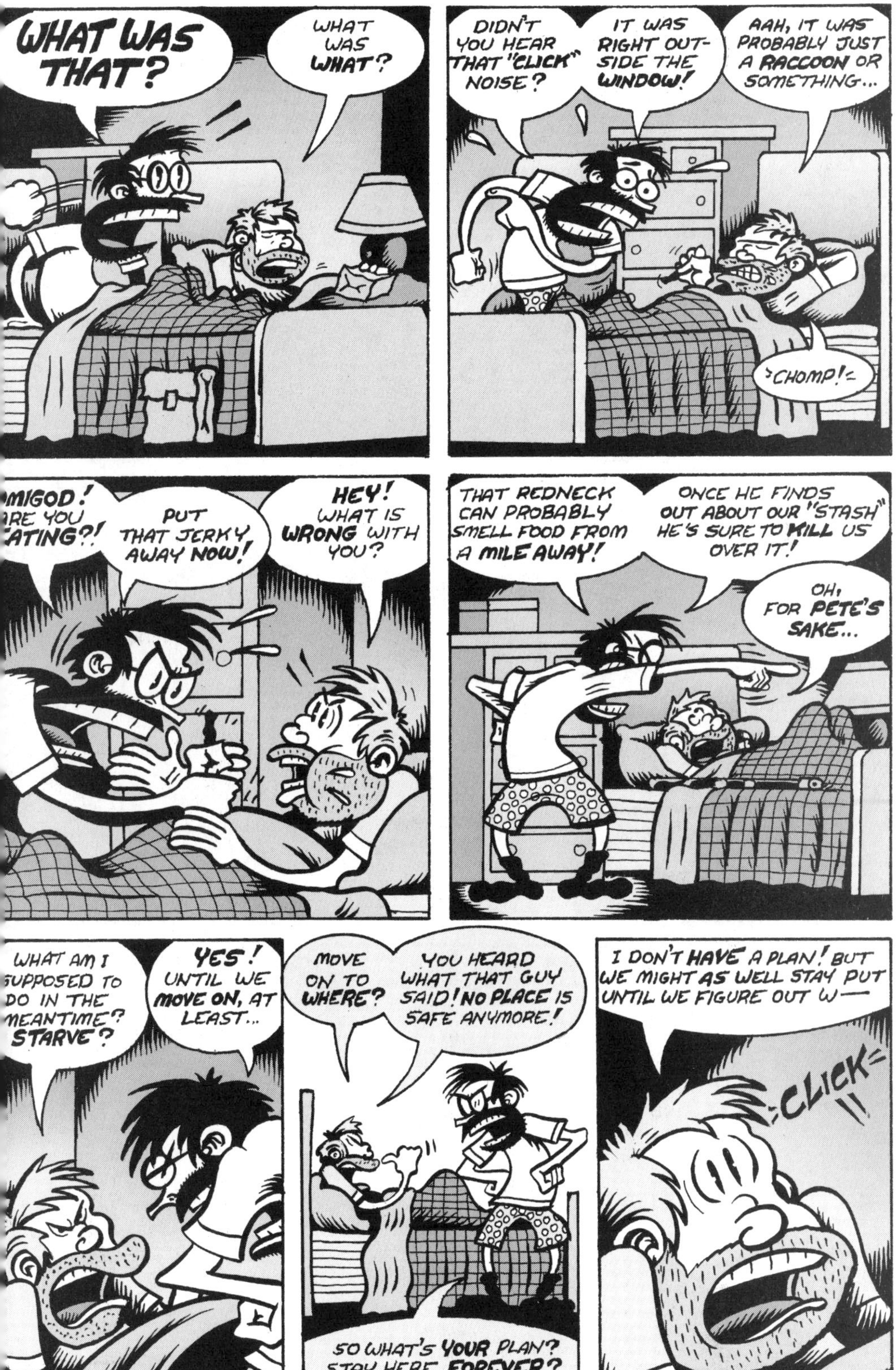
WHAT WAS THAT?
WHAT WAS WHAT?
DIDN'T YOU HEAR THAT "CLICK" NOISE?
IT WAS RIGHT OUT-SIDE THE WINDOW!
AAH, IT WAS PROBABLY JUST A RACCOON OR SOMETHING...
CHOMP!
OMIGOD! ARE YOU EATING?!
PUT THAT JERKY AWAY NOW!
HEY! WHAT IS WRONG WITH YOU?
THAT REDNECK CAN PROBABLY SMELL FOOD FROM A MILE AWAY!
ONCE HE FINDS OUT ABOUT OUR "STASH" HE'S SURE TO KILL US OVER IT!
OH, FOR PETE'S SAKE...
WHAT AM I SUPPOSED TO DO IN THE MEANTIME? STARVE?
YES! UNTIL WE MOVE ON, AT LEAST...
MOVE ON TO WHERE?
YOU HEARD WHAT THAT GUY SAID! NO PLACE IS SAFE ANYMORE!
SO WHAT'S YOUR PLAN? STAY HERE FOREVER?
I DON'T HAVE A PLAN! BUT WE MIGHT AS WELL STAY PUT UNTIL WE FIGURE OUT W—
CLICK

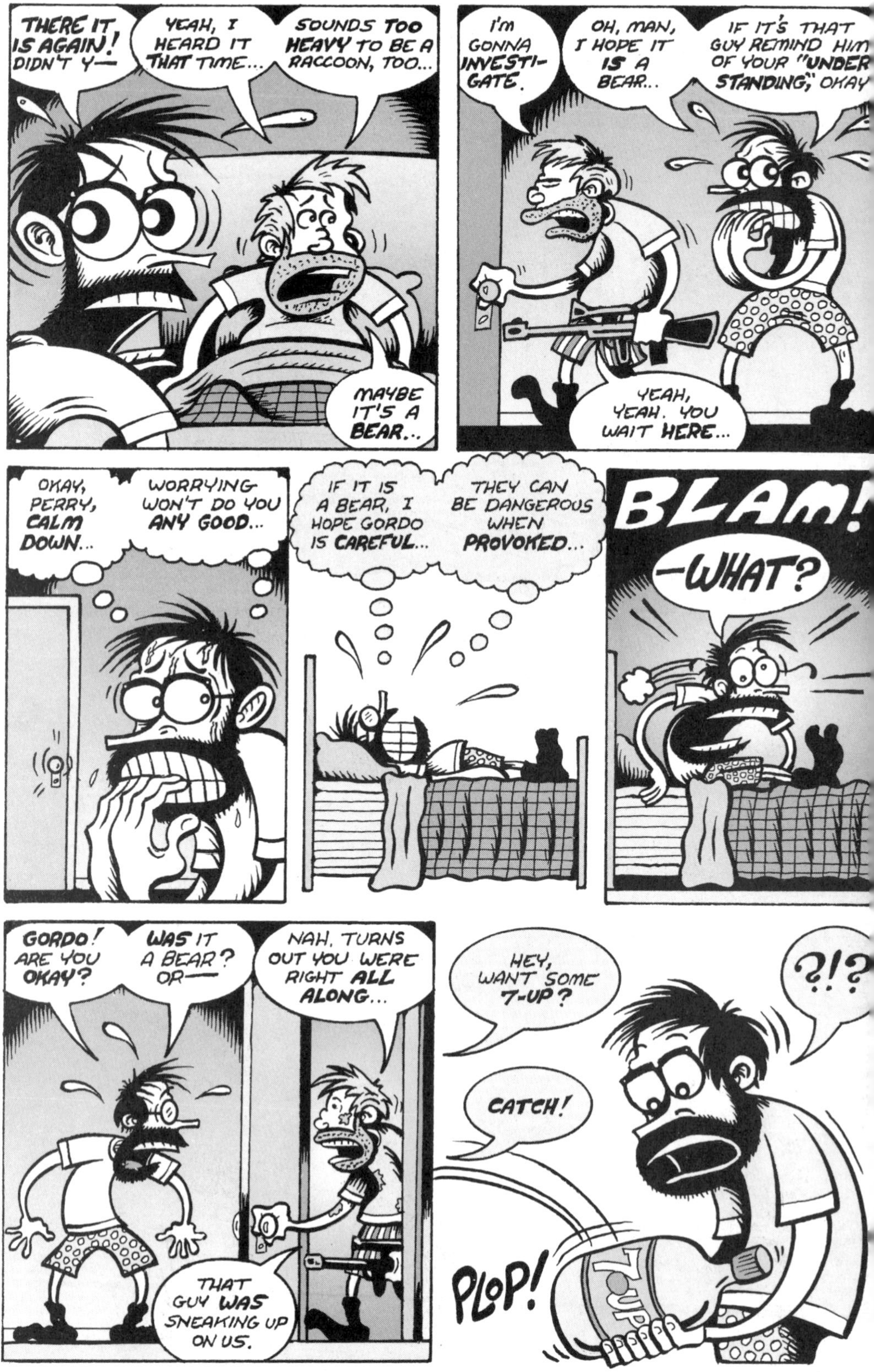

THERE IT IS AGAIN! DIDN'T Y—
YEAH, I HEARD IT THAT TIME...
SOUNDS TOO HEAVY TO BE A RACCOON, TOO...
MAYBE IT'S A BEAR...
I'M GONNA INVESTI-GATE.
OH, MAN, I HOPE IT IS A BEAR...
IF IT'S THAT GUY REMIND HIM OF YOUR "UNDER STANDING," OKAY
YEAH, YEAH. YOU WAIT HERE...
OKAY, PERRY, CALM DOWN...
WORRYING WON'T DO YOU ANY GOOD...
IF IT IS A BEAR, I HOPE GORDO IS CAREFUL...
THEY CAN BE DANGEROUS WHEN PROVOKED...
BLAM!
—WHAT?
GORDO! ARE YOU OKAY?
WAS IT A BEAR? OR—
NAH, TURNS OUT YOU WERE RIGHT ALL ALONG...
THAT GUY WAS SNEAKING UP ON US.
HEY, WANT SOME 7-UP?
?!?
CATCH!
PLOP!
7UP

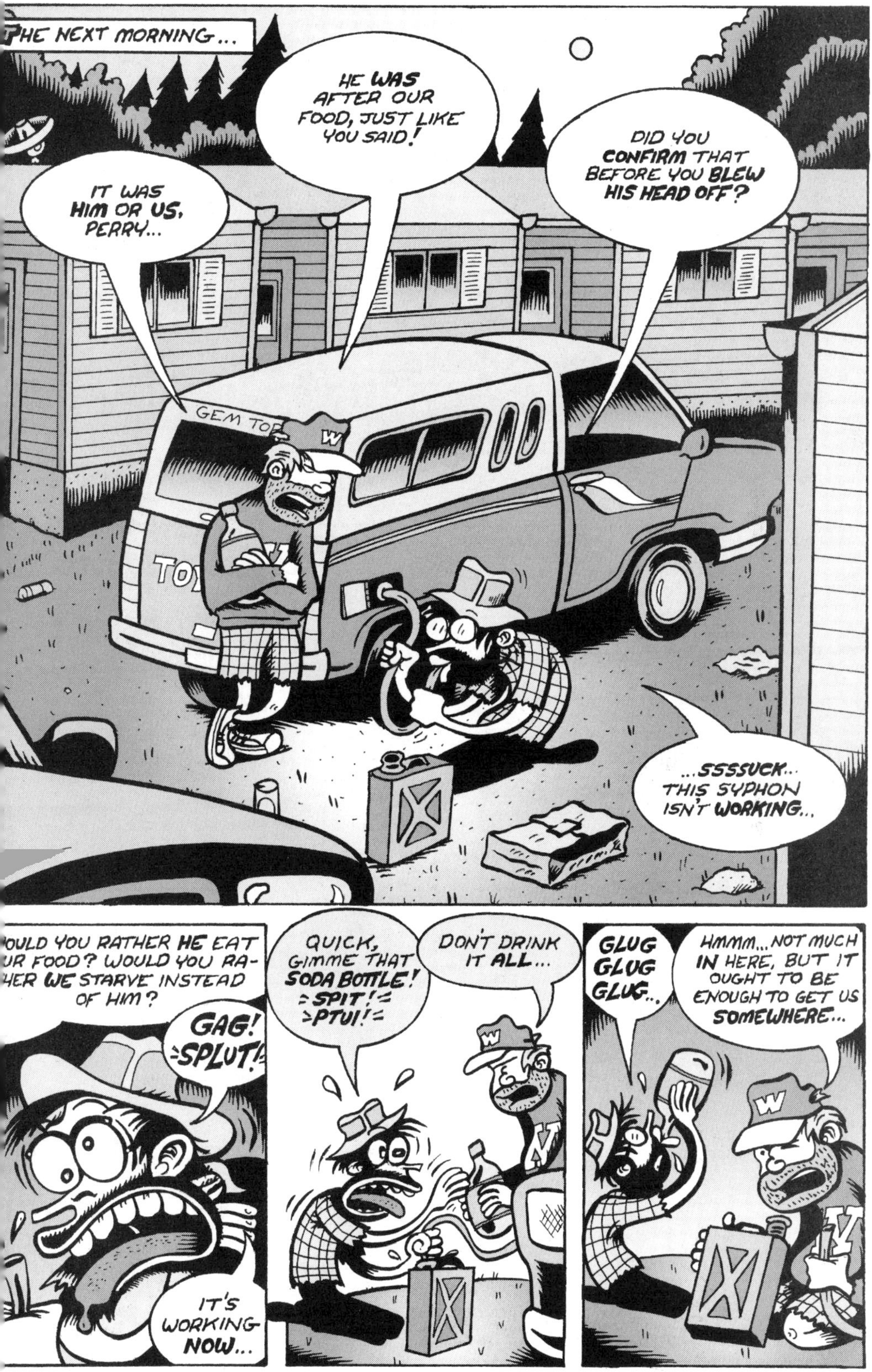
THE NEXT MORNING...
IT WAS HIM OR US, PERRY...
HE WAS AFTER OUR FOOD, JUST LIKE YOU SAID!
DID YOU CONFIRM THAT BEFORE YOU BLEW HIS HEAD OFF?
...SSSSUCK... THIS SYPHON ISN'T WORKING...
OULD YOU RATHER HE EAT UR FOOD? WOULD YOU RA- HER WE STARVE INSTEAD OF HIM?
GAG! SPLUT!
IT'S WORKING NOW...
QUICK, GIMME THAT SODA BOTTLE! SPIT! PTUI!
DON'T DRINK IT ALL...
GLUG GLUG GLUG...
HMMM... NOT MUCH IN HERE, BUT IT OUGHT TO BE ENOUGH TO GET US SOMEWHERE...

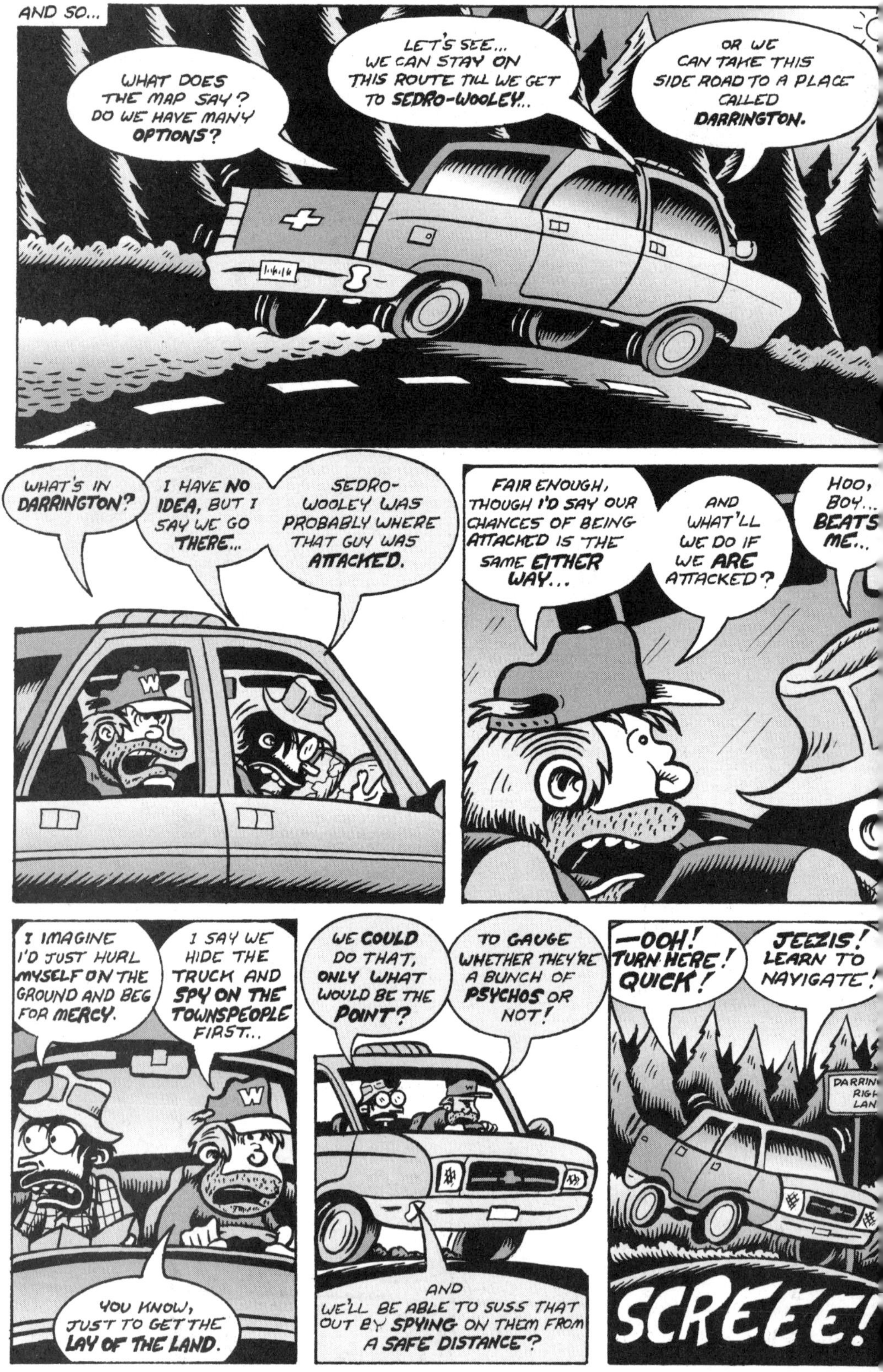
AND SO...
WHAT DOES THE MAP SAY? DO WE HAVE MANY OPTIONS?
LET'S SEE... WE CAN STAY ON THIS ROUTE TILL WE GET TO SEDRO-WOOLEY...
OR WE CAN TAKE THIS SIDE ROAD TO A PLACE CALLED DARRINGTON.
WHAT'S IN DARRINGTON?
I HAVE NO IDEA, BUT I SAY WE GO THERE...
SEDRO-WOOLEY WAS PROBABLY WHERE THAT GUY WAS ATTACKED.
FAIR ENOUGH, THOUGH I'D SAY OUR CHANCES OF BEING ATTACKED IS THE SAME EITHER WAY...
AND WHAT'LL WE DO IF WE ARE ATTACKED?
HOO, BOY... BEATS ME...
I IMAGINE I'D JUST HURL MYSELF ON THE GROUND AND BEG FOR MERCY.
I SAY WE HIDE THE TRUCK AND SPY ON THE TOWNSPEOPLE FIRST...
YOU KNOW, JUST TO GET THE LAY OF THE LAND.
WE COULD DO THAT, ONLY WHAT WOULD BE THE POINT?
TO GAUGE WHETHER THEY'RE A BUNCH OF PSYCHOS OR NOT!
AND WE'LL BE ABLE TO SUSS THAT OUT BY SPYING ON THEM FROM A SAFE DISTANCE?
—OOH! TURN HERE! QUICK!
JEEZIS! LEARN TO NAVIGATE!
SCREEE!

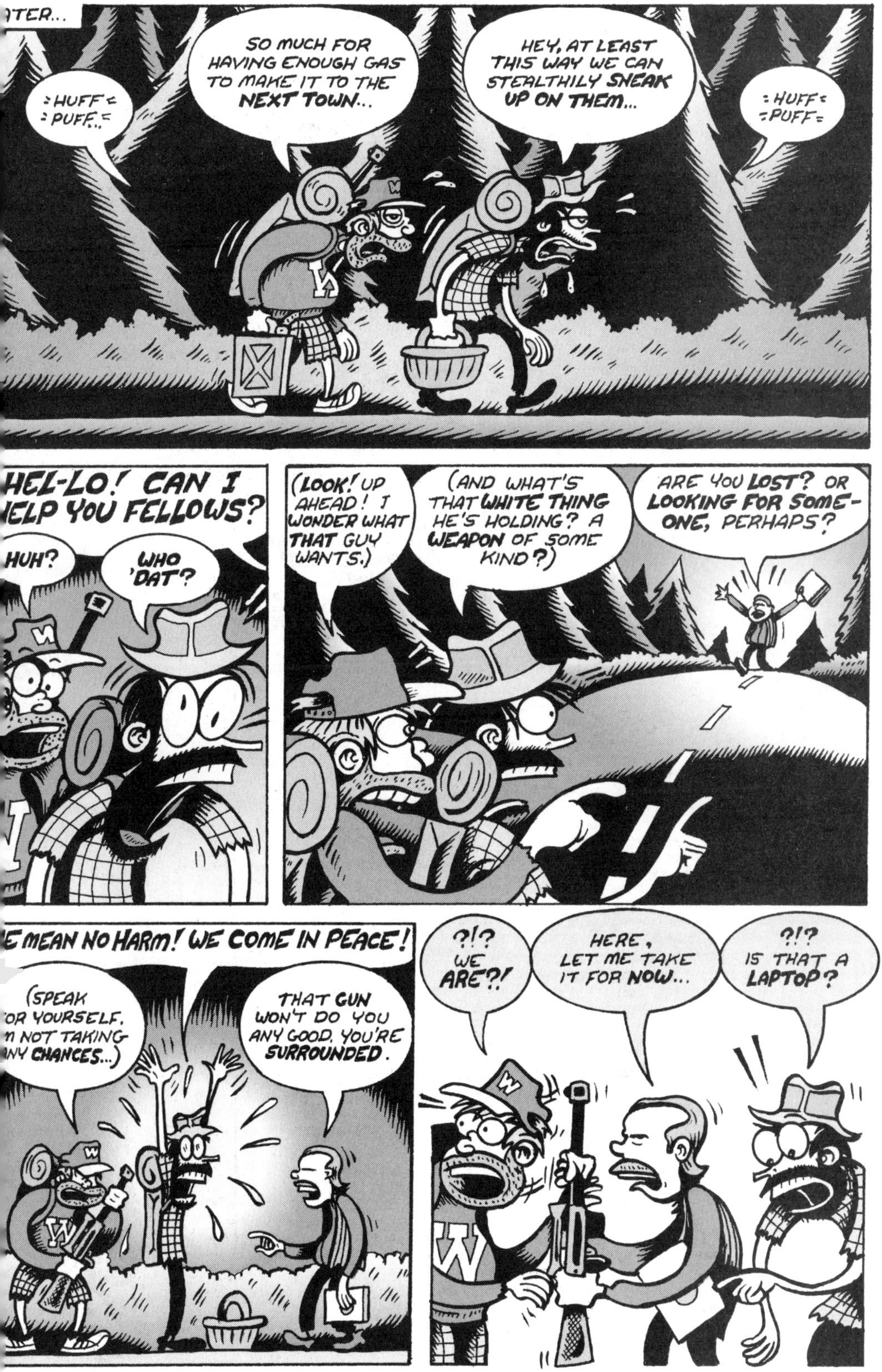

TER...
HUFF PUFF...
SO MUCH FOR HAVING ENOUGH GAS TO MAKE IT TO THE NEXT TOWN...
HEY, AT LEAST THIS WAY WE CAN STEALTHILY SNEAK UP ON THEM...
HUFF PUFF
HEL-LO! CAN I ELP YOU FELLOWS?
HUH?
WHO 'DAT'?
(LOOK! UP AHEAD! I WONDER WHAT THAT GUY WANTS.)
(AND WHAT'S THAT WHITE THING HE'S HOLDING? A WEAPON OF SOME KIND?)
ARE YOU LOST? OR LOOKING FOR SOME-ONE, PERHAPS?
E MEAN NO HARM! WE COME IN PEACE!
(SPEAK OR YOURSELF. M NOT TAKING NY CHANCES...)
THAT GUN WON'T DO YOU ANY GOOD. YOU'RE SURROUNDED.
?!? WE ARE?!
HERE, LET ME TAKE IT FOR NOW...
?!? IS THAT A LAPTOP?

WHERE ARE YOU TWO FROM?

UH... THE WOODS...

?! "THE WOODS"?

YOUR COMPUTER IS ON?

OH, YEAH. I'M SUPPOSED TO IM THE OTHERS AS TO WHAT'S GOING ON...

"IM"?

BUT.. HOW'

GENERATORS. PLUS THE MIRACLE OF WI-FI...

MY NAME'S EARNEST, BY THE WAY.

I'M GORDO...

PERRY...

WOW, ELECTRICITY. I'M IMPRESSED.

SO, HOW LONG HAVE YOU BEEN IN THE WOODS?

SINCE JUST BEFORE THE BOMB HIT...

WE'RE ORIGINALLY FROM THE CITY.

WE WERE CAMPING DEEP IN TH MOUNTAIN WHEN DISASTE STRUCK.

CONSIDER YOURSELVES LUCKY...

YOU'RE IN FAR BETTER SHAPE THAN MOST STRAGGLERS WE'VE COME ACROSS.

IN FACT, WE'VE HAD TO DO SEVERAL MERCY KILLINGS.

REALLY?

WHO IS THIS "WE" YOU KEEP REFERRING TO?

ME AND SOME FRIENDS HAVE A COMPOUND NEAR-BY...

I'LL TAKE YOU THERE IF YOU'D LIKE.

SURE! WHAT KIND OF FOOD DO YOU HAVE THERE?

I THOUGHT YO SAID WE WER SURROUNDEI

I LIED.

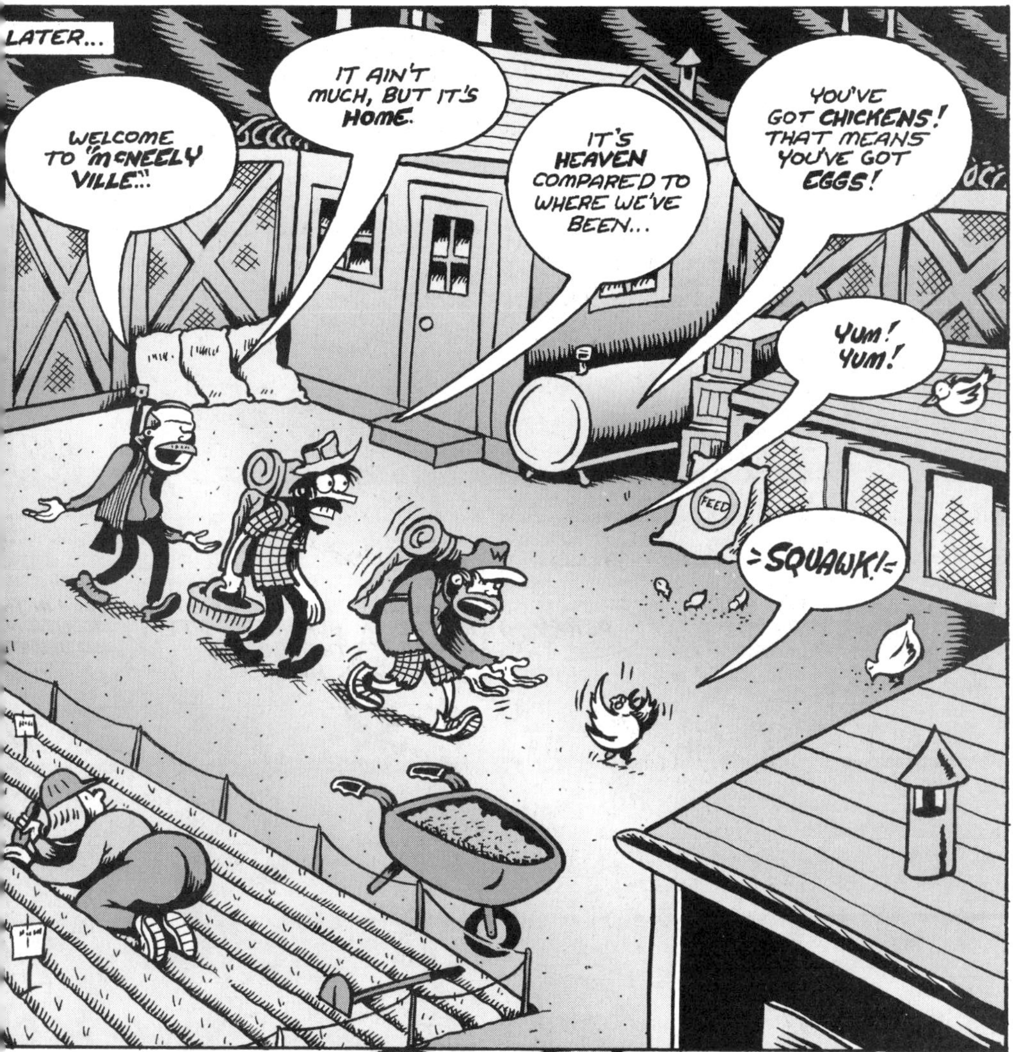
LATER...
WELCOME TO "McNEELY VILLE"!
IT AIN'T MUCH, BUT IT'S HOME.
IT'S HEAVEN COMPARED TO WHERE WE'VE BEEN...
YOU'VE GOT CHICKENS! THAT MEANS YOU'VE GOT EGGS!
YUM! YUM!
SQUAWK!
FEED

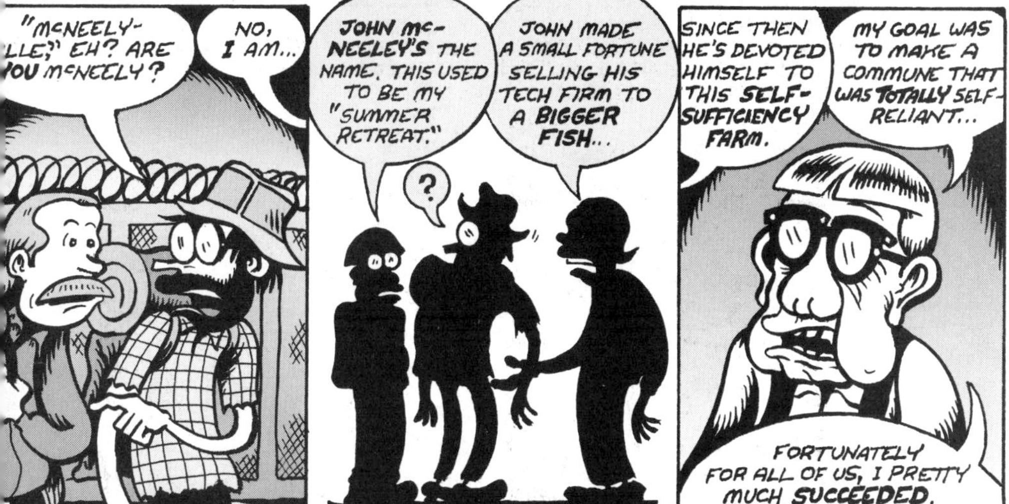
"McNEELY-LLE," EH? ARE YOU McNEELY?
NO, I AM...
JOHN McNEELEY'S THE NAME. THIS USED TO BE MY "SUMMER RETREAT."
?
JOHN MADE A SMALL FORTUNE SELLING HIS TECH FIRM TO A BIGGER FISH...
SINCE THEN HE'S DEVOTED HIMSELF TO THIS SELF-SUFFICIENCY FARM.
MY GOAL WAS TO MAKE A COMMUNE THAT WAS TOTALLY SELF-RELIANT...
FORTUNATELY FOR ALL OF US, I PRETTY MUCH SUCCEEDED.

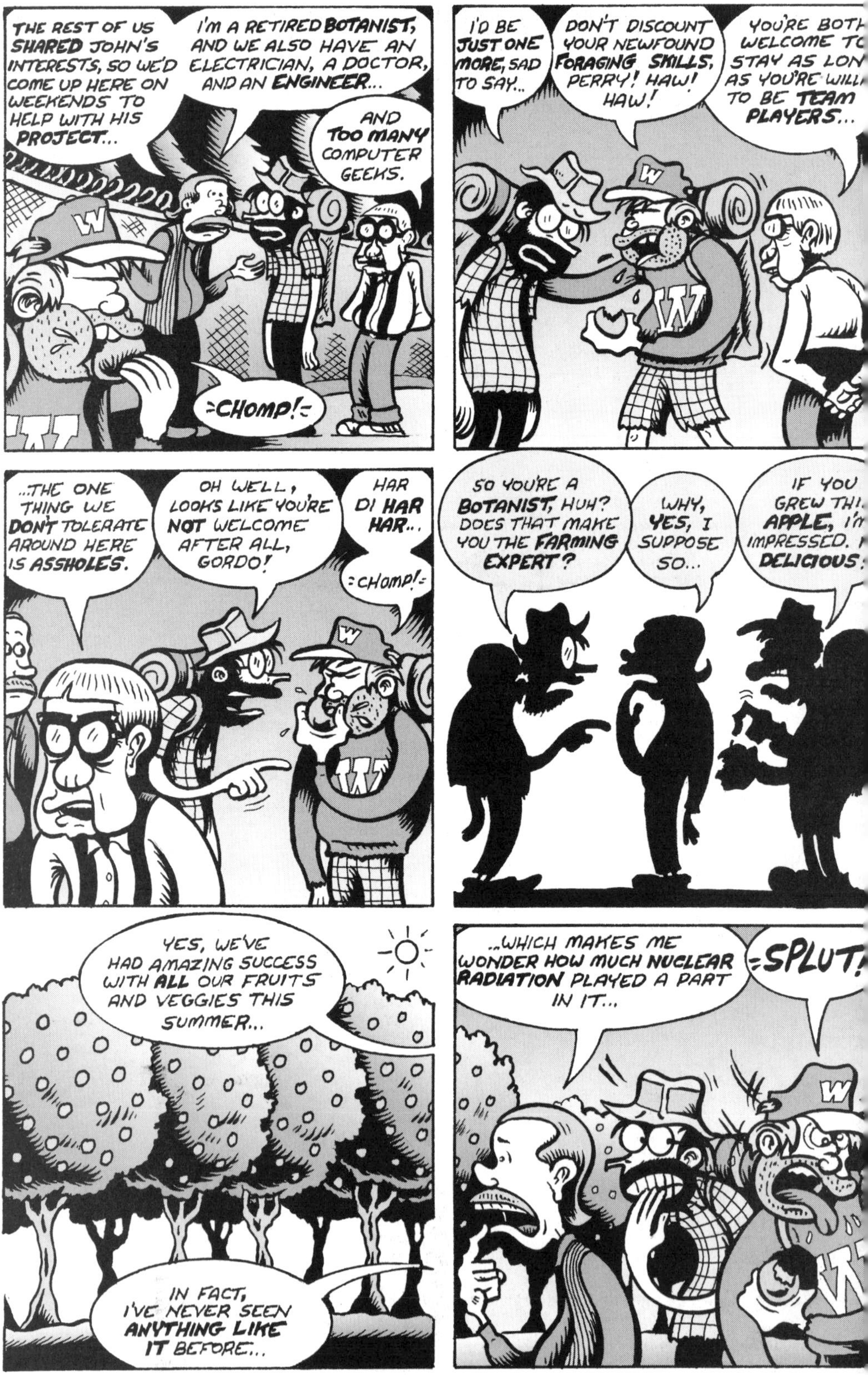
THE REST OF US SHARED JOHN'S INTERESTS, SO WE'D COME UP HERE ON WEEKENDS TO HELP WITH HIS PROJECT...
I'M A RETIRED BOTANIST, AND WE ALSO HAVE AN ELECTRICIAN, A DOCTOR, AND AN ENGINEER...
AND TOO MANY COMPUTER GEEKS.
CHOMP!
I'D BE JUST ONE MORE, SAD TO SAY...
DON'T DISCOUNT YOUR NEWFOUND FORAGING SKILLS, PERRY! HAW! HAW!
YOU'RE BOT WELCOME T STAY AS LON AS YOU'RE WILL TO BE TEAM PLAYERS...
...THE ONE THING WE DON'T TOLERATE AROUND HERE IS ASSHOLES.
OH WELL, LOOKS LIKE YOU'RE NOT WELCOME AFTER ALL, GORDO!
HAR DI HAR HAR...
CHOMP!
SO YOU'RE A BOTANIST, HUH? DOES THAT MAKE YOU THE FARMING EXPERT?
WHY, YES, I SUPPOSE SO...
IF YOU GREW THI APPLE, I' IMPRESSED. DELICIOUS
YES, WE'VE HAD AMAZING SUCCESS WITH ALL OUR FRUITS AND VEGGIES THIS SUMMER...
IN FACT, I'VE NEVER SEEN ANYTHING LIKE IT BEFORE...
...WHICH MAKES ME WONDER HOW MUCH NUCLEAR RADIATION PLAYED A PART IN IT...
SPLUT!

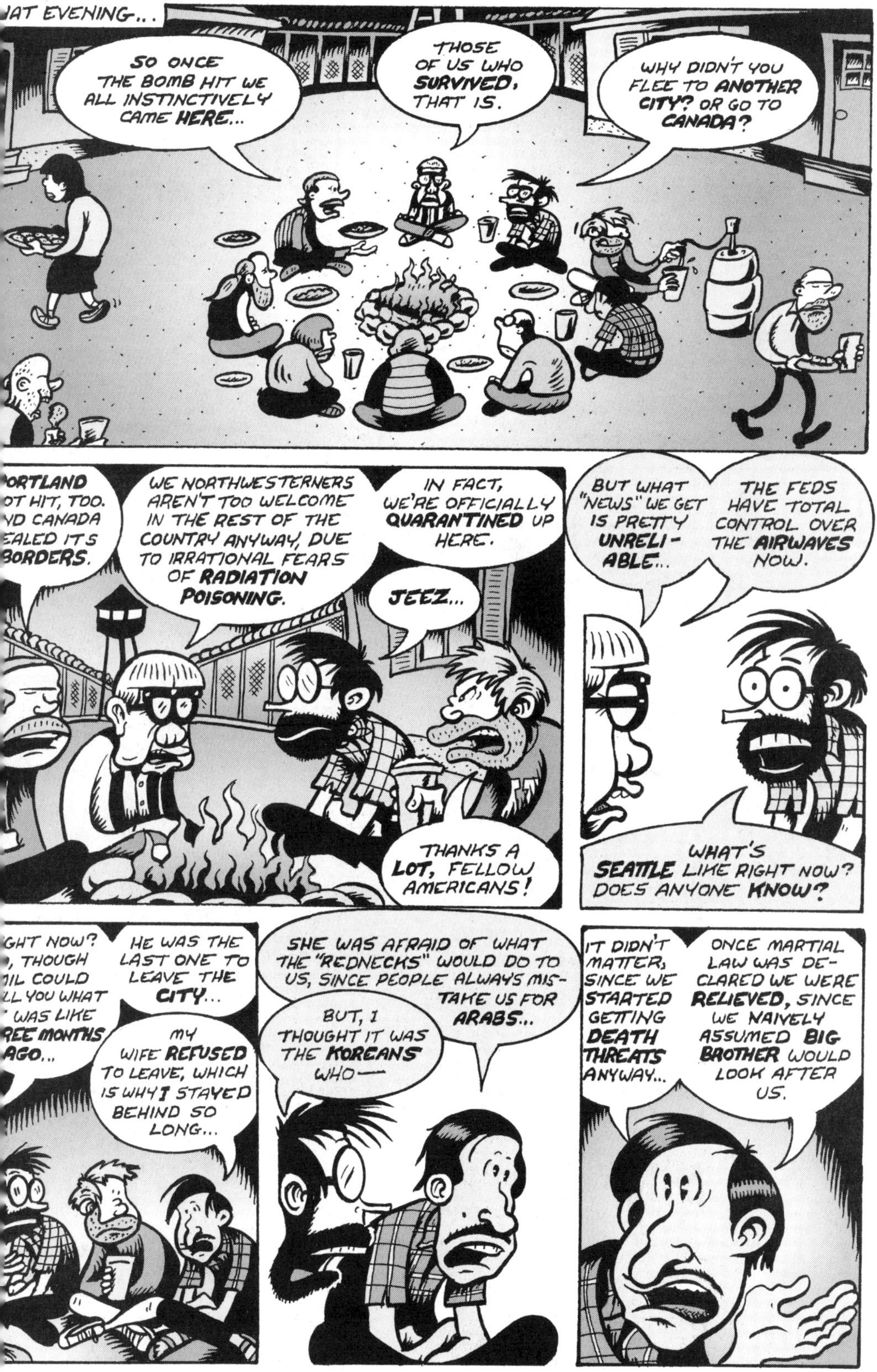

AT EVENING...
SO ONCE THE BOMB HIT WE ALL INSTINCTIVELY CAME HERE...
THOSE OF US WHO SURVIVED, THAT IS.
WHY DIDN'T YOU FLEE TO ANOTHER CITY? OR GO TO CANADA?
ORTLAND OT HIT, TOO. ND CANADA EALED ITS BORDERS.
WE NORTHWESTERNERS AREN'T TOO WELCOME IN THE REST OF THE COUNTRY ANYWAY, DUE TO IRRATIONAL FEARS OF RADIATION POISONING.
IN FACT, WE'RE OFFICIALLY QUARANTINED UP HERE.
JEEZ...
THANKS A LOT, FELLOW AMERICANS!
BUT WHAT "NEWS" WE GET IS PRETTY UNRELI-ABLE...
THE FEDS HAVE TOTAL CONTROL OVER THE AIRWAVES NOW.
WHAT'S SEATTLE LIKE RIGHT NOW? DOES ANYONE KNOW?
GHT NOW? , THOUGH IL COULD LL YOU WHAT WAS LIKE REE MONTHS AGO...
HE WAS THE LAST ONE TO LEAVE THE CITY...
MY WIFE REFUSED TO LEAVE, WHICH IS WHY I STAYED BEHIND SO LONG...
SHE WAS AFRAID OF WHAT THE "REDNECKS" WOULD DO TO US, SINCE PEOPLE ALWAYS MIS-TAKE US FOR ARABS...
BUT, I THOUGHT IT WAS THE KOREANS WHO—
IT DIDN'T MATTER, SINCE WE STARTED GETTING DEATH THREATS ANYWAY...
ONCE MARTIAL LAW WAS DE-CLARED WE WERE RELIEVED, SINCE WE NAIVELY ASSUMED BIG BROTHER WOULD LOOK AFTER US.

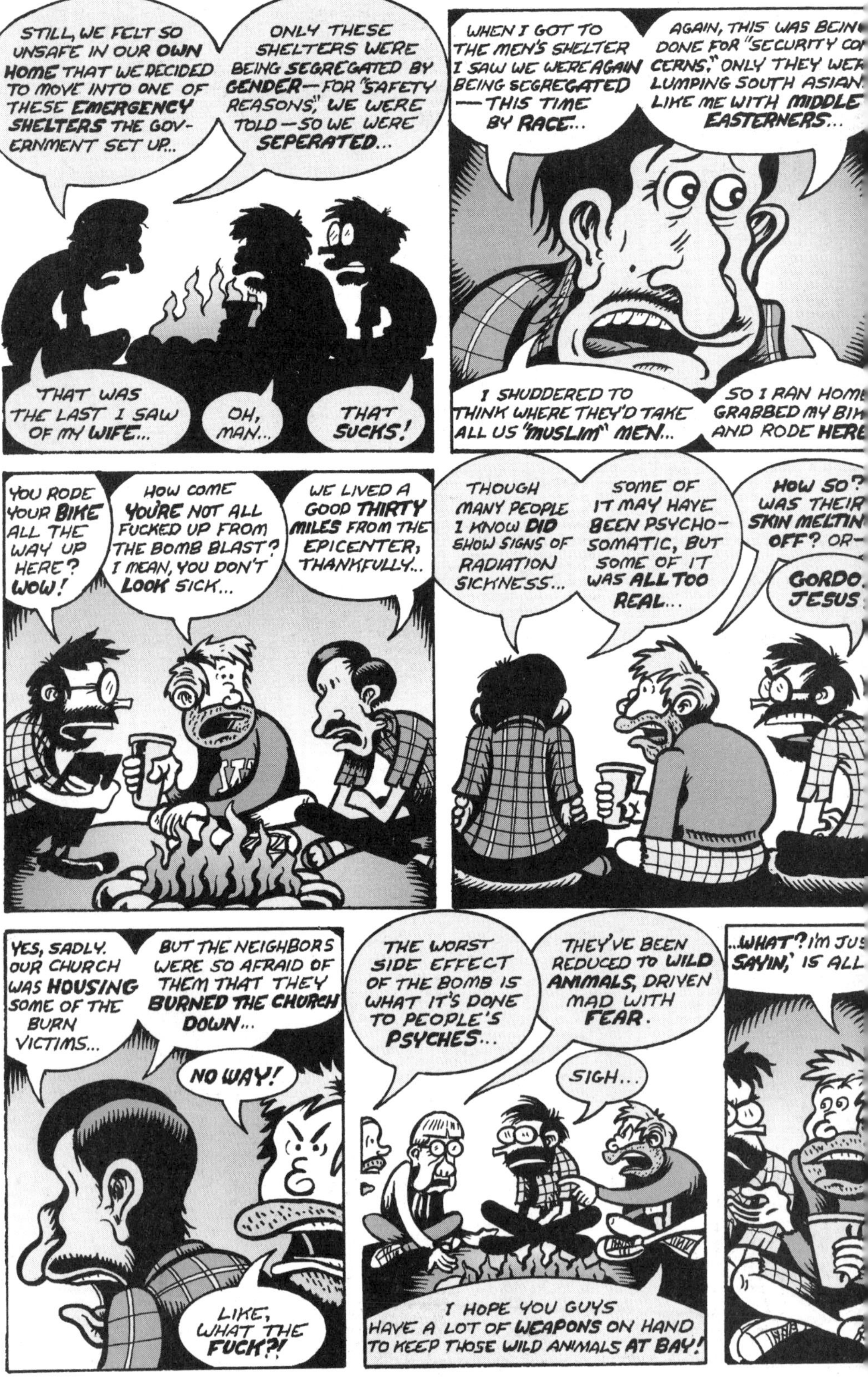

STILL, WE FELT SO UNSAFE IN OUR OWN HOME THAT WE DECIDED TO MOVE INTO ONE OF THESE EMERGENCY SHELTERS THE GOVERNMENT SET UP...
ONLY THESE SHELTERS WERE BEING SEGREGATED BY GENDER— FOR "SAFETY REASONS," WE WERE TOLD—SO WE WERE SEPERATED...
THAT WAS THE LAST I SAW OF MY WIFE...
OH, MAN...
THAT SUCKS!
WHEN I GOT TO THE MEN'S SHELTER I SAW WE WERE AGAIN BEING SEGREGATED —THIS TIME BY RACE...
AGAIN, THIS WAS BEIN DONE FOR "SECURITY CO CERNS." ONLY THEY WER LUMPING SOUTH ASIAN LIKE ME WITH MIDDLE EASTERNERS...
I SHUDDERED TO THINK WHERE THEY'D TAKE ALL US "MUSLIM" MEN...
SO I RAN HOM GRABBED MY BI AND RODE HERE
YOU RODE YOUR BIKE ALL THE WAY UP HERE? WOW!
HOW COME YOU'RE NOT ALL FUCKED UP FROM THE BOMB BLAST? I MEAN, YOU DON'T LOOK SICK...
WE LIVED A GOOD THIRTY MILES FROM THE EPICENTER, THANKFULLY...
THOUGH MANY PEOPLE I KNOW DID SHOW SIGNS OF RADIATION SICKNESS...
SOME OF IT MAY HAVE BEEN PSYCHOSOMATIC, BUT SOME OF IT WAS ALL TOO REAL...
HOW SO? WAS THEIR SKIN MELTIN OFF? OR—
GORDO. JESUS
YES, SADLY. OUR CHURCH WAS HOUSING SOME OF THE BURN VICTIMS...
BUT THE NEIGHBORS WERE SO AFRAID OF THEM THAT THEY BURNED THE CHURCH DOWN...
NO WAY!
LIKE, WHAT THE FUCK?!
THE WORST SIDE EFFECT OF THE BOMB IS WHAT IT'S DONE TO PEOPLE'S PSYCHES...
THEY'VE BEEN REDUCED TO WILD ANIMALS, DRIVEN MAD WITH FEAR.
SIGH...
I HOPE YOU GUYS HAVE A LOT OF WEAPONS ON HAND TO KEEP THOSE WILD ANIMALS AT BAY!
...WHAT? I'M JUS SAYIN,' IS ALL

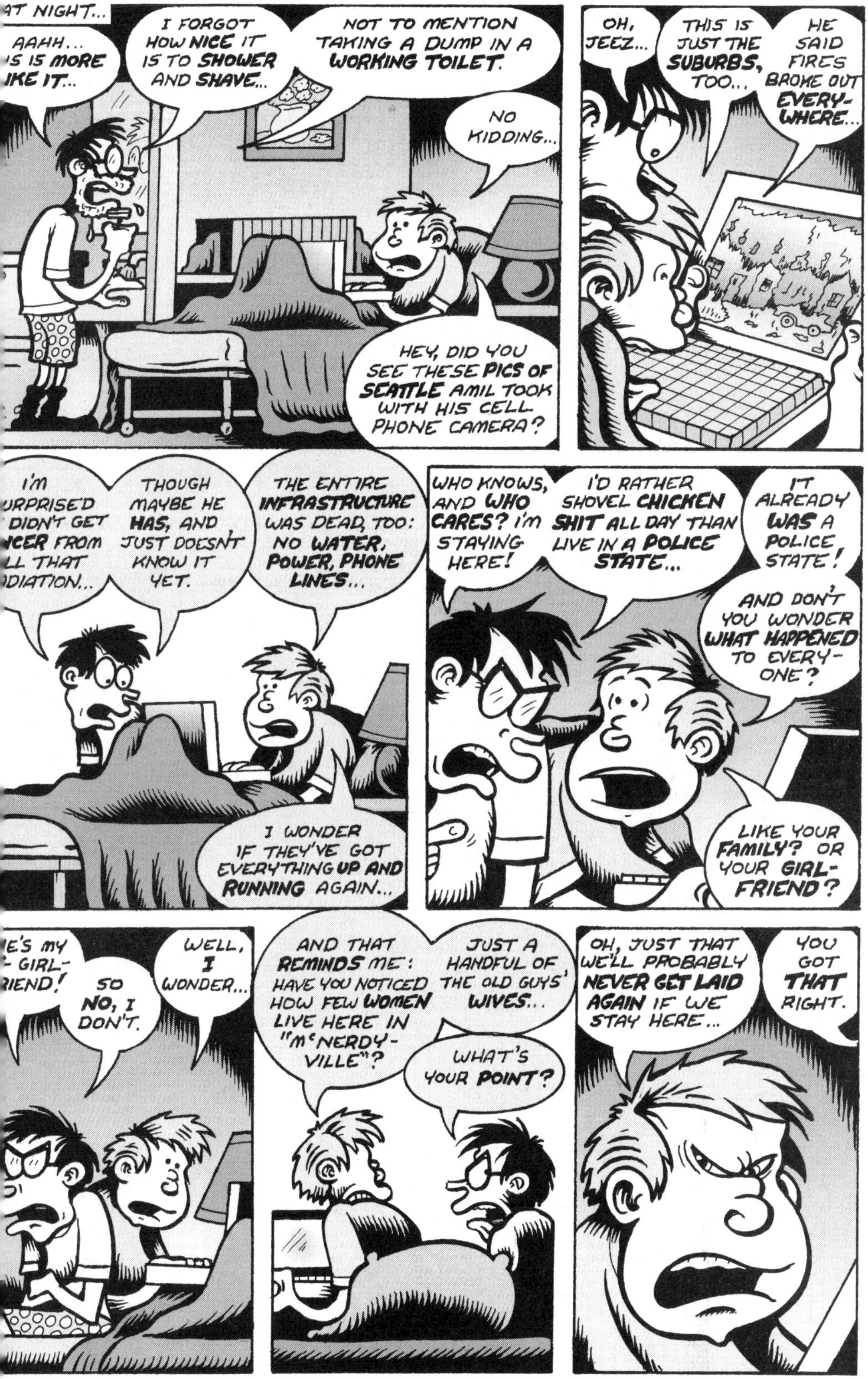
AT NIGHT...
AAHH... 'S IS MORE IKE IT...
I FORGOT HOW NICE IT IS TO SHOWER AND SHAVE...
NOT TO MENTION TAKING A DUMP IN A WORKING TOILET.
NO KIDDING...
HEY, DID YOU SEE THESE PICS OF SEATTLE AMIL TOOK WITH HIS CELL PHONE CAMERA?
OH, JEEZ...
THIS IS JUST THE SUBURBS, TOO...
HE SAID FIRES BROKE OUT EVERYWHERE...
I'M URPRISED DIDN'T GET NCER FROM LL THAT DIATION...
THOUGH MAYBE HE HAS, AND JUST DOESN'T KNOW IT YET.
THE ENTIRE INFRASTRUCTURE WAS DEAD, TOO: NO WATER, POWER, PHONE LINES...
I WONDER IF THEY'VE GOT EVERYTHING UP AND RUNNING AGAIN...
WHO KNOWS, AND WHO CARES? I'M STAYING HERE!
I'D RATHER SHOVEL CHICKEN SHIT ALL DAY THAN LIVE IN A POLICE STATE...
IT ALREADY WAS A POLICE STATE!
AND DON'T YOU WONDER WHAT HAPPENED TO EVERYONE?
LIKE YOUR FAMILY? OR YOUR GIRLFRIEND?
E'S MY GIRL- RIEND!
SO NO, I DON'T.
WELL, I WONDER...
AND THAT REMINDS ME: HAVE YOU NOTICED HOW FEW WOMEN LIVE HERE IN "McNERDY-VILLE"?
JUST A HANDFUL OF THE OLD GUYS' WIVES...
WHAT'S YOUR POINT?
OH, JUST THAT WE'LL PROBABLY NEVER GET LAID AGAIN IF WE STAY HERE...
YOU GOT THAT RIGHT.

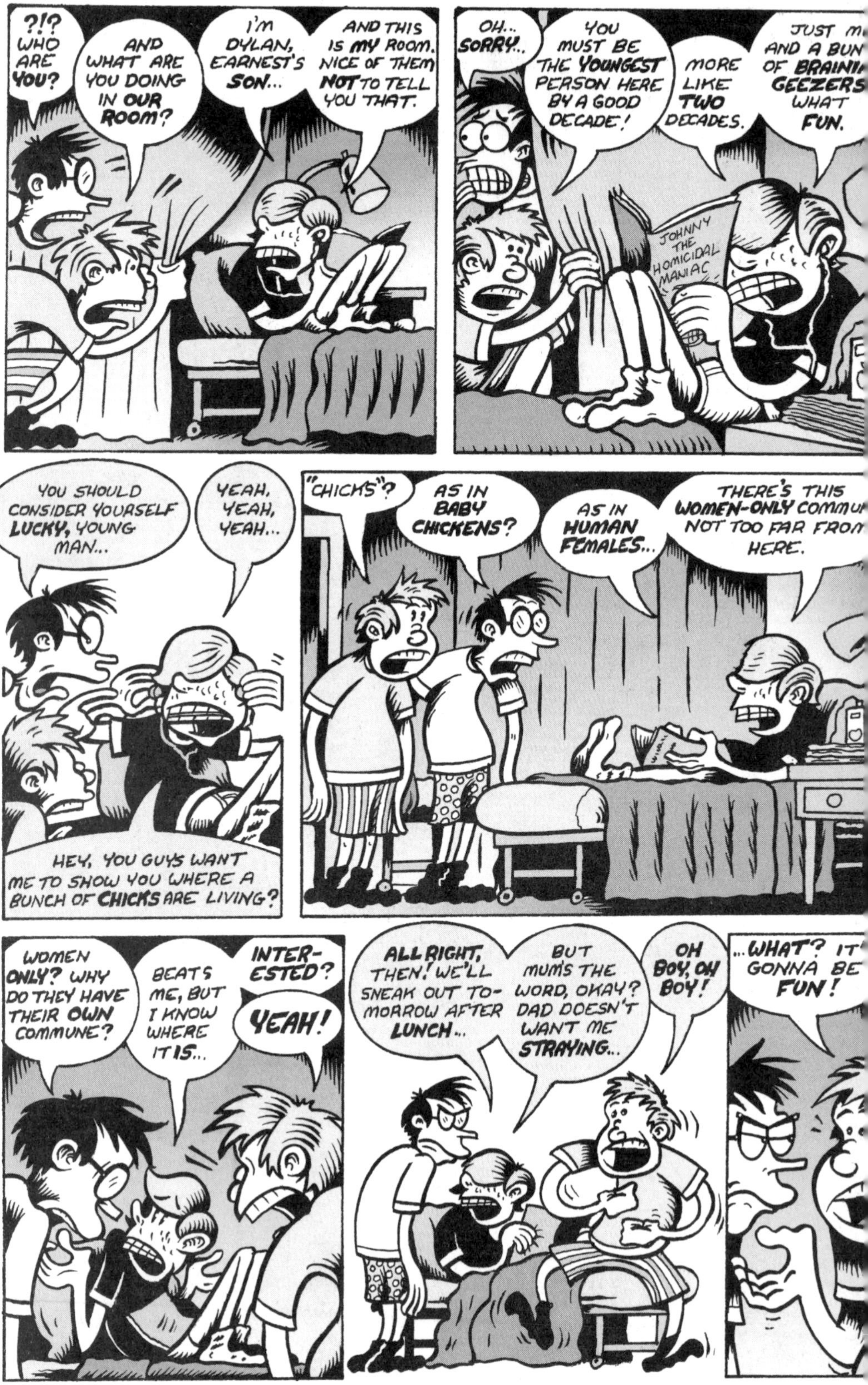
?!? WHO ARE YOU?
AND WHAT ARE YOU DOING IN OUR ROOM?
I'M DYLAN, EARNEST'S SON...
AND THIS IS MY ROOM. NICE OF THEM NOT TO TELL YOU THAT.
OH... SORRY...
YOU MUST BE THE YOUNGEST PERSON HERE BY A GOOD DECADE!
MORE LIKE TWO DECADES.
JOHNNY THE HOMICIDAL MANIAC
YOU SHOULD CONSIDER YOURSELF LUCKY, YOUNG MAN...
YEAH, YEAH, YEAH...
HEY, YOU GUYS WANT ME TO SHOW YOU WHERE A BUNCH OF CHICKS ARE LIVING?
"CHICKS"?
AS IN BABY CHICKENS?
AS IN HUMAN FEMALES...
WOMEN ONLY? WHY DO THEY HAVE THEIR OWN COMMUNE?
BEATS ME, BUT I KNOW WHERE IT IS...
INTER-ESTED?
YEAH!
ALL RIGHT, THEN! WE'LL SNEAK OUT TO-MORROW AFTER LUNCH...
BUT MUM'S THE WORD, OKAY? DAD DOESN'T WANT ME STRAYING...
OH BOY, OH BOY!

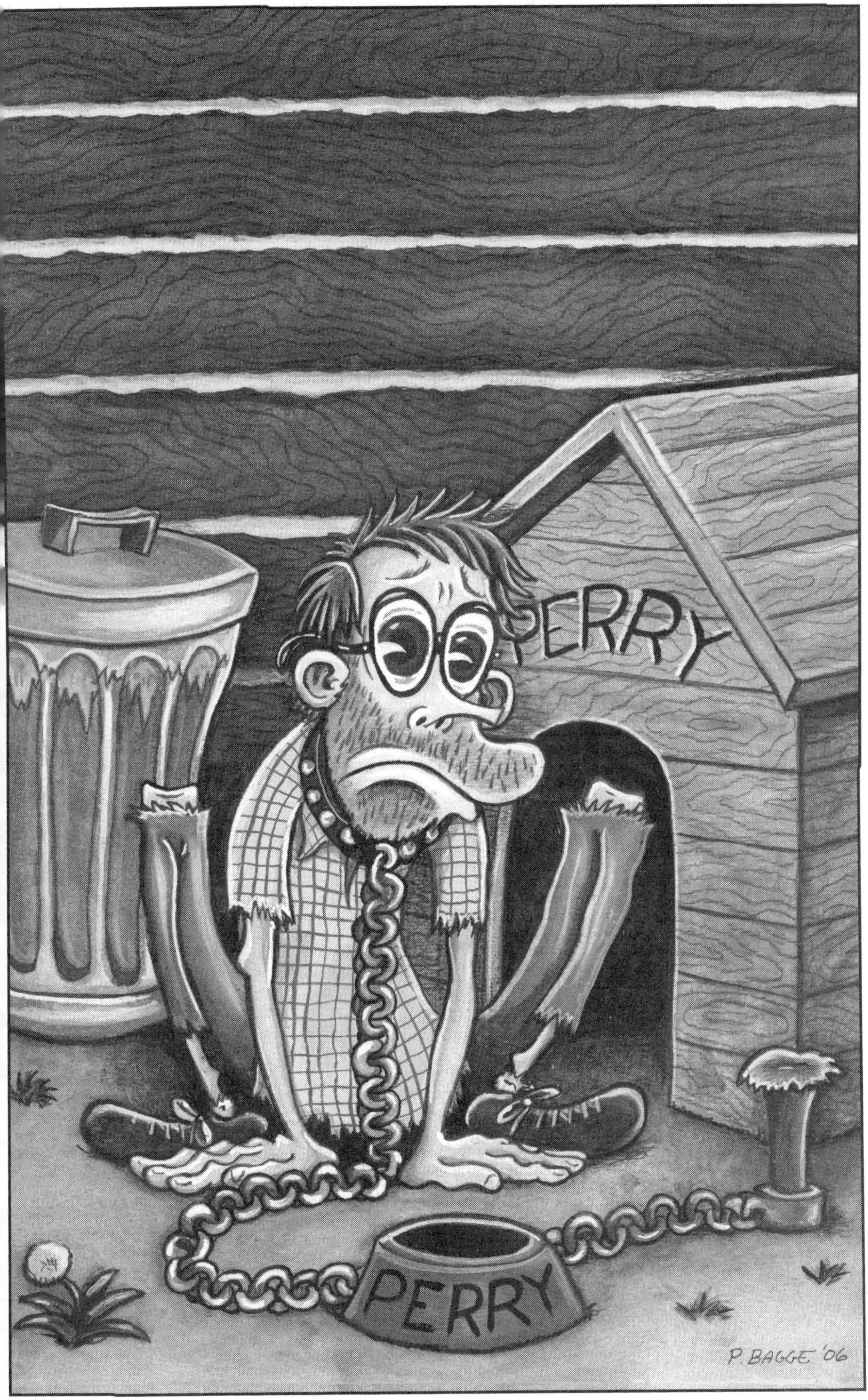
PERRY
PERRY
P. BAGGE '06

Chapter 4

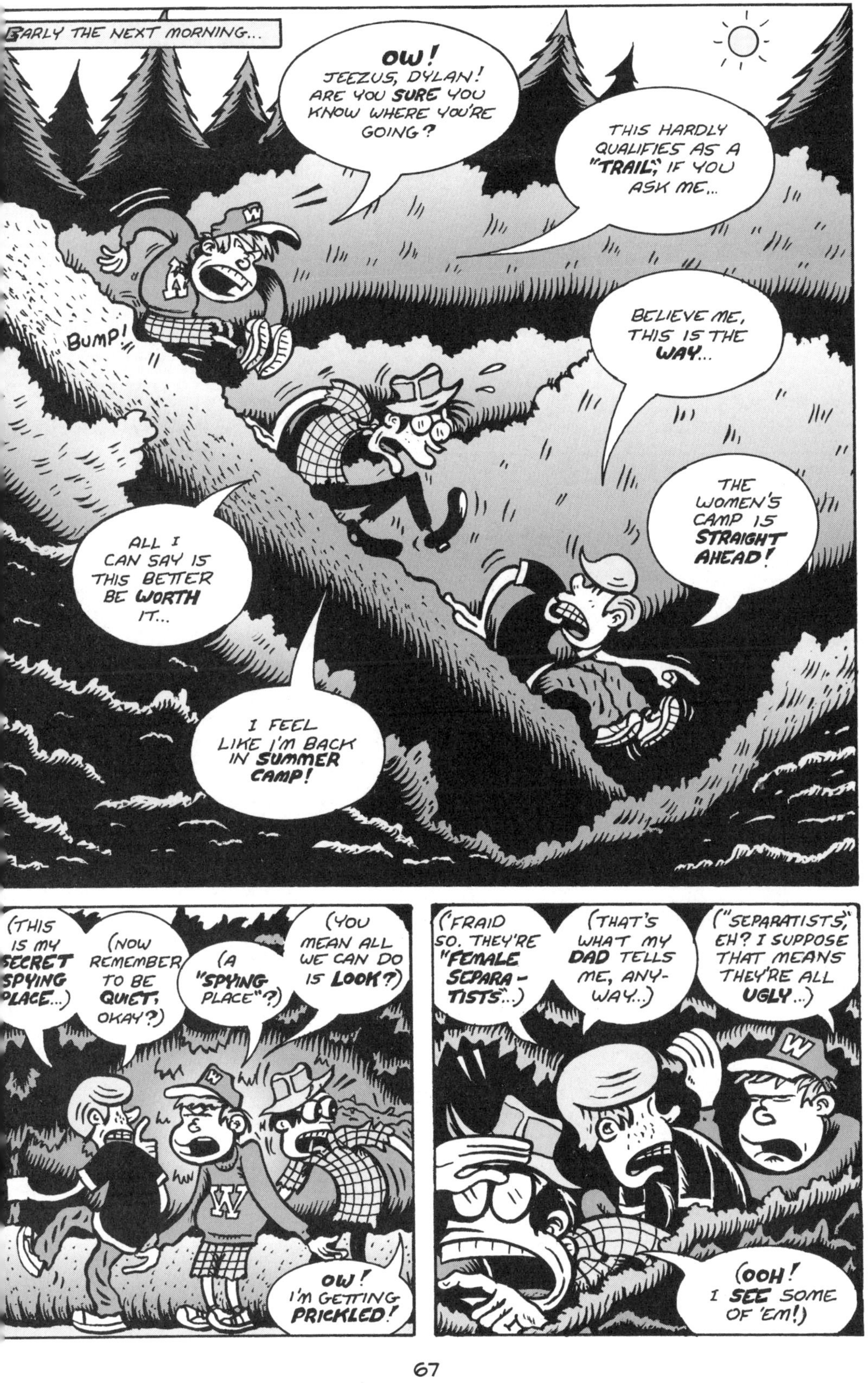
EARLY THE NEXT MORNING...
OW! JEEZUS, DYLAN! ARE YOU SURE YOU KNOW WHERE YOU'RE GOING?
THIS HARDLY QUALIFIES AS A "TRAIL," IF YOU ASK ME...
BUMP!
BELIEVE ME, THIS IS THE WAY...
THE WOMEN'S CAMP IS STRAIGHT AHEAD!
ALL I CAN SAY IS THIS BETTER BE WORTH IT...
I FEEL LIKE I'M BACK IN SUMMER CAMP!
(THIS IS MY SECRET SPYING PLACE...)
(NOW REMEMBER TO BE QUIET, OKAY?)
(A "SPYING PLACE"?)
(YOU MEAN ALL WE CAN DO IS LOOK?)
OW! I'M GETTING PRICKLED!
('FRAID SO. THEY'RE "FEMALE SEPARATISTS"...)
(THAT'S WHAT MY DAD TELLS ME, ANYWAY...)
("SEPARATISTS," EH? I SUPPOSE THAT MEANS THEY'RE ALL UGLY...)
(OOH! I SEE SOME OF 'EM!)

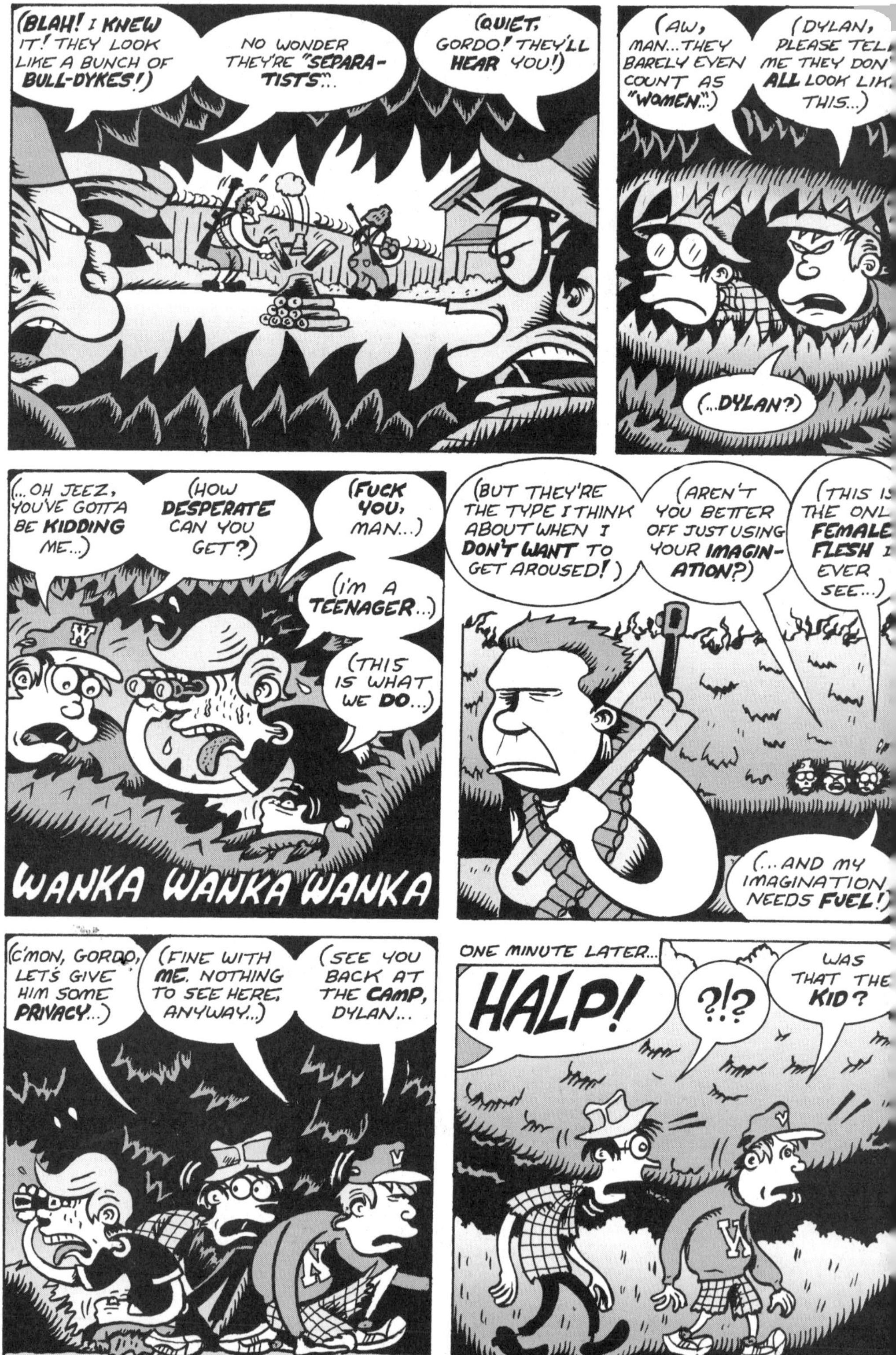

(BLAH! I KNEW IT! THEY LOOK LIKE A BUNCH OF BULL-DYKES!)
NO WONDER THEY'RE "SEPARATISTS"...
(QUIET, GORDO! THEY'LL HEAR YOU!)
(AW, MAN... THEY BARELY EVEN COUNT AS "WOMEN"...)
(DYLAN, PLEASE TEL ME THEY DON ALL LOOK LIK THIS...)
(...DYLAN?)
(...OH JEEZ, YOU'VE GOTTA BE KIDDING ME...)
(HOW DESPERATE CAN YOU GET?)
(FUCK YOU, MAN...)
(I'M A TEENAGER...)
(THIS IS WHAT WE DO...)
WANKA WANKA WANKA
(BUT THEY'RE THE TYPE I THINK ABOUT WHEN I DON'T WANT TO GET AROUSED!)
(AREN'T YOU BETTER OFF JUST USING YOUR IMAGINATION?)
(THIS IS THE ONL FEMALE FLESH I EVER SEE...)
(...AND MY IMAGINATION NEEDS FUEL!)
(C'MON, GORDO, LET'S GIVE HIM SOME PRIVACY...)
(FINE WITH ME. NOTHING TO SEE HERE, ANYWAY...)
(SEE YOU BACK AT THE CAMP, DYLAN...
ONE MINUTE LATER...
HALP!
?!?
WAS THAT THE KID?

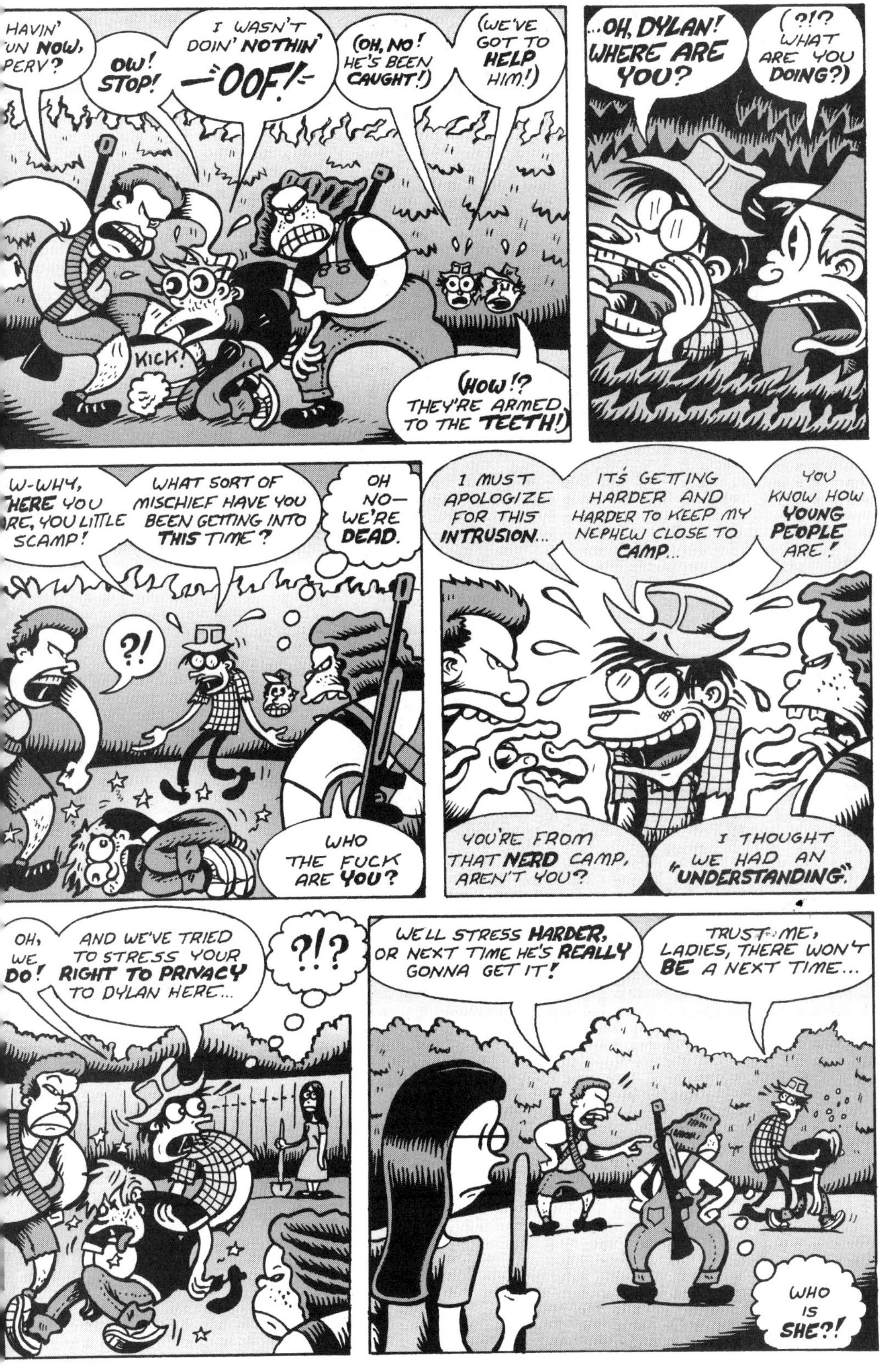
HAVIN' 'UN NOW, PERV?
OW! STOP!
I WASN'T DOIN' NOTHIN' —OOF!—
(OH, NO! HE'S BEEN CAUGHT!)
(WE'VE GOT TO HELP HIM!)
KICK!
(HOW!? THEY'RE ARMED TO THE TEETH!)
...OH, DYLAN! WHERE ARE YOU?
(?!? WHAT ARE YOU DOING?)
W-WHY, HERE YOU ARE, YOU LITTLE SCAMP!
WHAT SORT OF MISCHIEF HAVE YOU BEEN GETTING INTO THIS TIME?
OH NO— WE'RE DEAD.
?!
WHO THE FUCK ARE YOU?
I MUST APOLOGIZE FOR THIS INTRUSION...
IT'S GETTING HARDER AND HARDER TO KEEP MY NEPHEW CLOSE TO CAMP...
YOU KNOW HOW YOUNG PEOPLE ARE!
YOU'RE FROM THAT NERD CAMP, AREN'T YOU?
I THOUGHT WE HAD AN "UNDERSTANDING."
OH, WE DO!
AND WE'VE TRIED TO STRESS YOUR RIGHT TO PRIVACY TO DYLAN HERE...
?!?
WELL STRESS HARDER, OR NEXT TIME HE'S REALLY GONNA GET IT!
TRUST ME, LADIES, THERE WON'T BE A NEXT TIME...
WHO IS SHE?!

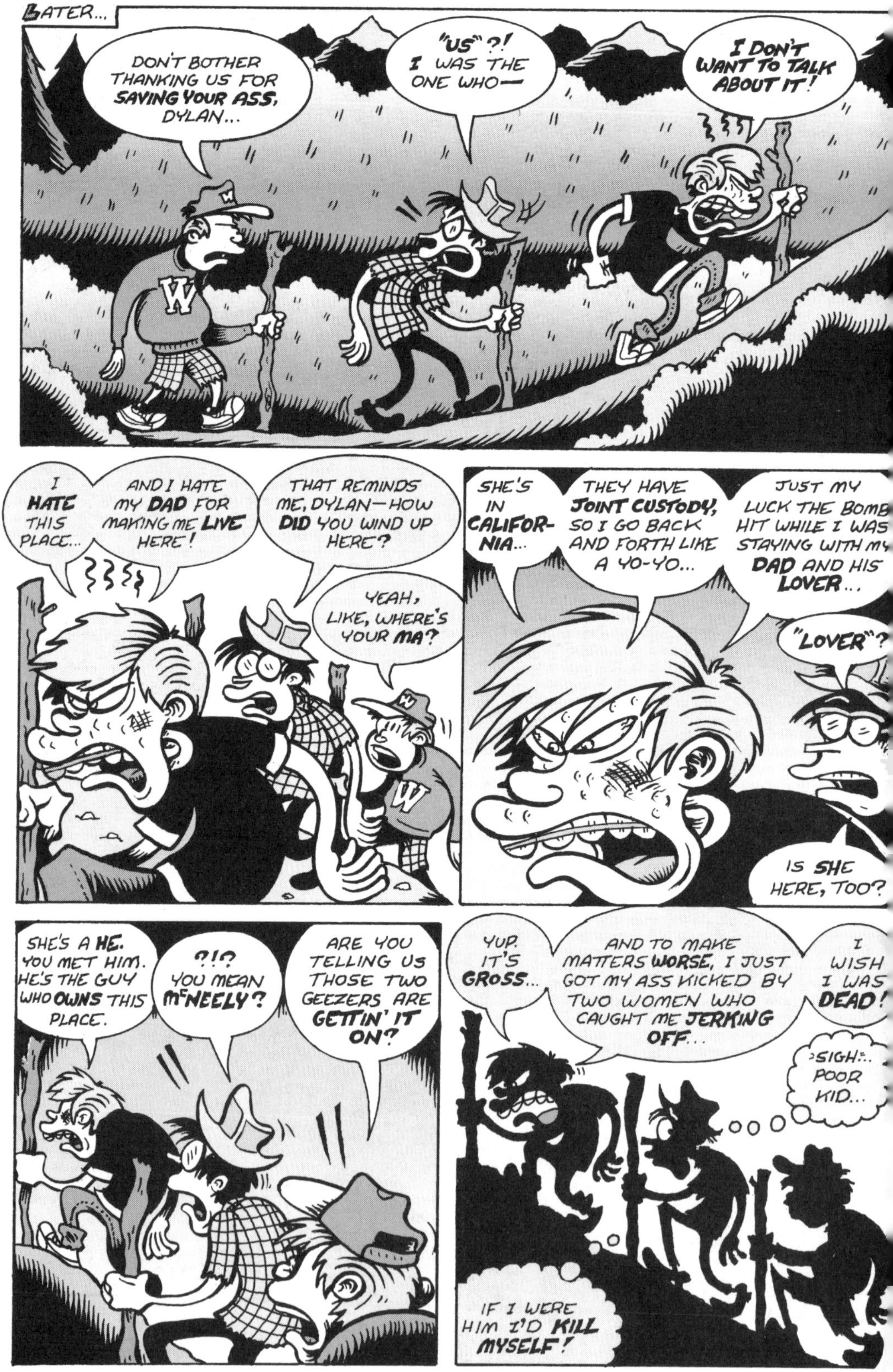
LATER...
DON'T BOTHER THANKING US FOR SAVING YOUR ASS, DYLAN...
"US"?! I WAS THE ONE WHO—
I DON'T WANT TO TALK ABOUT IT!
I HATE THIS PLACE...
AND I HATE MY DAD FOR MAKING ME LIVE HERE!
THAT REMINDS ME, DYLAN—HOW DID YOU WIND UP HERE?
YEAH, LIKE, WHERE'S YOUR MA?
SHE'S IN CALIFOR-NIA...
THEY HAVE JOINT CUSTODY, SO I GO BACK AND FORTH LIKE A YO-YO...
JUST MY LUCK THE BOMB HIT WHILE I WAS STAYING WITH MY DAD AND HIS LOVER...
"LOVER"?
IS SHE HERE, TOO?
SHE'S A HE. YOU MET HIM. HE'S THE GUY WHO OWNS THIS PLACE.
?!? YOU MEAN McNEELY?
ARE YOU TELLING US THOSE TWO GEEZERS ARE GETTIN' IT ON?
YUP. IT'S GROSS...
AND TO MAKE MATTERS WORSE, I JUST GOT MY ASS KICKED BY TWO WOMEN WHO CAUGHT ME JERKING OFF...
I WISH I WAS DEAD!
SIGH... POOR KID...
IF I WERE HIM I'D KILL MYSELF!

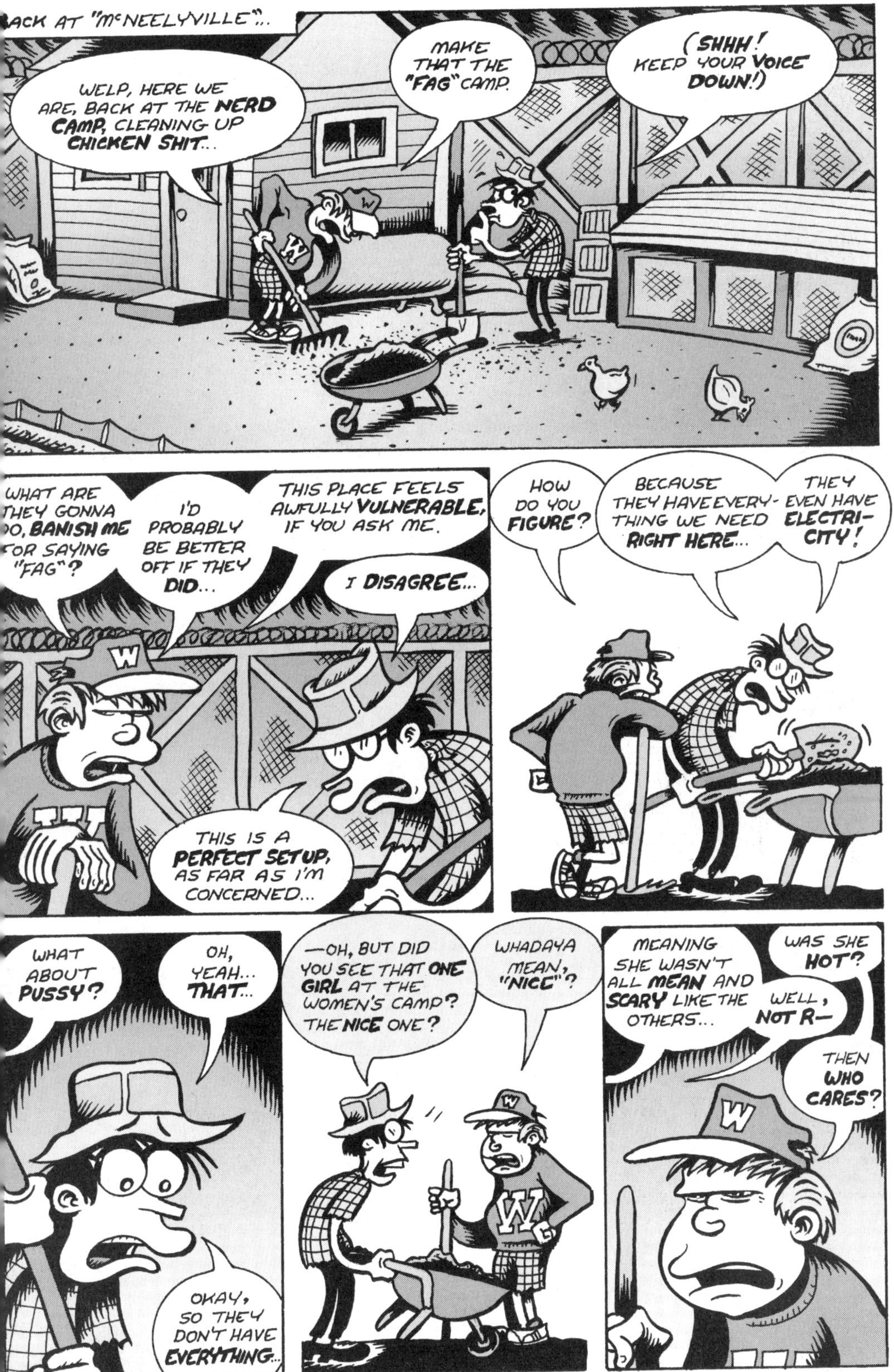

BACK AT "McNEELYVILLE"...
WELP, HERE WE ARE, BACK AT THE NERD CAMP, CLEANING UP CHICKEN SHIT...
MAKE THAT THE "FAG" CAMP.
(SHHH! KEEP YOUR VOICE DOWN!)
WHAT ARE THEY GONNA DO, BANISH ME FOR SAYING "FAG"?
I'D PROBABLY BE BETTER OFF IF THEY DID...
THIS PLACE FEELS AWFULLY VULNERABLE, IF YOU ASK ME.
I DISAGREE...
THIS IS A PERFECT SETUP, AS FAR AS I'M CONCERNED...
HOW DO YOU FIGURE?
BECAUSE THEY HAVE EVERYTHING WE NEED RIGHT HERE...
THEY EVEN HAVE ELECTRICITY!
WHAT ABOUT PUSSY?
OH, YEAH... THAT...
OKAY, SO THEY DON'T HAVE EVERYTHING...
—OH, BUT DID YOU SEE THAT ONE GIRL AT THE WOMEN'S CAMP? THE NICE ONE?
WHADAYA MEAN, "NICE"?
MEANING SHE WASN'T ALL MEAN AND SCARY LIKE THE OTHERS...
WAS SHE HOT?
WELL, NOT R—
THEN WHO CARES?

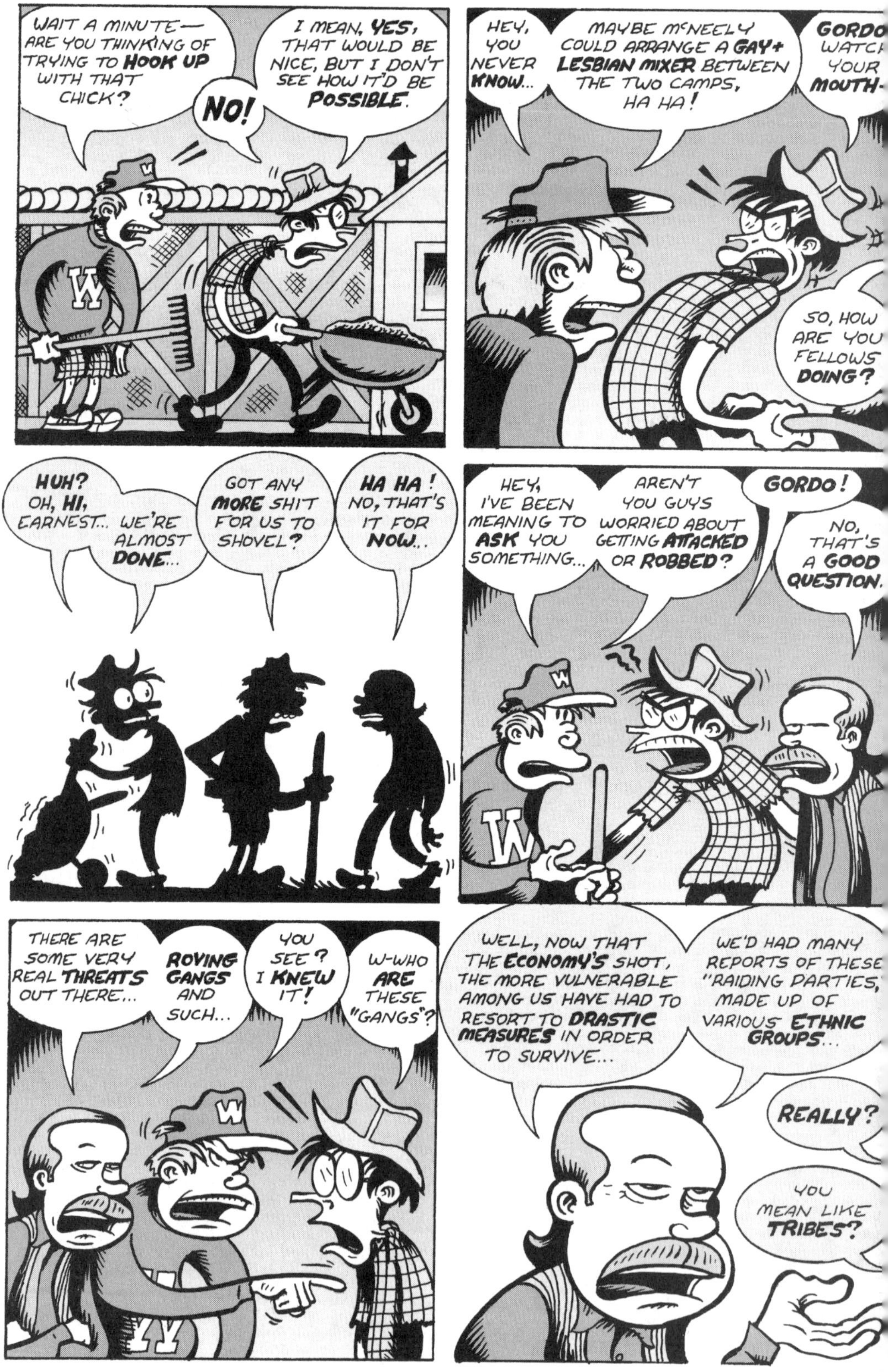

WAIT A MINUTE— ARE YOU THINKING OF TRYING TO HOOK UP WITH THAT CHICK?
NO!
I MEAN, YES, THAT WOULD BE NICE, BUT I DON'T SEE HOW IT'D BE POSSIBLE.
HEY, YOU NEVER KNOW...
MAYBE McNEELY COULD ARRANGE A GAY+ LESBIAN MIXER BETWEEN THE TWO CAMPS, HA HA!
GORDO WATCH YOUR MOUTH-
SO, HOW ARE YOU FELLOWS DOING?
HUH? OH, HI, EARNEST...
WE'RE ALMOST DONE...
GOT ANY MORE SHIT FOR US TO SHOVEL?
HA HA! NO, THAT'S IT FOR NOW...
HEY, I'VE BEEN MEANING TO ASK YOU SOMETHING...
AREN'T YOU GUYS WORRIED ABOUT GETTING ATTACKED OR ROBBED?
GORDO!
NO, THAT'S A GOOD QUESTION.
THERE ARE SOME VERY REAL THREATS OUT THERE...
ROVING GANGS AND SUCH...
YOU SEE? I KNEW IT!
W-WHO ARE THESE "GANGS"?
WELL, NOW THAT THE ECONOMY'S SHOT, THE MORE VULNERABLE AMONG US HAVE HAD TO RESORT TO DRASTIC MEASURES IN ORDER TO SURVIVE...
WE'D HAD MANY REPORTS OF THESE "RAIDING PARTIES," MADE UP OF VARIOUS ETHNIC GROUPS...
REALLY?
YOU MEAN LIKE TRIBES?

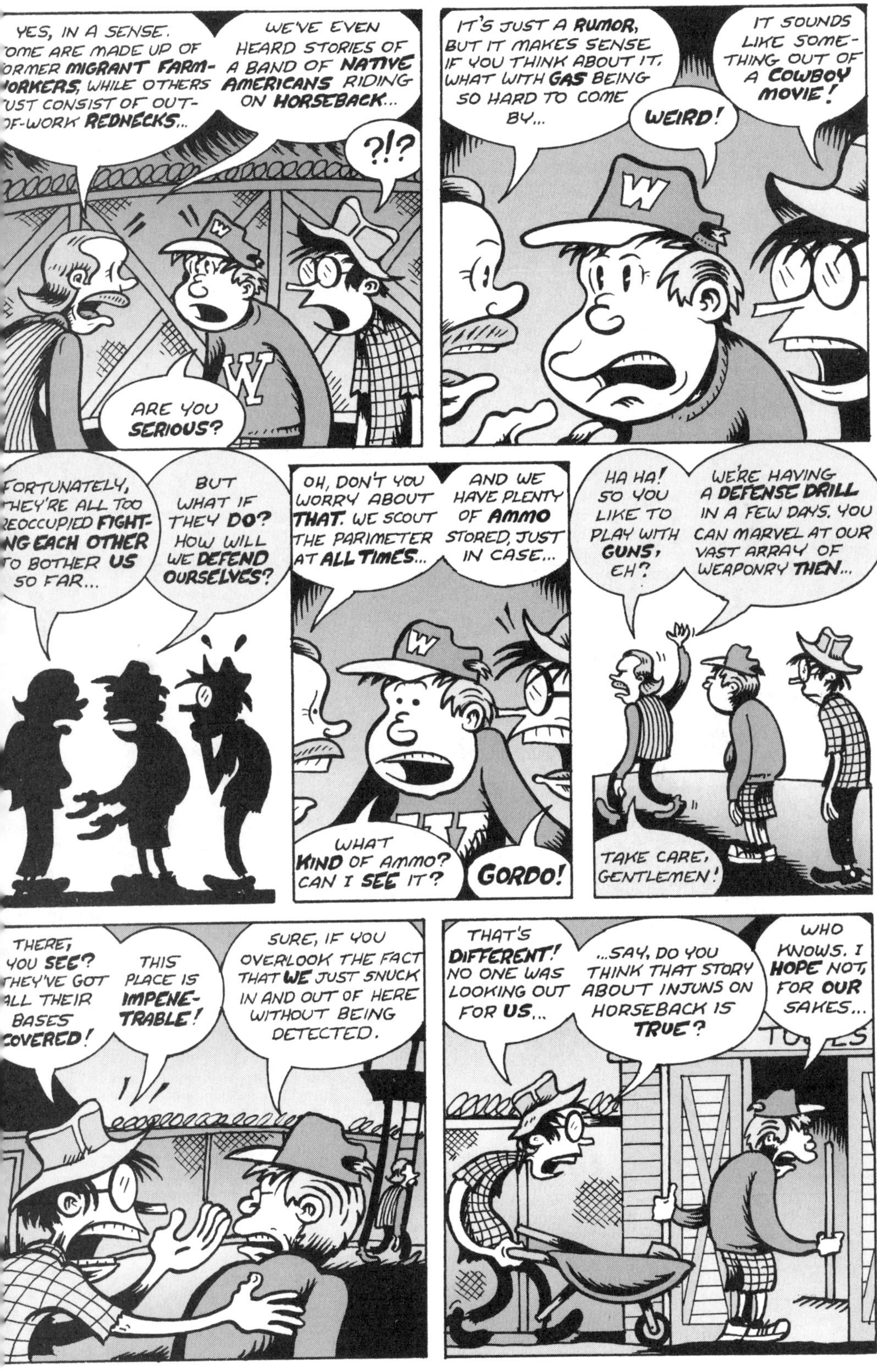
YES, IN A SENSE. SOME ARE MADE UP OF FORMER MIGRANT FARM-WORKERS, WHILE OTHERS JUST CONSIST OF OUT-OF-WORK REDNECKS...
WE'VE EVEN HEARD STORIES OF A BAND OF NATIVE AMERICANS RIDING ON HORSEBACK...
?!?
ARE YOU SERIOUS?
IT'S JUST A RUMOR, BUT IT MAKES SENSE IF YOU THINK ABOUT IT, WHAT WITH GAS BEING SO HARD TO COME BY...
WEIRD!
IT SOUNDS LIKE SOME-THING OUT OF A COWBOY MOVIE!
FORTUNATELY, THEY'RE ALL TOO PREOCCUPIED FIGHT-ING EACH OTHER TO BOTHER US SO FAR...
BUT WHAT IF THEY DO? HOW WILL WE DEFEND OURSELVES?
OH, DON'T YOU WORRY ABOUT THAT. WE SCOUT THE PARIMETER AT ALL TIMES...
AND WE HAVE PLENTY OF AMMO STORED, JUST IN CASE...
WHAT KIND OF AMMO? CAN I SEE IT?
GORDO!
HA HA! SO YOU LIKE TO PLAY WITH GUNS, EH?
WE'RE HAVING A DEFENSE DRILL IN A FEW DAYS. YOU CAN MARVEL AT OUR VAST ARRAY OF WEAPONRY THEN...
TAKE CARE, GENTLEMEN!
THERE, YOU SEE? THEY'VE GOT ALL THEIR BASES COVERED!
THIS PLACE IS IMPENE-TRABLE!
SURE, IF YOU OVERLOOK THE FACT THAT WE JUST SNUCK IN AND OUT OF HERE WITHOUT BEING DETECTED.
THAT'S DIFFERENT! NO ONE WAS LOOKING OUT FOR US...
...SAY, DO YOU THINK THAT STORY ABOUT INJUNS ON HORSEBACK IS TRUE?
WHO KNOWS. I HOPE NOT, FOR OUR SAKES...

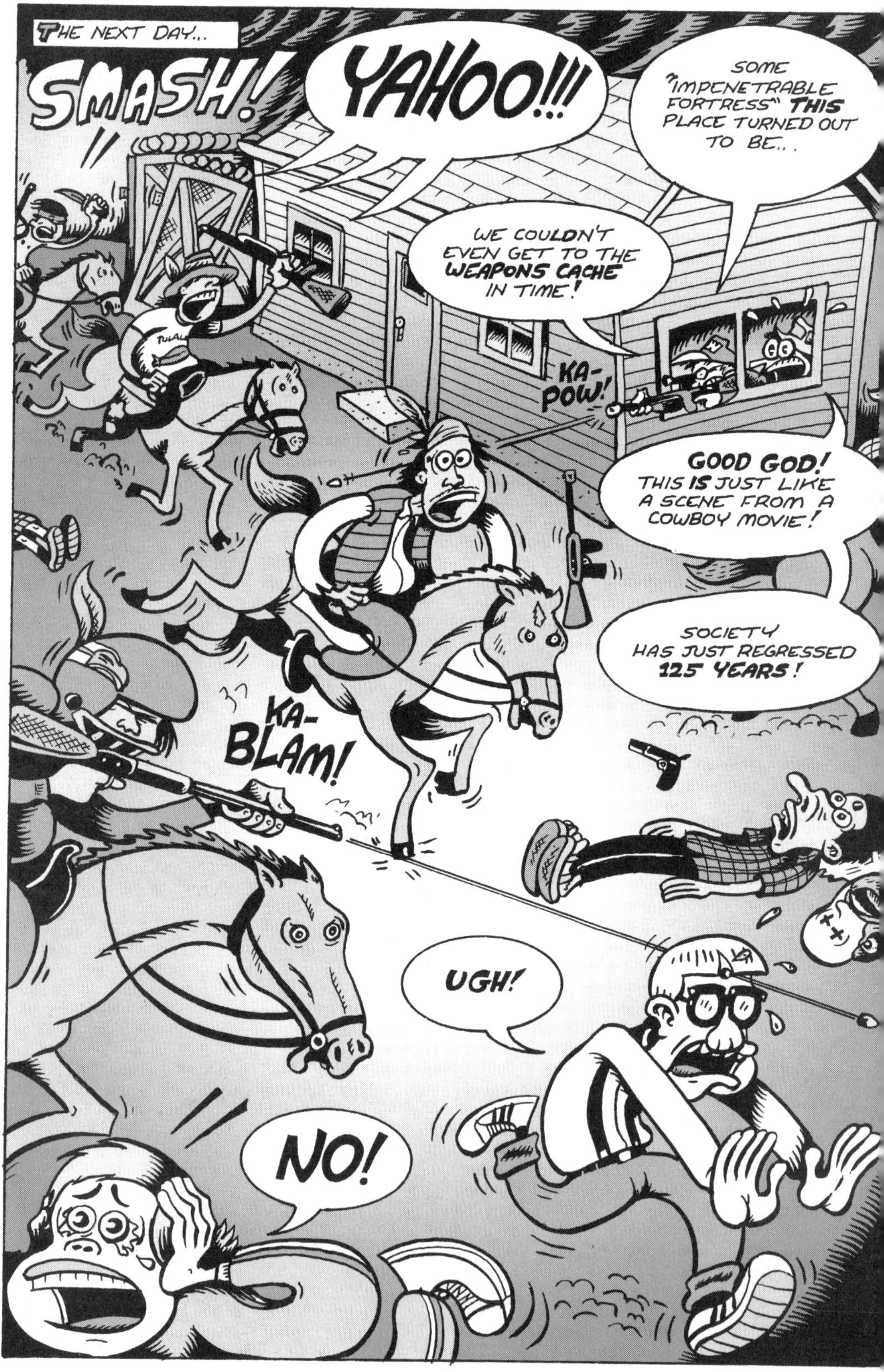
THE NEXT DAY...
SMASH!
YAHOO!!!
SOME "IMPENETRABLE FORTRESS" THIS PLACE TURNED OUT TO BE...
WE COULDN'T EVEN GET TO THE WEAPONS CACHE IN TIME!
KA-POW!
GOOD GOD! THIS IS JUST LIKE A SCENE FROM A COWBOY MOVIE!
SOCIETY HAS JUST REGRESSED 125 YEARS!
KA-BLAM!
UGH!
NO!

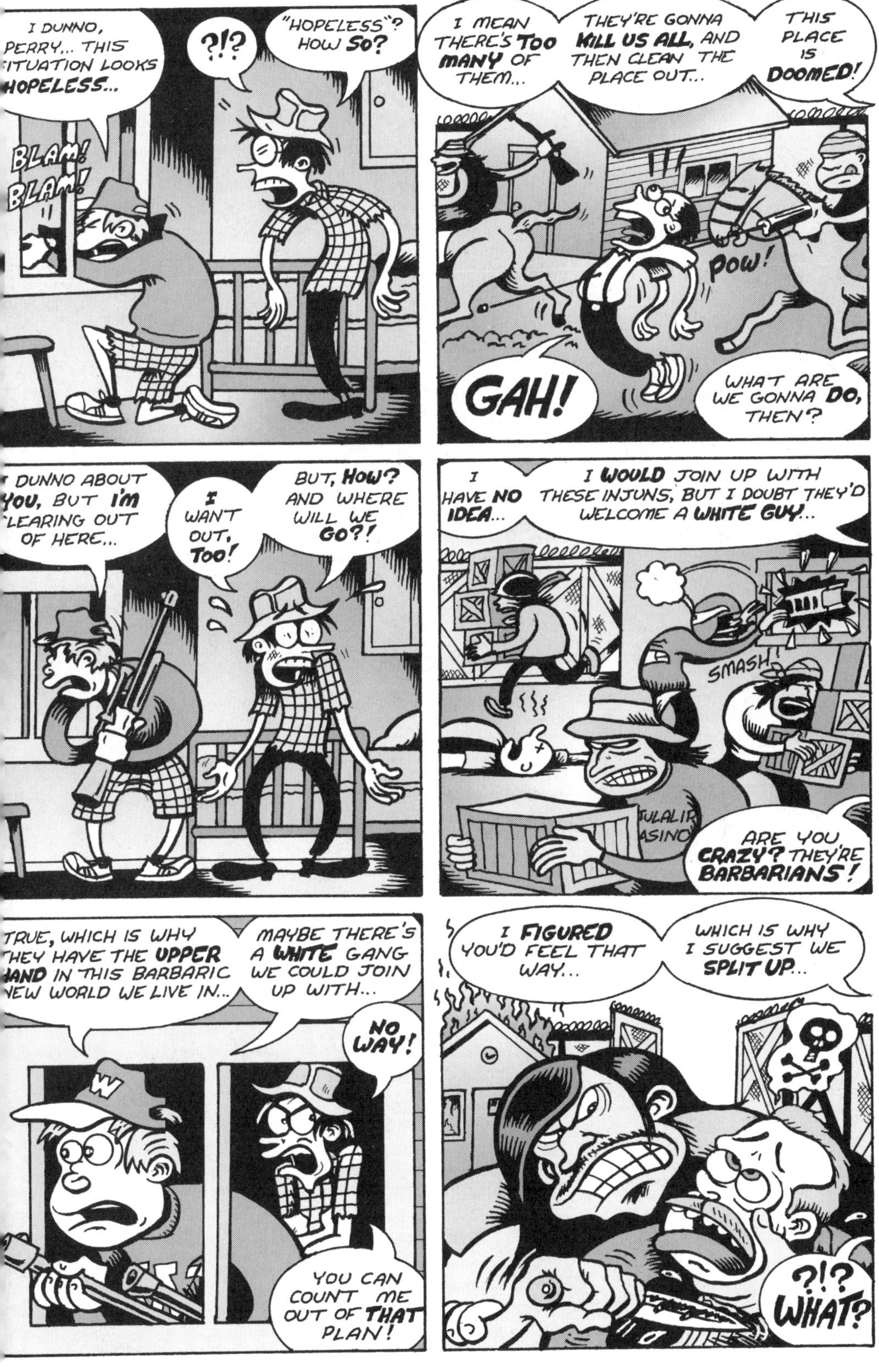
I DUNNO, PERRY... THIS SITUATION LOOKS HOPELESS...
BLAM! BLAM!
?!?
"HOPELESS"? HOW SO?
I MEAN THERE'S TOO MANY OF THEM...
THEY'RE GONNA KILL US ALL, AND THEN CLEAN THE PLACE OUT...
THIS PLACE IS DOOMED!
POW!
GAH!
WHAT ARE WE GONNA DO, THEN?
I DUNNO ABOUT YOU, BUT I'M CLEARING OUT OF HERE...
I WANT OUT, TOO!
BUT, HOW? AND WHERE WILL WE GO?!
I HAVE NO IDEA...
I WOULD JOIN UP WITH THESE INJUNS, BUT I DOUBT THEY'D WELCOME A WHITE GUY...
SMASH!
ARE YOU CRAZY? THEY'RE BARBARIANS!
TRUE, WHICH IS WHY THEY HAVE THE UPPER HAND IN THIS BARBARIC NEW WORLD WE LIVE IN...
MAYBE THERE'S A WHITE GANG WE COULD JOIN UP WITH...
NO WAY!
YOU CAN COUNT ME OUT OF THAT PLAN!
I FIGURED YOU'D FEEL THAT WAY...
WHICH IS WHY I SUGGEST WE SPLIT UP...
?!? WHAT?

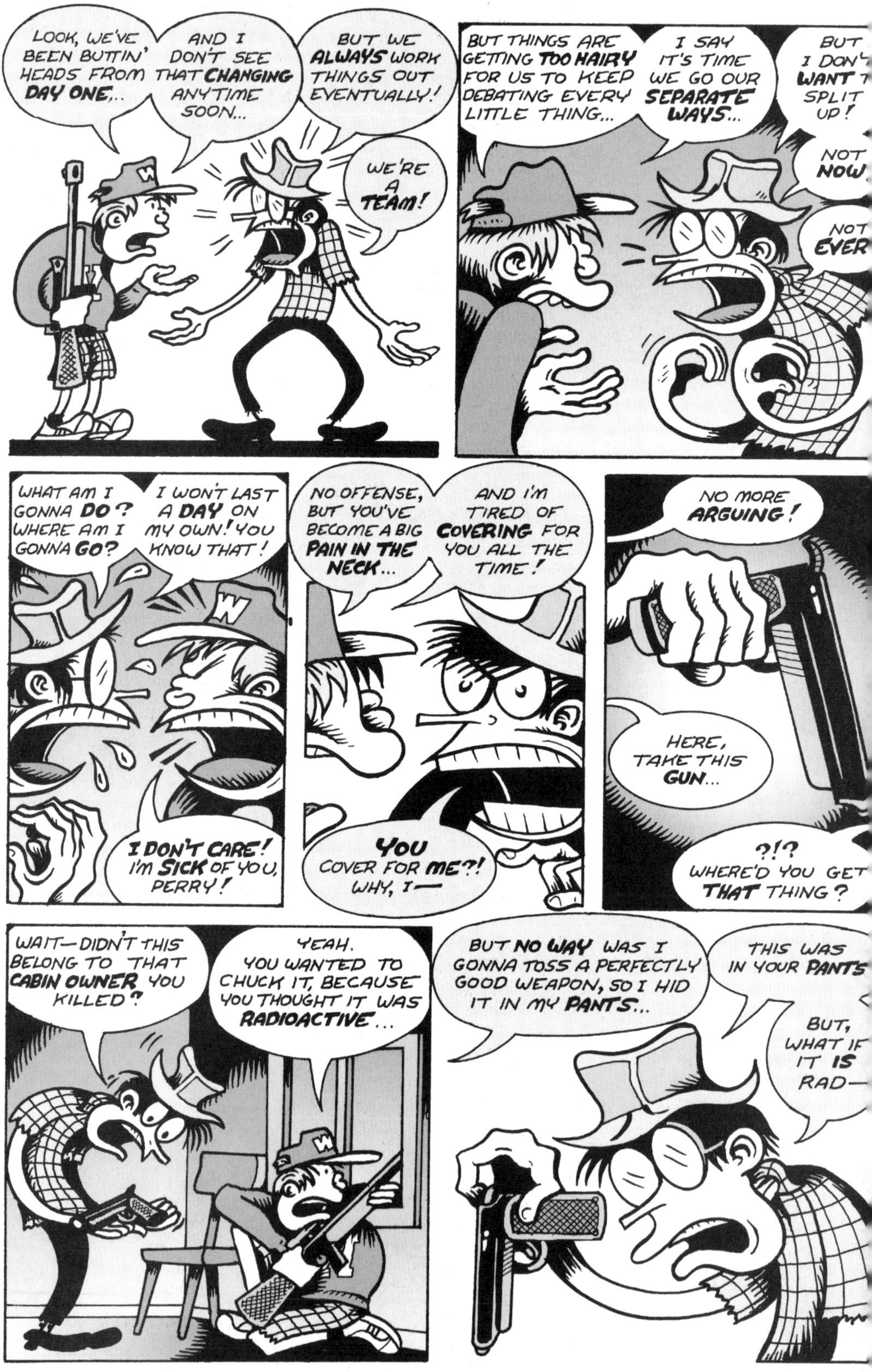

LOOK, WE'VE BEEN BUTTIN' HEADS FROM DAY ONE,..
AND I DON'T SEE THAT CHANGING ANYTIME SOON...
BUT WE ALWAYS WORK THINGS OUT EVENTUALLY!
WE'RE A TEAM!
BUT THINGS ARE GETTING TOO HAIRY FOR US TO KEEP DEBATING EVERY LITTLE THING...
I SAY IT'S TIME WE GO OUR SEPARATE WAYS...
BUT I DON'T WANT T SPLIT UP!
NOT NOW
NOT EVER
WHAT AM I GONNA DO? WHERE AM I GONNA GO?
I WON'T LAST A DAY ON MY OWN! YOU KNOW THAT!
I DON'T CARE! I'M SICK OF YOU, PERRY!
NO OFFENSE, BUT YOU'VE BECOME A BIG PAIN IN THE NECK...
AND I'M TIRED OF COVERING FOR YOU ALL THE TIME!
YOU COVER FOR ME?! WHY, I—
NO MORE ARGUING!
HERE, TAKE THIS GUN...
?!? WHERE'D YOU GET THAT THING?
WAIT—DIDN'T THIS BELONG TO THAT CABIN OWNER YOU KILLED?
YEAH. YOU WANTED TO CHUCK IT, BECAUSE YOU THOUGHT IT WAS RADIOACTIVE...
BUT NO WAY WAS I GONNA TOSS A PERFECTLY GOOD WEAPON, SO I HID IT IN MY PANTS...
THIS WAS IN YOUR PANTS
BUT, WHAT IF IT IS RAD—

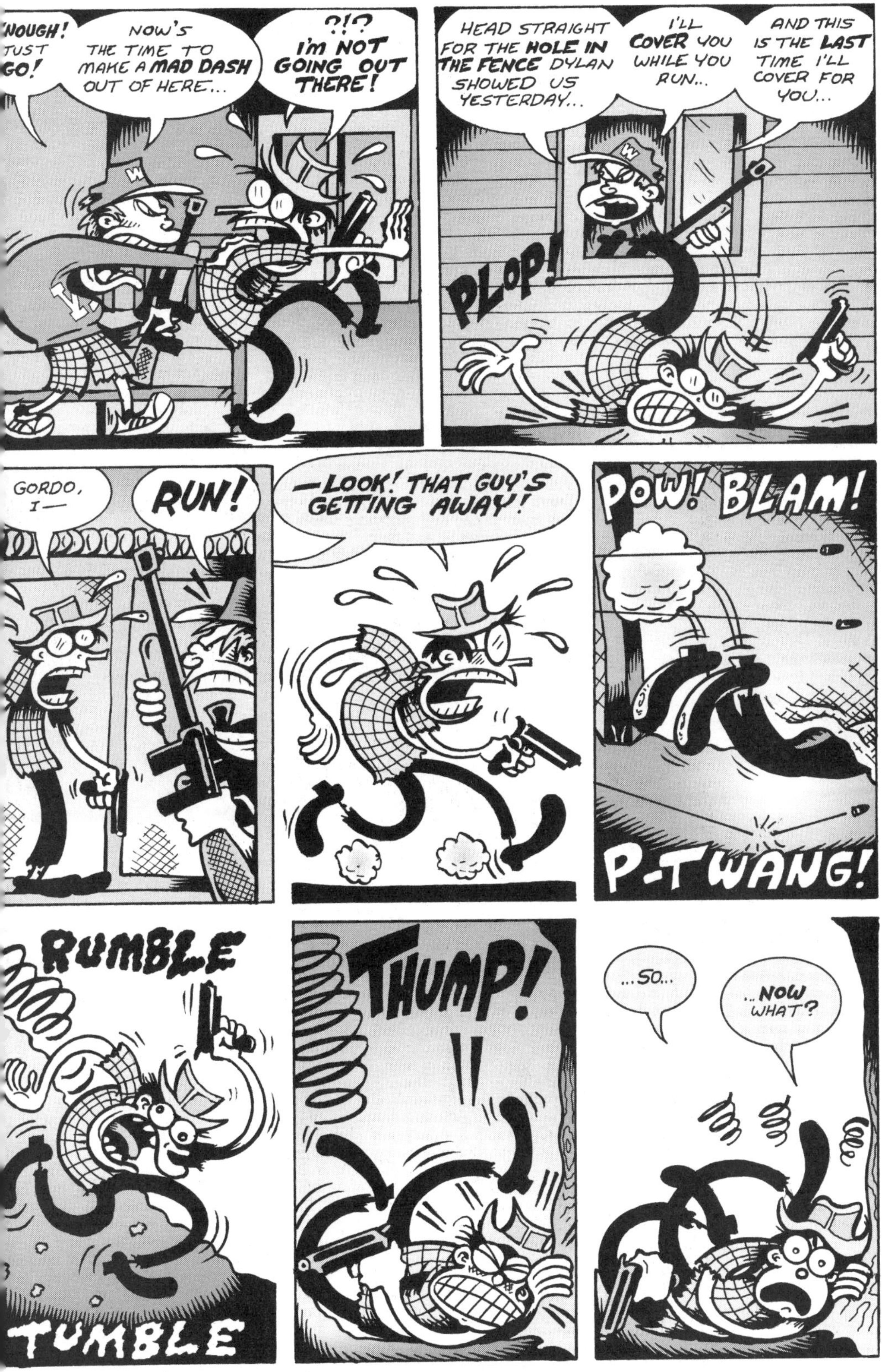
'NOUGH! JUST GO!
NOW'S THE TIME TO MAKE A MAD DASH OUT OF HERE...
?!? I'M NOT GOING OUT THERE!
HEAD STRAIGHT FOR THE HOLE IN THE FENCE DYLAN SHOWED US YESTERDAY...
I'LL COVER YOU WHILE YOU RUN...
AND THIS IS THE LAST TIME I'LL COVER FOR YOU...
PLOP!
GORDO, I—
RUN!
—LOOK! THAT GUY'S GETTING AWAY!
POW! BLAM!
P-TWANG!
RUMBLE
TUMBLE
THUMP!
...SO...
...NOW WHAT?

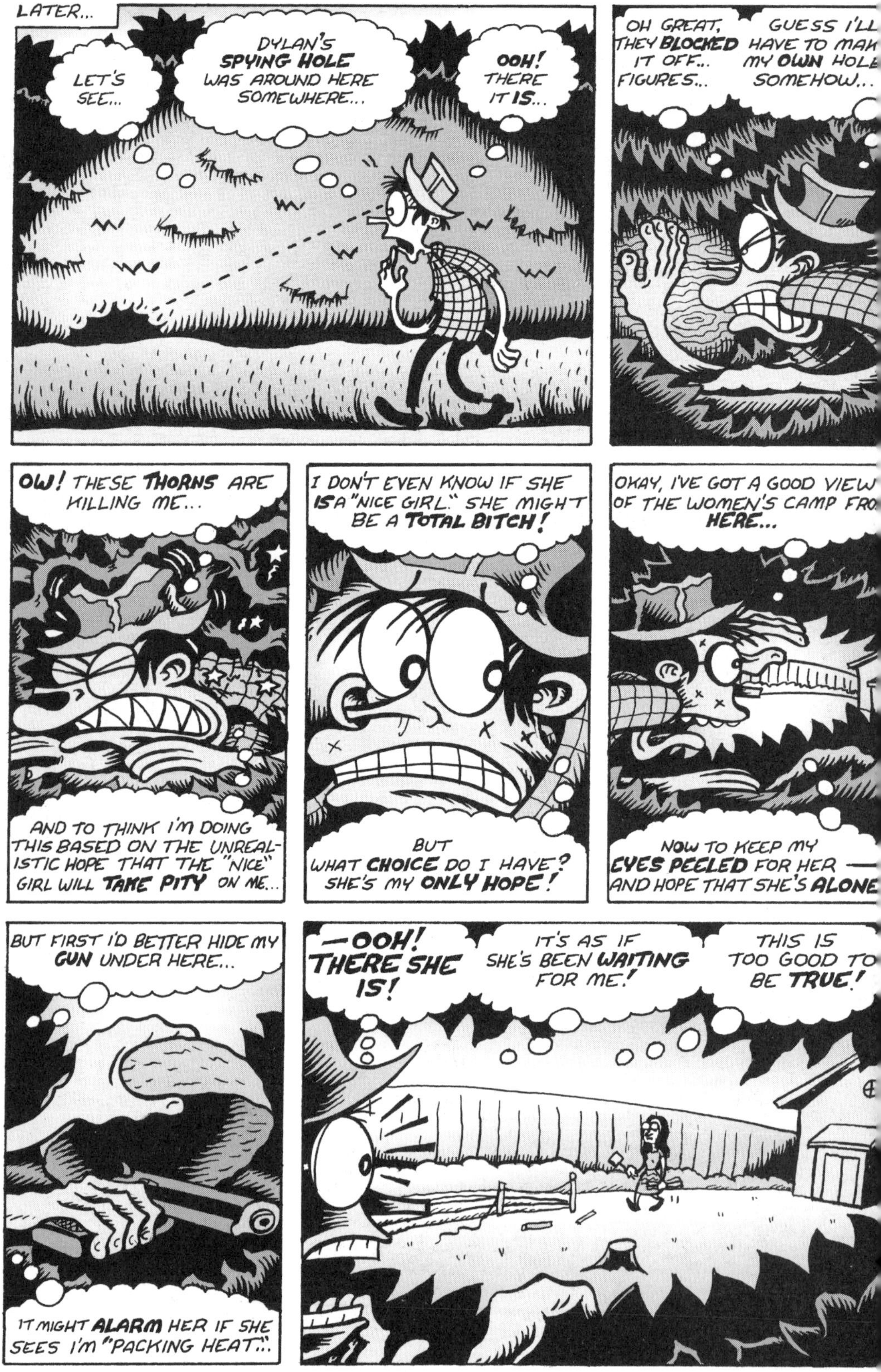
LATER...
LET'S SEE...
DYLAN'S SPYING HOLE WAS AROUND HERE SOMEWHERE...
OOH! THERE IT IS...
OH GREAT, THEY BLOCKED IT OFF.. FIGURES...
GUESS I'LL HAVE TO MAK MY OWN HOLE SOMEHOW...
OW! THESE THORNS ARE KILLING ME...
AND TO THINK I'M DOING THIS BASED ON THE UNREALISTIC HOPE THAT THE "NICE" GIRL WILL TAKE PITY ON ME...
I DON'T EVEN KNOW IF SHE IS A "NICE GIRL." SHE MIGHT BE A TOTAL BITCH!
BUT WHAT CHOICE DO I HAVE? SHE'S MY ONLY HOPE!
OKAY, I'VE GOT A GOOD VIEW OF THE WOMEN'S CAMP FRO HERE...
NOW TO KEEP MY EYES PEELED FOR HER — AND HOPE THAT SHE'S ALONE
BUT FIRST I'D BETTER HIDE MY GUN UNDER HERE...
IT MIGHT ALARM HER IF SHE SEES I'M "PACKING HEAT."
—OOH! THERE SHE IS!
IT'S AS IF SHE'S BEEN WAITING FOR ME!
THIS IS TOO GOOD TO BE TRUE!

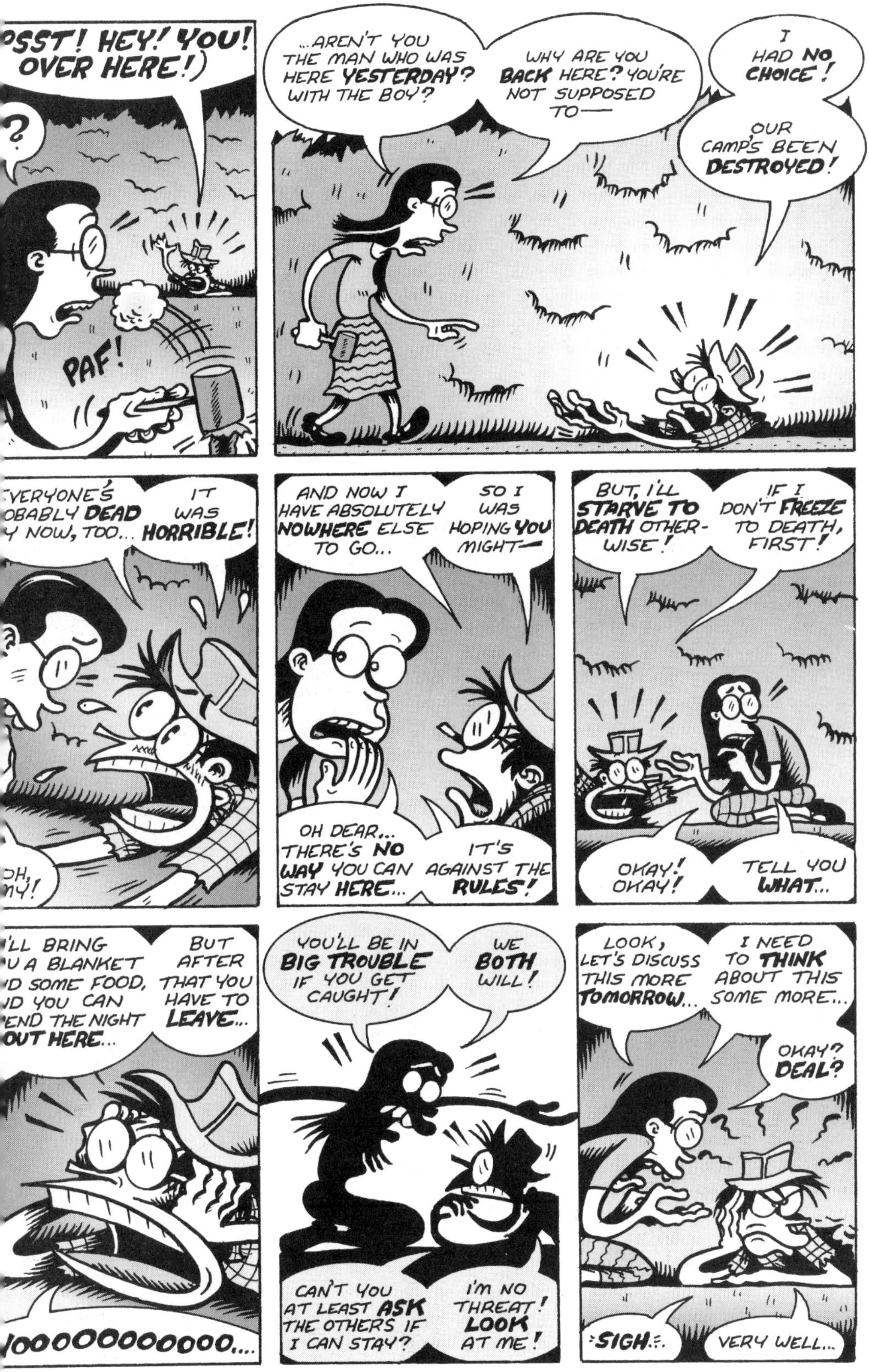
PSST! HEY! YOU! OVER HERE!)
?
PAF!
...AREN'T YOU THE MAN WHO WAS HERE YESTERDAY? WITH THE BOY?
WHY ARE YOU BACK HERE? YOU'RE NOT SUPPOSED TO—
I HAD NO CHOICE!
OUR CAMP'S BEEN DESTROYED!
EVERYONE'S PROBABLY DEAD BY NOW, TOO...
IT WAS HORRIBLE!
OH, MY!
AND NOW I HAVE ABSOLUTELY NOWHERE ELSE TO GO...
SO I WAS HOPING YOU MIGHT—
OH DEAR... THERE'S NO WAY YOU CAN STAY HERE...
IT'S AGAINST THE RULES!
BUT, I'LL STARVE TO DEATH OTHER-WISE!
IF I DON'T FREEZE TO DEATH, FIRST!
OKAY! OKAY!
TELL YOU WHAT...
I'LL BRING YOU A BLANKET AND SOME FOOD, AND YOU CAN SPEND THE NIGHT OUT HERE...
BUT AFTER THAT YOU HAVE TO LEAVE...
NOOOOOOOOOOOO....
YOU'LL BE IN BIG TROUBLE IF YOU GET CAUGHT!
WE BOTH WILL!
CAN'T YOU AT LEAST ASK THE OTHERS IF I CAN STAY?
I'M NO THREAT! LOOK AT ME!
LOOK, LET'S DISCUSS THIS MORE TOMORROW...
I NEED TO THINK ABOUT THIS SOME MORE...
OKAY? DEAL?
SIGH
VERY WELL...

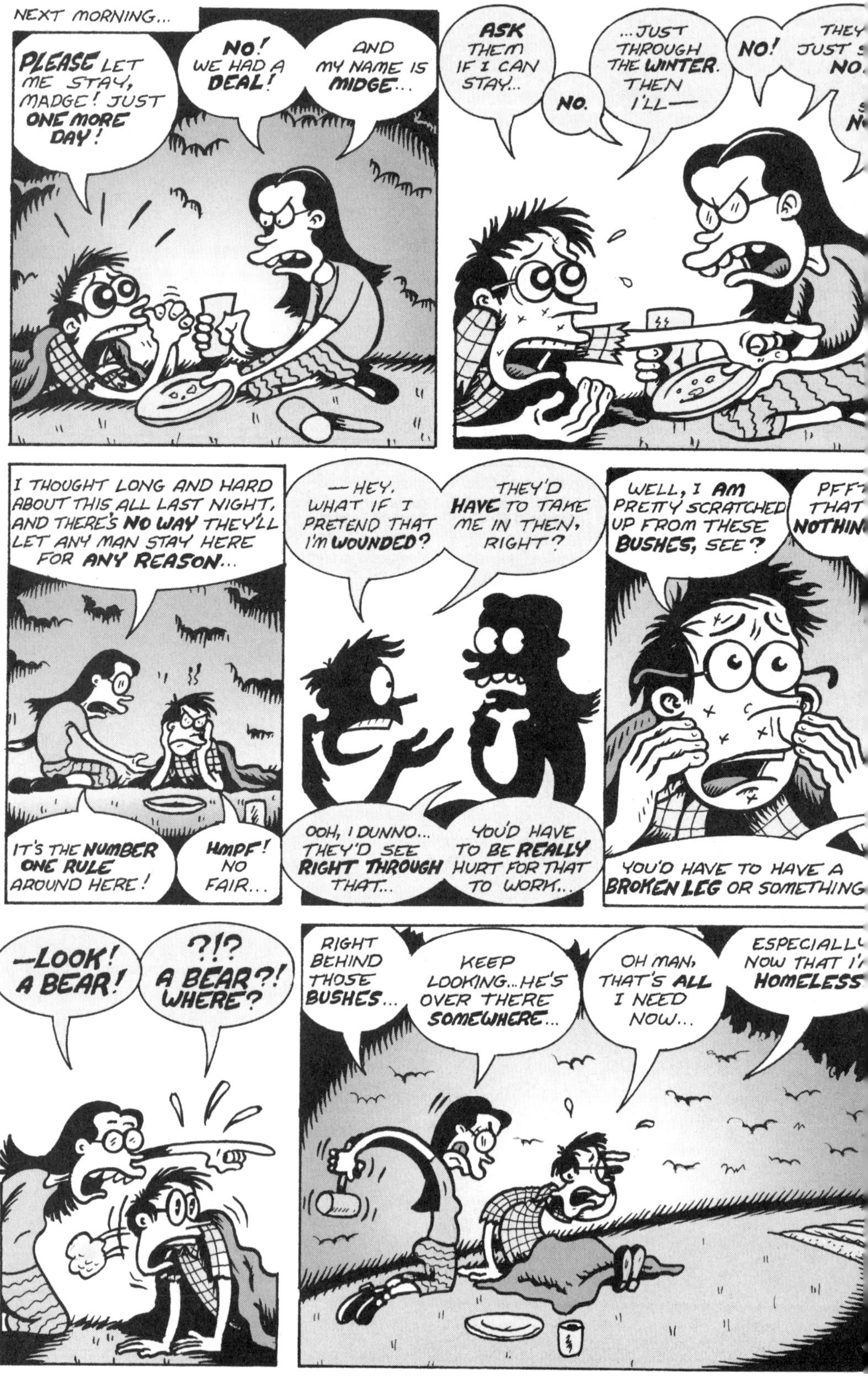
NEXT MORNING...
PLEASE LET ME STAY, MADGE! JUST ONE MORE DAY!
NO! WE HAD A DEAL!
AND MY NAME IS MIDGE...
ASK THEM IF I CAN STAY...
NO.
...JUST THROUGH THE WINTER. THEN I'LL—
NO!
I THOUGHT LONG AND HARD ABOUT THIS ALL LAST NIGHT, AND THERE'S NO WAY THEY'LL LET ANY MAN STAY HERE FOR ANY REASON...
IT'S THE NUMBER ONE RULE AROUND HERE!
HMPF! NO FAIR...
—HEY. WHAT IF I PRETEND THAT I'M WOUNDED?
THEY'D HAVE TO TAKE ME IN THEN, RIGHT?
OOH, I DUNNO... THEY'D SEE RIGHT THROUGH THAT...
YOU'D HAVE TO BE REALLY HURT FOR THAT TO WORK...
WELL, I AM PRETTY SCRATCHED UP FROM THESE BUSHES, SEE?
YOU'D HAVE TO HAVE A BROKEN LEG OR SOMETHING
—LOOK! A BEAR!
?!? A BEAR?! WHERE?
RIGHT BEHIND THOSE BUSHES...
KEEP LOOKING... HE'S OVER THERE SOMEWHERE...
OH MAN, THAT'S ALL I NEED NOW...

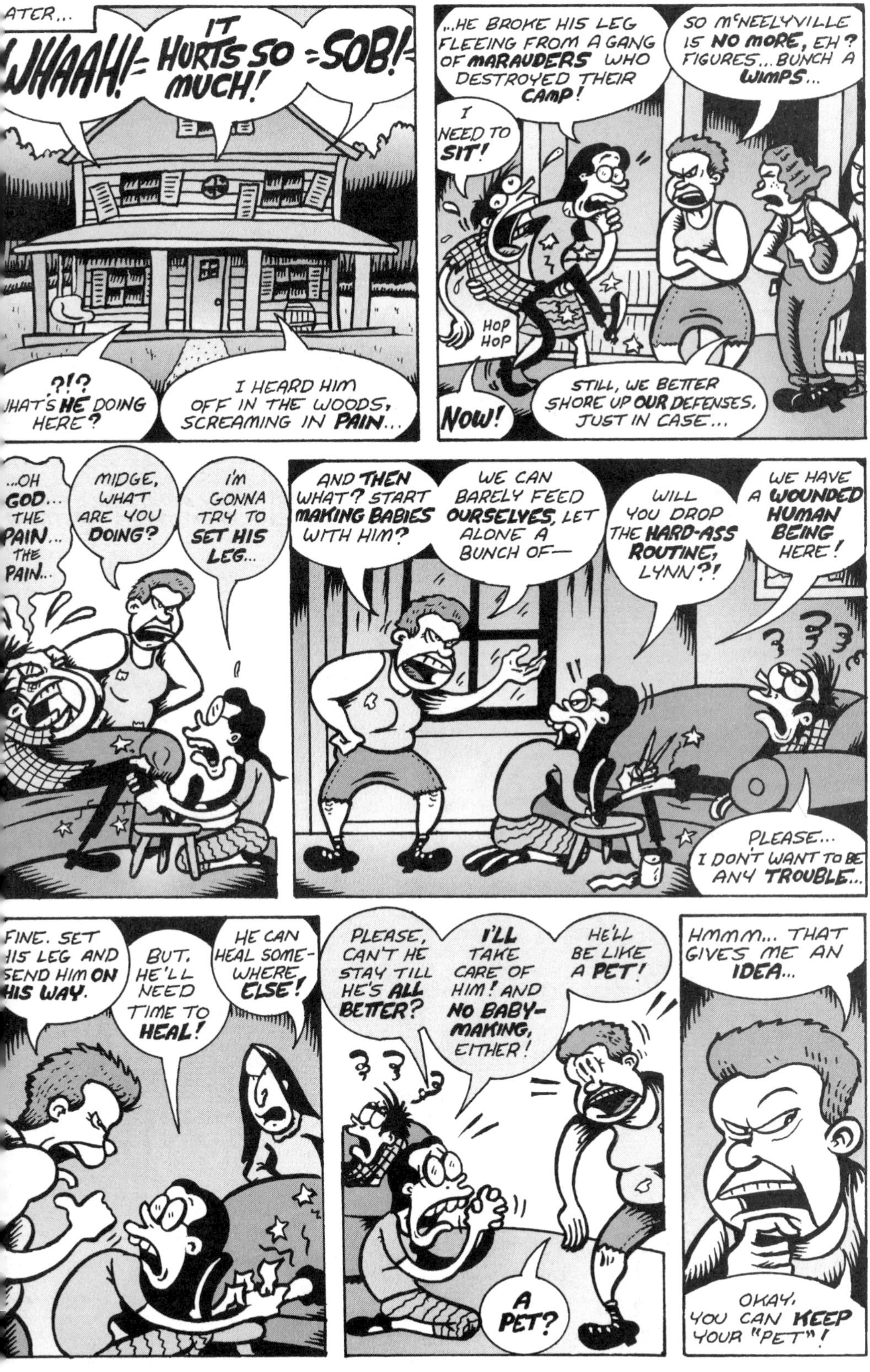
ATER...
WHAAH!
IT HURTS SO MUCH!
SOB!
?!?
HAT'S HE DOING HERE?
I HEARD HIM OFF IN THE WOODS, SCREAMING IN PAIN...
...HE BROKE HIS LEG FLEEING FROM A GANG OF MARAUDERS WHO DESTROYED THEIR CAMP!
I NEED TO SIT!
HOP HOP
NOW!
SO MᶜNEELYVILLE IS NO MORE, EH? FIGURES... BUNCH A WIMPS...
STILL, WE BETTER SHORE UP OUR DEFENSES, JUST IN CASE...
...OH GOD... THE PAIN... THE PAIN...
MIDGE, WHAT ARE YOU DOING?
I'M GONNA TRY TO SET HIS LEG...
AND THEN WHAT? START MAKING BABIES WITH HIM?
WE CAN BARELY FEED OURSELVES, LET ALONE A BUNCH OF—
WILL YOU DROP THE HARD-ASS ROUTINE, LYNN?!
WE HAVE A WOUNDED HUMAN BEING HERE!
PLEASE... I DON'T WANT TO BE ANY TROUBLE...
FINE. SET HIS LEG AND SEND HIM ON HIS WAY.
BUT, HE'LL NEED TIME TO HEAL!
HE CAN HEAL SOME-WHERE ELSE!
PLEASE, CAN'T HE STAY TILL HE'S ALL BETTER?
I'LL TAKE CARE OF HIM! AND NO BABY-MAKING, EITHER!
HE'LL BE LIKE A PET!
A PET?
HMMM... THAT GIVES ME AN IDEA...
OKAY, YOU CAN KEEP YOUR "PET"!

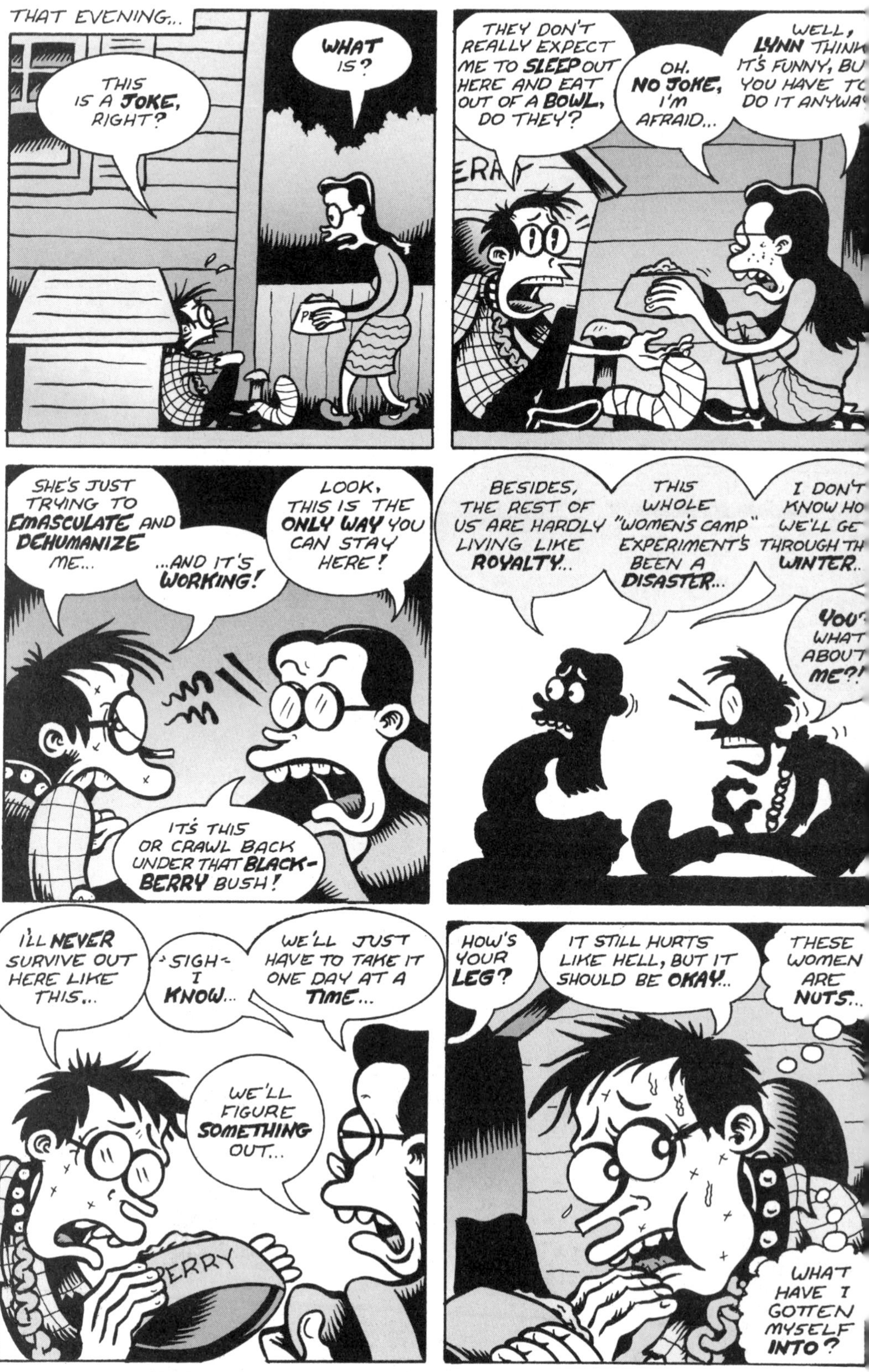
THAT EVENING...
THIS IS A JOKE, RIGHT?
WHAT IS?
THEY DON'T REALLY EXPECT ME TO SLEEP OUT HERE AND EAT OUT OF A BOWL, DO THEY?
OH. NO JOKE, I'M AFRAID...
WELL, LYNN THINK IT'S FUNNY, BU YOU HAVE TO DO IT ANYWA
SHE'S JUST TRYING TO EMASCULATE AND DEHUMANIZE ME...
...AND IT'S WORKING!
LOOK, THIS IS THE ONLY WAY YOU CAN STAY HERE!
IT'S THIS OR CRAWL BACK UNDER THAT BLACK-BERRY BUSH!
BESIDES, THE REST OF US ARE HARDLY LIVING LIKE ROYALTY...
THIS WHOLE "WOMEN'S CAMP" EXPERIMENT'S BEEN A DISASTER...
I DON'T KNOW HO WE'LL GE THROUGH TH WINTER...
WHAT ABOUT ME?!
I'LL NEVER SURVIVE OUT HERE LIKE THIS...
-SIGH- I KNOW...
WE'LL JUST HAVE TO TAKE IT ONE DAY AT A TIME...
WE'LL FIGURE SOMETHING OUT...
HOW'S YOUR LEG?
IT STILL HURTS LIKE HELL, BUT IT SHOULD BE OKAY...
THESE WOMEN ARE NUTS...
WHAT HAVE I GOTTEN MYSELF INTO?

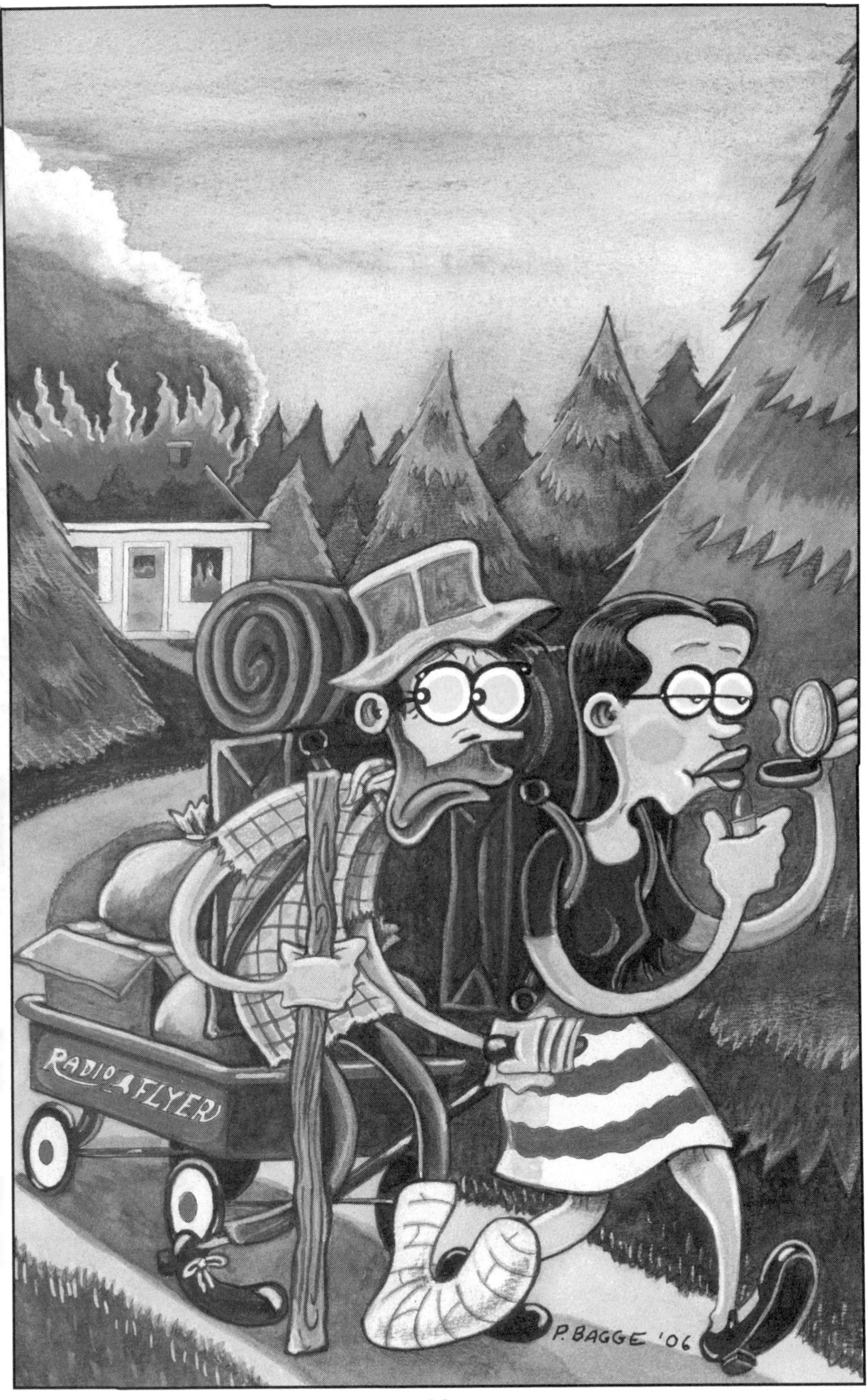
RADIO FLYER
P. BAGGE '06

Chapter 5

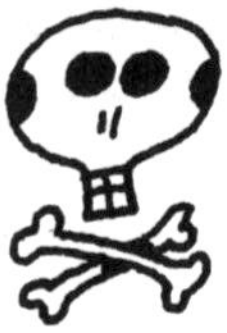

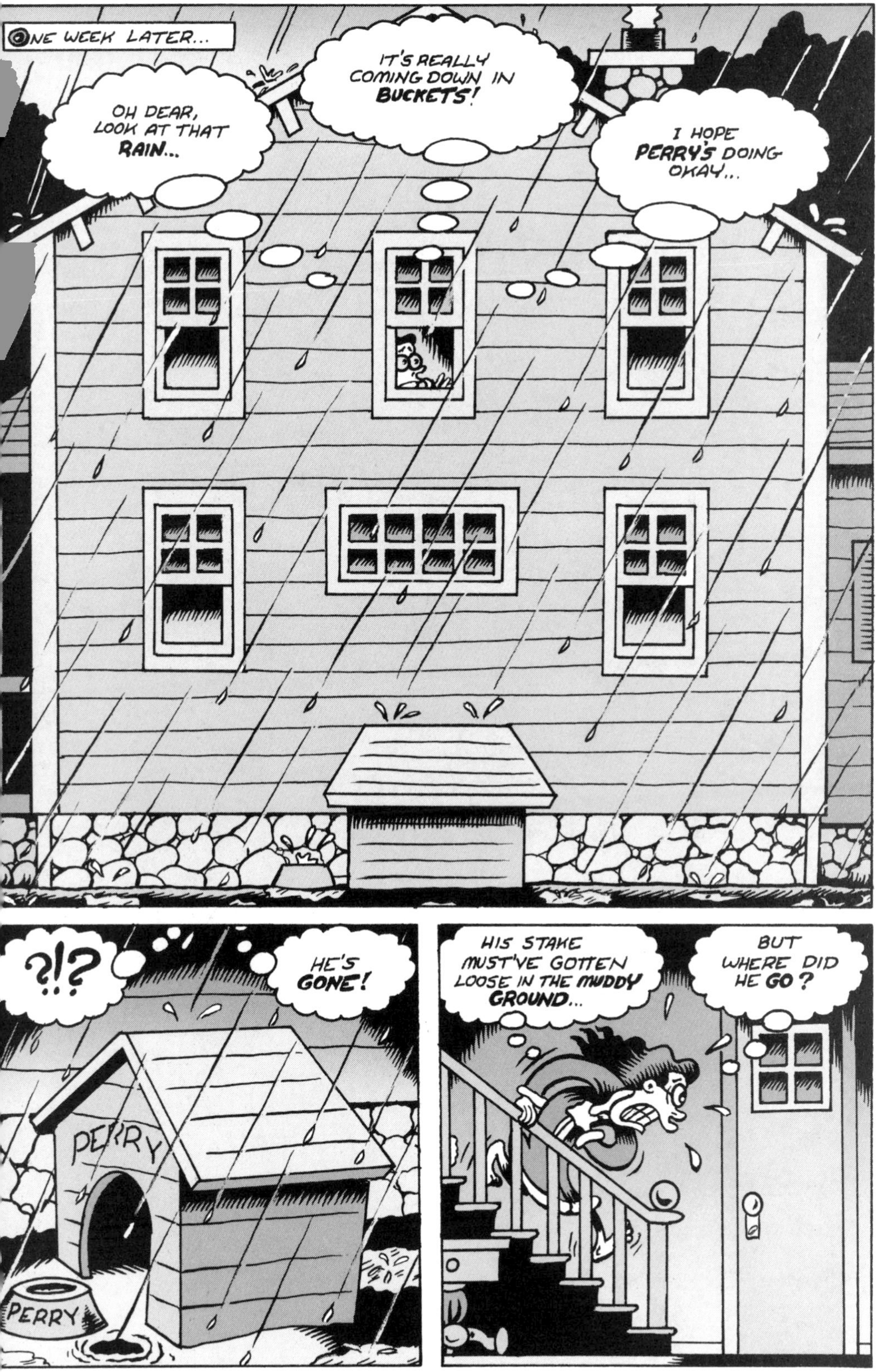
ONE WEEK LATER...
OH DEAR, LOOK AT THAT RAIN...
IT'S REALLY COMING DOWN IN BUCKETS!
I HOPE PERRY'S DOING OKAY...
?!?
HE'S GONE!
PERRY
PERRY
HIS STAKE MUST'VE GOTTEN LOOSE IN THE MUDDY GROUND...
BUT WHERE DID HE GO?

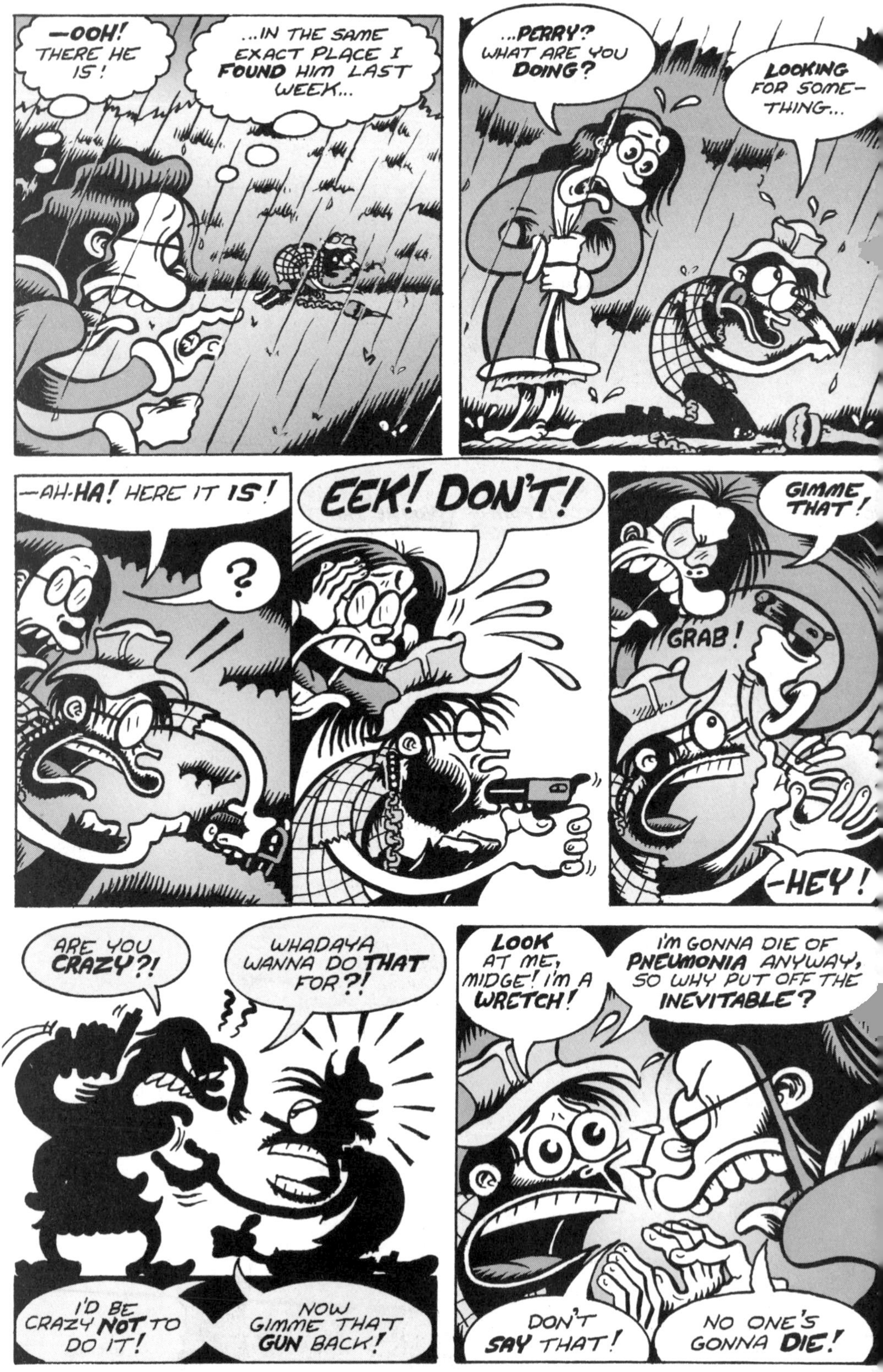

—OOH! THERE HE IS!
...IN THE SAME EXACT PLACE I FOUND HIM LAST WEEK...
...PERRY? WHAT ARE YOU DOING?
LOOKING FOR SOME-THING...
—AH-HA! HERE IT IS!
?
EEK! DON'T!
GIMME THAT!
GRAB!
-HEY!
ARE YOU CRAZY?!
WHADAYA WANNA DO THAT FOR?!
I'D BE CRAZY NOT TO DO IT!
NOW GIMME THAT GUN BACK!
LOOK AT ME, MIDGE! I'M A WRETCH!
I'M GONNA DIE OF PNEUMONIA ANYWAY, SO WHY PUT OFF THE INEVITABLE?
DON'T SAY THAT!
NO ONE'S GONNA DIE!

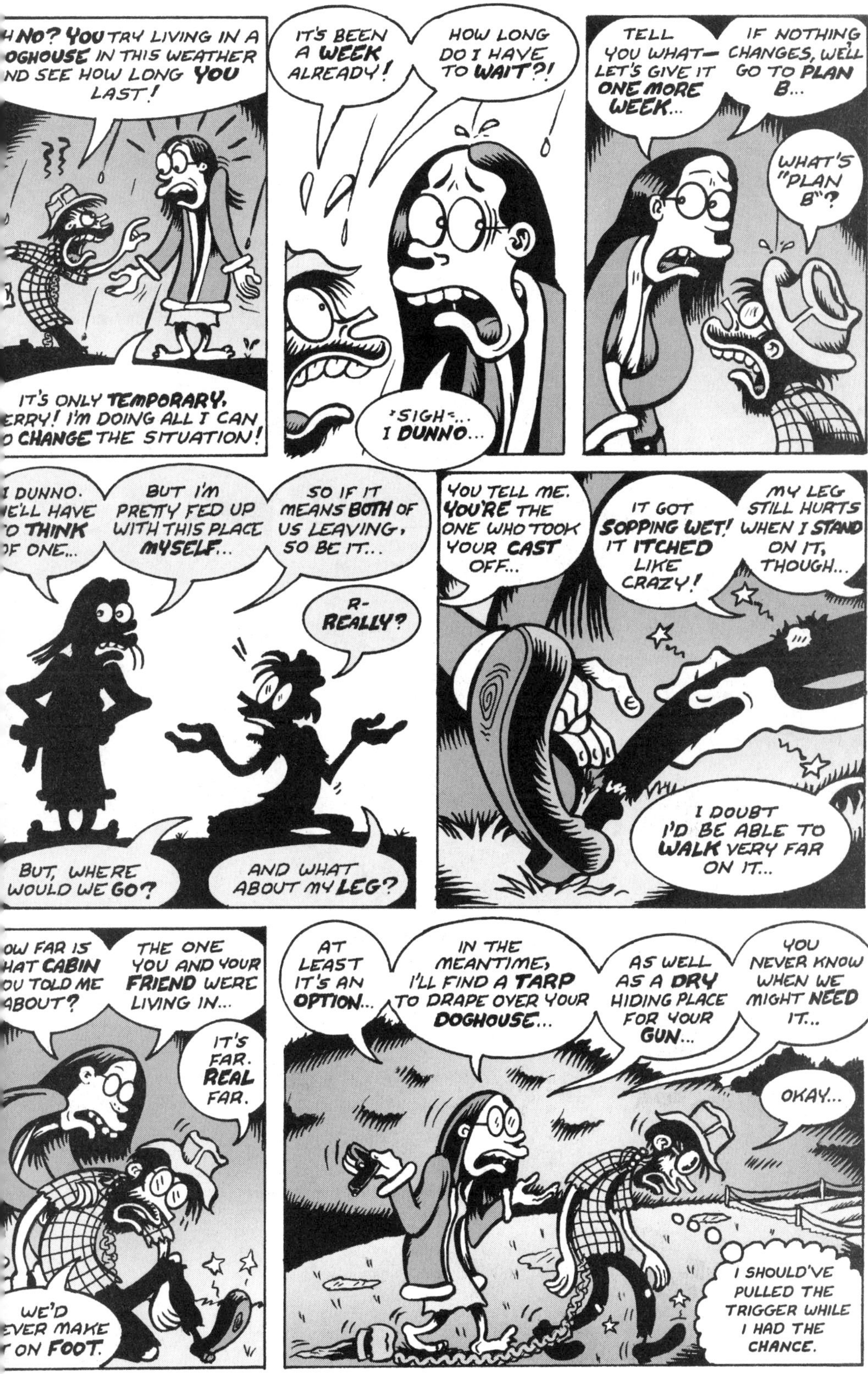
H NO? YOU TRY LIVING IN A OGHOUSE IN THIS WEATHER ND SEE HOW LONG YOU LAST!
IT'S ONLY TEMPORARY, ERRY! I'M DOING ALL I CAN O CHANGE THE SITUATION!
IT'S BEEN A WEEK ALREADY!
HOW LONG DO I HAVE TO WAIT?!
SIGH... I DUNNO...
TELL YOU WHAT— LET'S GIVE IT ONE MORE WEEK...
IF NOTHING CHANGES, WE'LL GO TO PLAN B...
WHAT'S "PLAN B"?
I DUNNO. WE'LL HAVE TO THINK OF ONE...
BUT I'M PRETTY FED UP WITH THIS PLACE MYSELF...
SO IF IT MEANS BOTH OF US LEAVING, SO BE IT...
R-REALLY?
BUT, WHERE WOULD WE GO?
AND WHAT ABOUT MY LEG?
YOU TELL ME. YOU'RE THE ONE WHO TOOK YOUR CAST OFF...
IT GOT SOPPING WET! IT ITCHED LIKE CRAZY!
MY LEG STILL HURTS WHEN I STAND ON IT, THOUGH...
I DOUBT I'D BE ABLE TO WALK VERY FAR ON IT...
OW FAR IS HAT CABIN OU TOLD ME ABOUT?
THE ONE YOU AND YOUR FRIEND WERE LIVING IN...
IT'S FAR. REAL FAR.
WE'D EVER MAKE T ON FOOT.
AT LEAST IT'S AN OPTION...
IN THE MEANTIME, I'LL FIND A TARP TO DRAPE OVER YOUR DOGHOUSE...
AS WELL AS A DRY HIDING PLACE FOR YOUR GUN...
YOU NEVER KNOW WHEN WE MIGHT NEED IT...
OKAY...
I SHOULD'VE PULLED THE TRIGGER WHILE I HAD THE CHANCE.

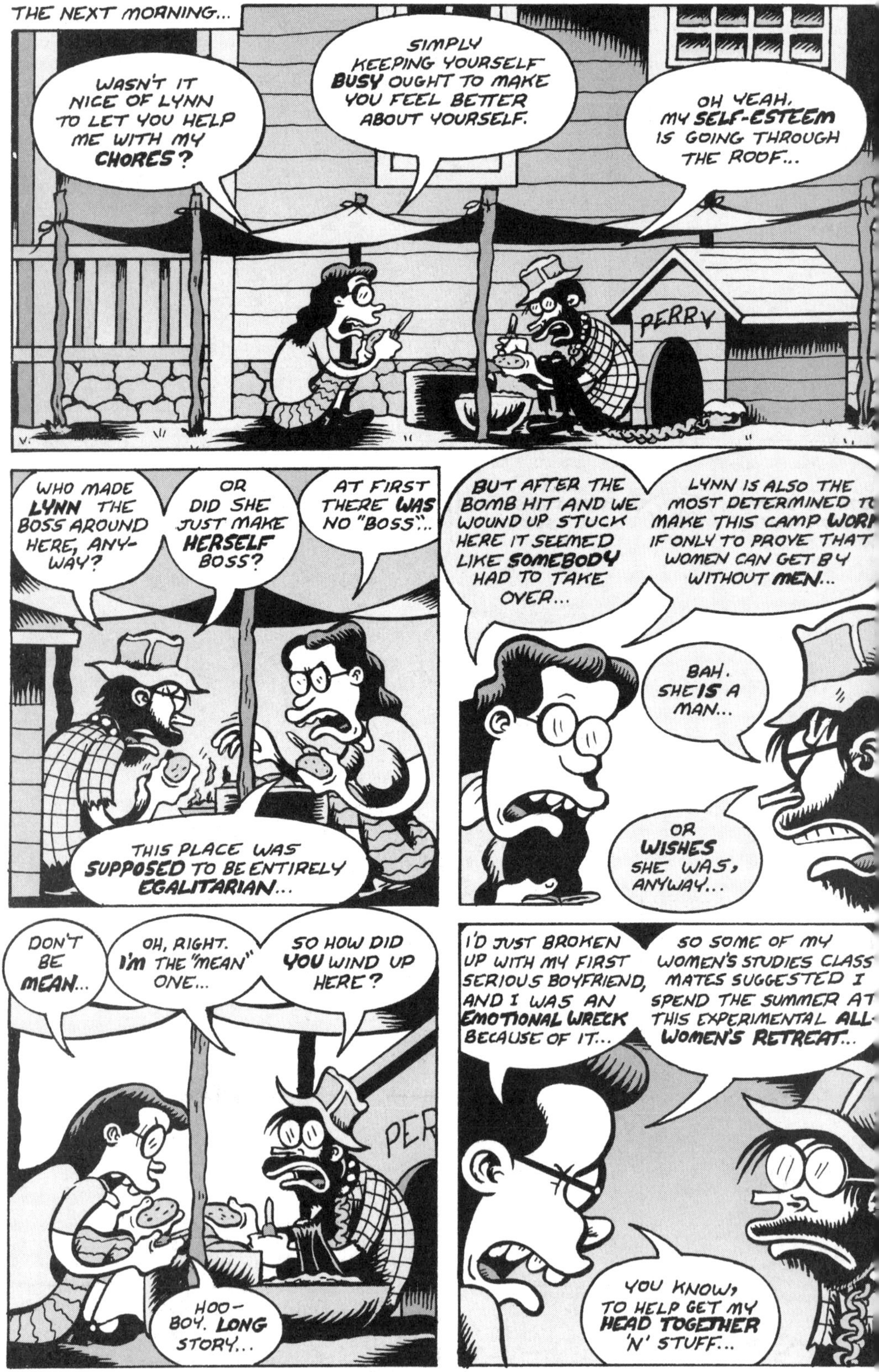
THE NEXT MORNING...
WASN'T IT NICE OF LYNN TO LET YOU HELP ME WITH MY CHORES?
SIMPLY KEEPING YOURSELF BUSY OUGHT TO MAKE YOU FEEL BETTER ABOUT YOURSELF.
OH YEAH. MY SELF-ESTEEM IS GOING THROUGH THE ROOF...
PERRY
WHO MADE LYNN THE BOSS AROUND HERE, ANYWAY?
OR DID SHE JUST MAKE HERSELF BOSS?
AT FIRST THERE WAS NO "BOSS"...
THIS PLACE WAS SUPPOSED TO BE ENTIRELY EGALITARIAN...
BUT AFTER THE BOMB HIT AND WE WOUND UP STUCK HERE IT SEEMED LIKE SOMEBODY HAD TO TAKE OVER...
LYNN IS ALSO THE MOST DETERMINED TO MAKE THIS CAMP WORK IF ONLY TO PROVE THAT WOMEN CAN GET BY WITHOUT MEN...
BAH. SHE IS A MAN...
OR WISHES SHE WAS, ANYWAY...
DON'T BE MEAN...
OH, RIGHT. I'M THE "MEAN" ONE...
SO HOW DID YOU WIND UP HERE?
HOO-BOY. LONG STORY...
I'D JUST BROKEN UP WITH MY FIRST SERIOUS BOYFRIEND, AND I WAS AN EMOTIONAL WRECK BECAUSE OF IT...
SO SOME OF MY WOMEN'S STUDIES CLASSMATES SUGGESTED I SPEND THE SUMMER AT THIS EXPERIMENTAL ALL-WOMEN'S RETREAT...
YOU KNOW, TO HELP GET MY HEAD TOGETHER 'N' STUFF...

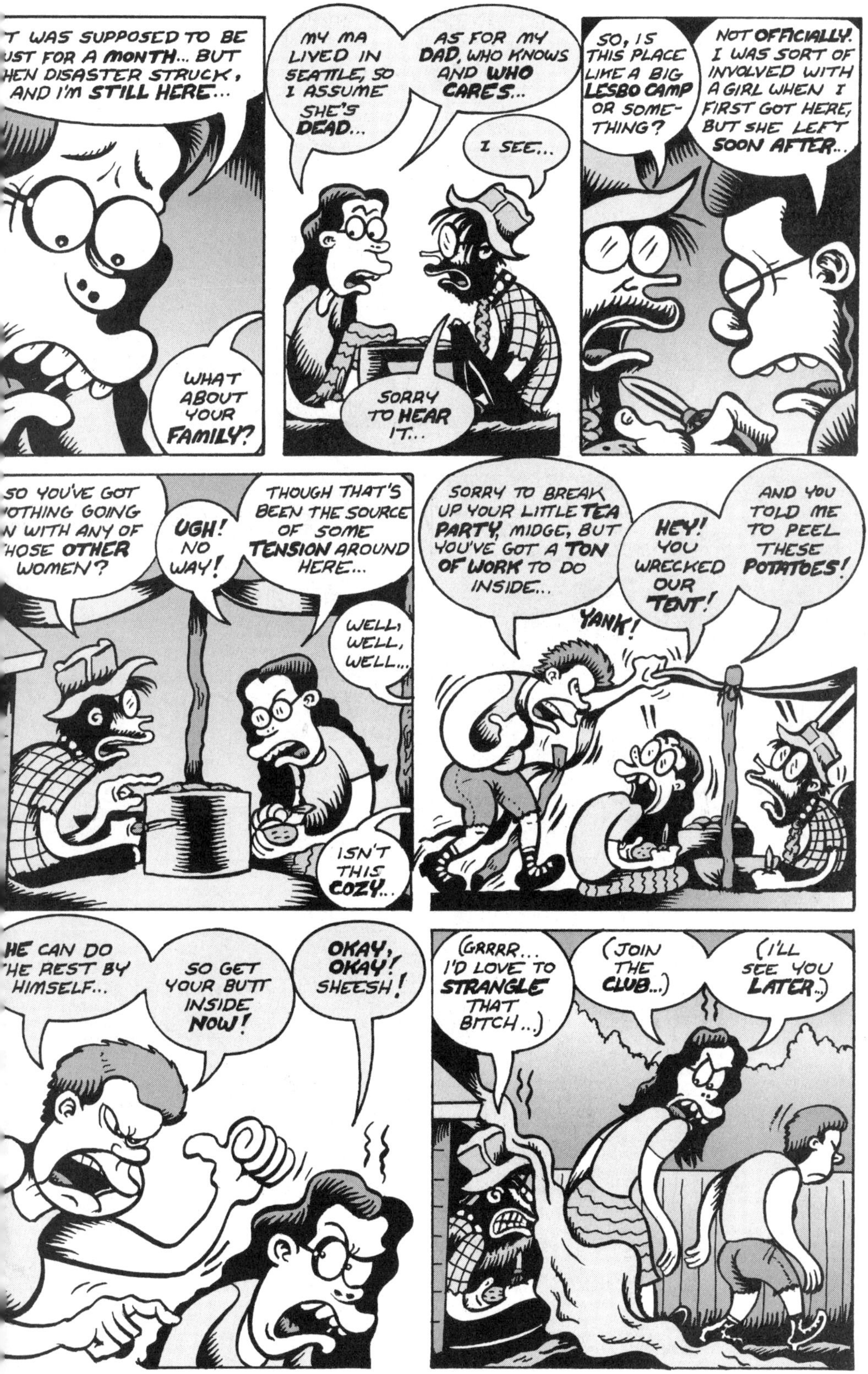

T WAS SUPPOSED TO BE UST FOR A MONTH... BUT HEN DISASTER STRUCK, AND I'M STILL HERE...
WHAT ABOUT YOUR FAMILY?
MY MA LIVED IN SEATTLE, SO I ASSUME SHE'S DEAD...
AS FOR MY DAD, WHO KNOWS AND WHO CARES...
I SEE...
SORRY TO HEAR IT...
SO, IS THIS PLACE LIKE A BIG LESBO CAMP OR SOME-THING?
NOT OFFICIALLY. I WAS SORT OF INVOLVED WITH A GIRL WHEN I FIRST GOT HERE, BUT SHE LEFT SOON AFTER...
SO YOU'VE GOT OTHING GOING N WITH ANY OF HOSE OTHER WOMEN?
UGH! NO WAY!
THOUGH THAT'S BEEN THE SOURCE OF SOME TENSION AROUND HERE...
WELL, WELL, WELL...
ISN'T THIS COZY...
SORRY TO BREAK UP YOUR LITTLE TEA PARTY, MIDGE, BUT YOU'VE GOT A TON OF WORK TO DO INSIDE...
YANK!
HEY! YOU WRECKED OUR TENT!
AND YOU TOLD ME TO PEEL THESE POTATOES!
HE CAN DO HE REST BY HIMSELF...
SO GET YOUR BUTT INSIDE NOW!
OKAY, OKAY! SHEESH!
(GRRRR... I'D LOVE TO STRANGLE THAT BITCH...)
(JOIN THE CLUB...)
(I'LL SEE YOU LATER...)

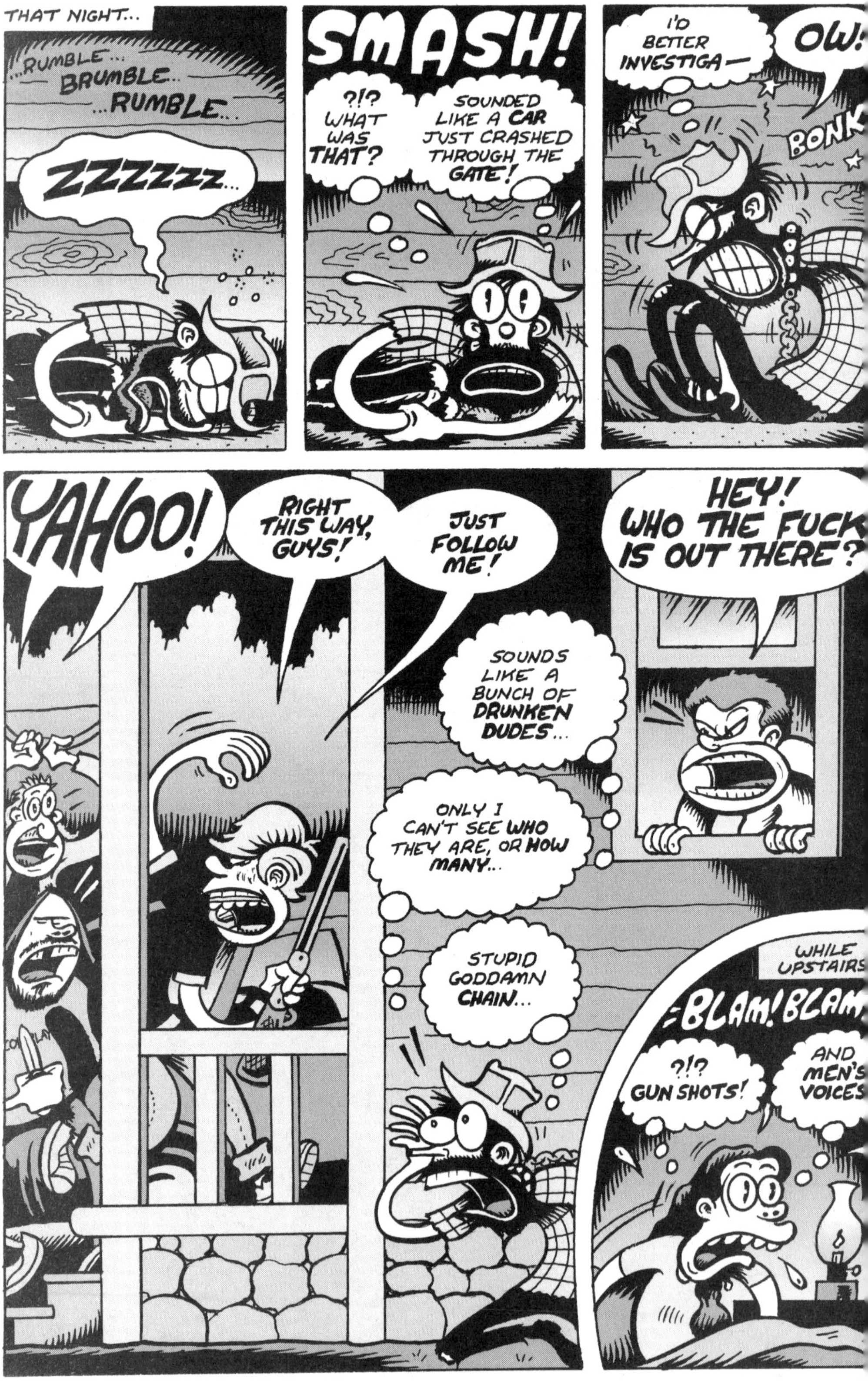
THAT NIGHT...
...RUMBLE... BRUMBLE... ...RUMBLE...
ZZZZZZ...
SMASH!
?!? WHAT WAS THAT?
SOUNDED LIKE A CAR JUST CRASHED THROUGH THE GATE!
I'D BETTER INVESTIGA—
OW!
BONK
YAHOO!
RIGHT THIS WAY, GUYS!
JUST FOLLOW ME!
HEY! WHO THE FUCK IS OUT THERE?
SOUNDS LIKE A BUNCH OF DRUNKEN DUDES...
ONLY I CAN'T SEE WHO THEY ARE, OR HOW MANY...
STUPID GODDAMN CHAIN...
WHILE UPSTAIRS
BLAM! BLAM
?!? GUN SHOTS!
AND MEN'S VOICES

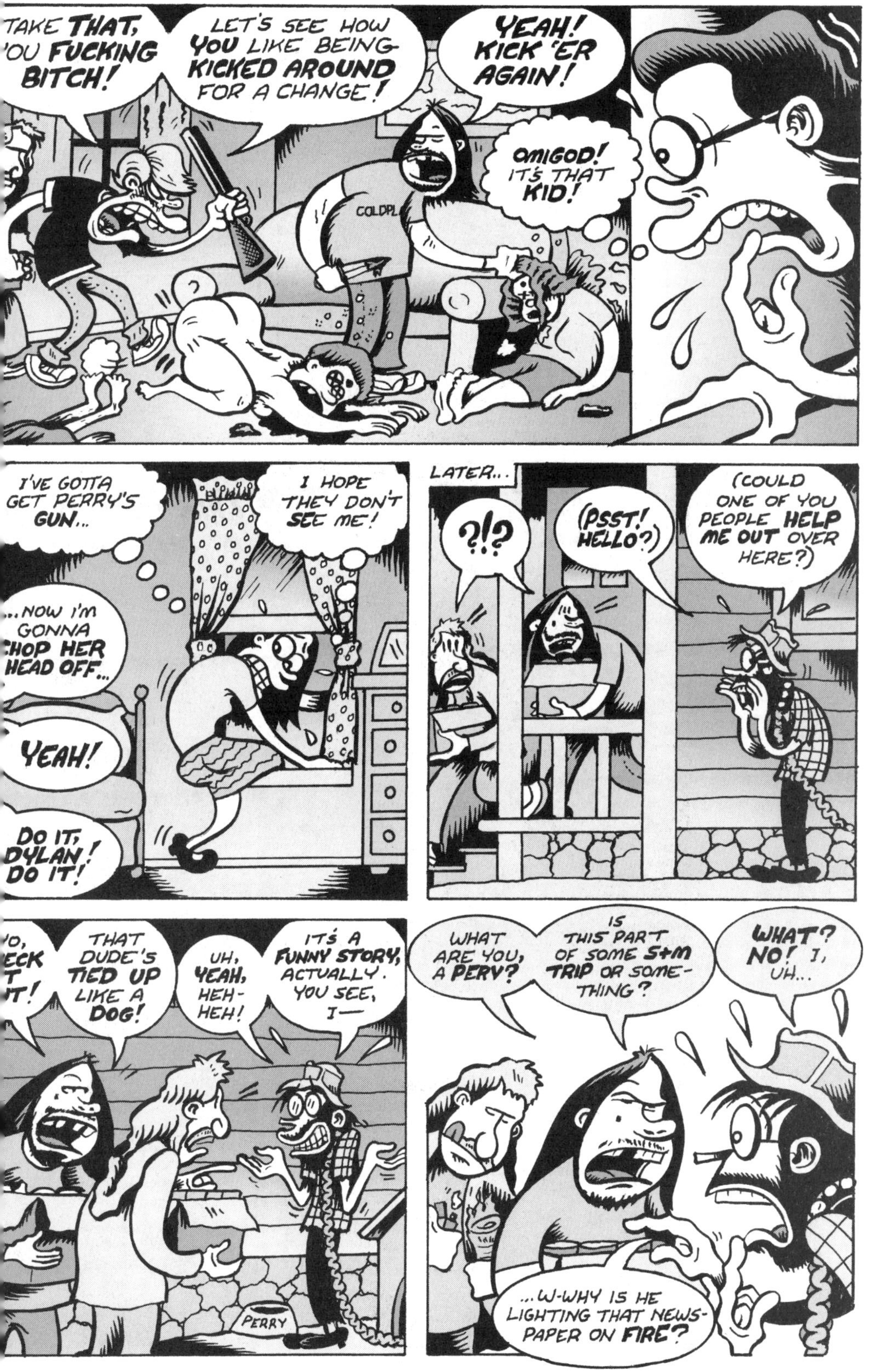
TAKE THAT, YOU FUCKING BITCH!
LET'S SEE HOW YOU LIKE BEING KICKED AROUND FOR A CHANGE!
YEAH! KICK 'ER AGAIN!
OMIGOD! IT'S THAT KID!
COLDPL
I'VE GOTTA GET PERRY'S GUN...
I HOPE THEY DON'T SEE ME!
...NOW I'M GONNA CHOP HER HEAD OFF...
YEAH!
DO IT, DYLAN! DO IT!
LATER...
?!?
(PSST! HELLO?)
(COULD ONE OF YOU PEOPLE HELP ME OUT OVER HERE?)
THAT DUDE'S TIED UP LIKE A DOG!
UH, YEAH, HEH-HEH!
IT'S A FUNNY STORY, ACTUALLY. YOU SEE, I—
PERRY
WHAT ARE YOU, A PERV?
IS THIS PART OF SOME S+M TRIP OR SOME-THING?
WHAT? NO! I, UH...
...W-WHY IS HE LIGHTING THAT NEWS-PAPER ON FIRE?

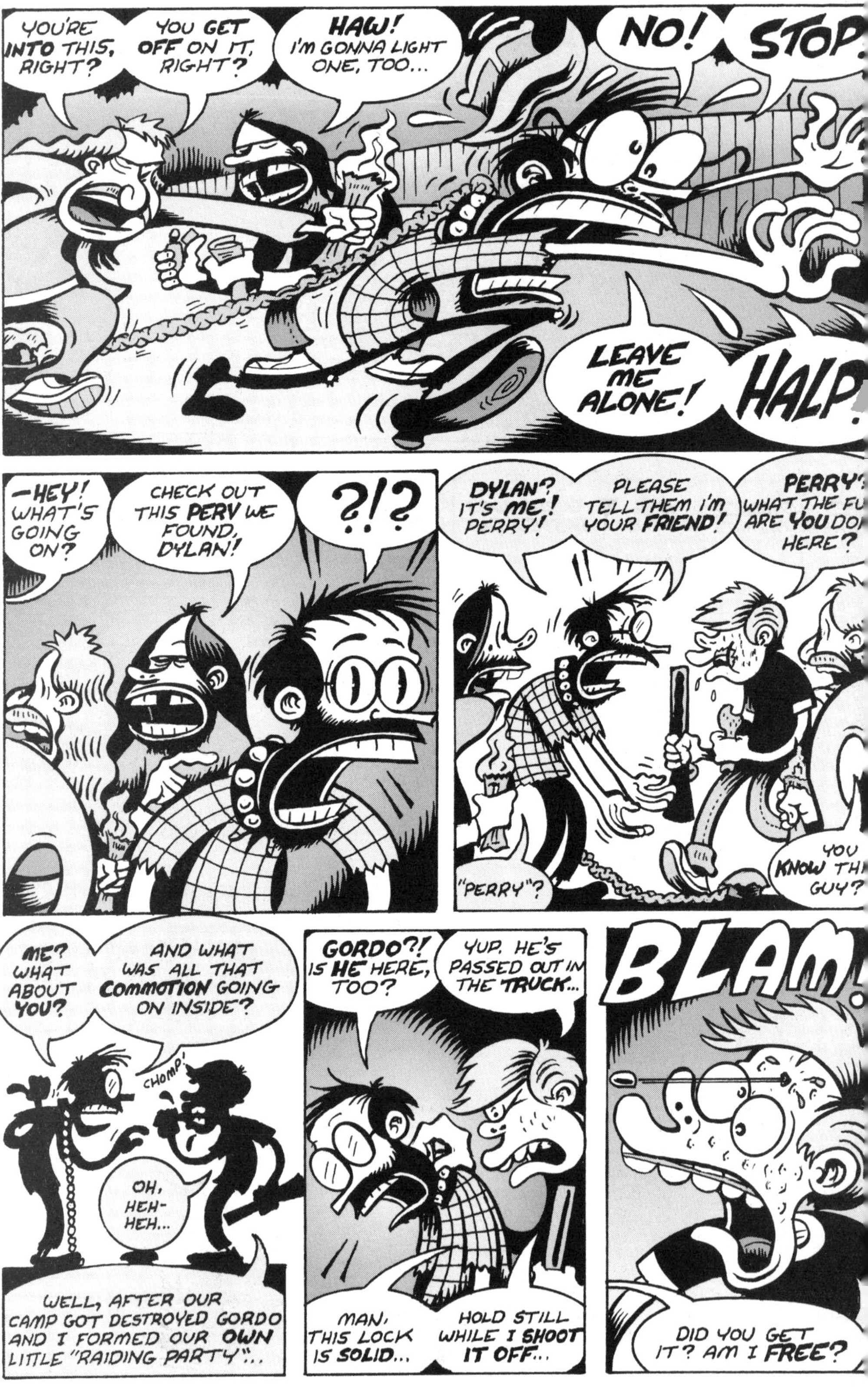

YOU'RE INTO THIS, RIGHT?
YOU GET OFF ON IT, RIGHT?
HAW! I'M GONNA LIGHT ONE, TOO...
NO!
STOP!
LEAVE ME ALONE!
HALP!
—HEY! WHAT'S GOING ON?
CHECK OUT THIS PERV WE FOUND, DYLAN!
?!?
DYLAN? IT'S ME! PERRY!
PLEASE TELL THEM I'M YOUR FRIEND!
PERRY?
WHAT THE FU
ARE YOU DO
HERE?
"PERRY"?
YOU KNOW THI
GUY?
ME? WHAT ABOUT YOU?
AND WHAT WAS ALL THAT COMMOTION GOING ON INSIDE?
CHOMP!
OH, HEH-HEH...
WELL, AFTER OUR CAMP GOT DESTROYED GORDO AND I FORMED OUR OWN LITTLE "RAIDING PARTY"...
GORDO?! IS HE HERE, TOO?
YUP. HE'S PASSED OUT IN THE TRUCK...
MAN, THIS LOCK IS SOLID...
HOLD STILL WHILE I SHOOT IT OFF...
BLAM!
DID YOU GET IT? AM I FREE?

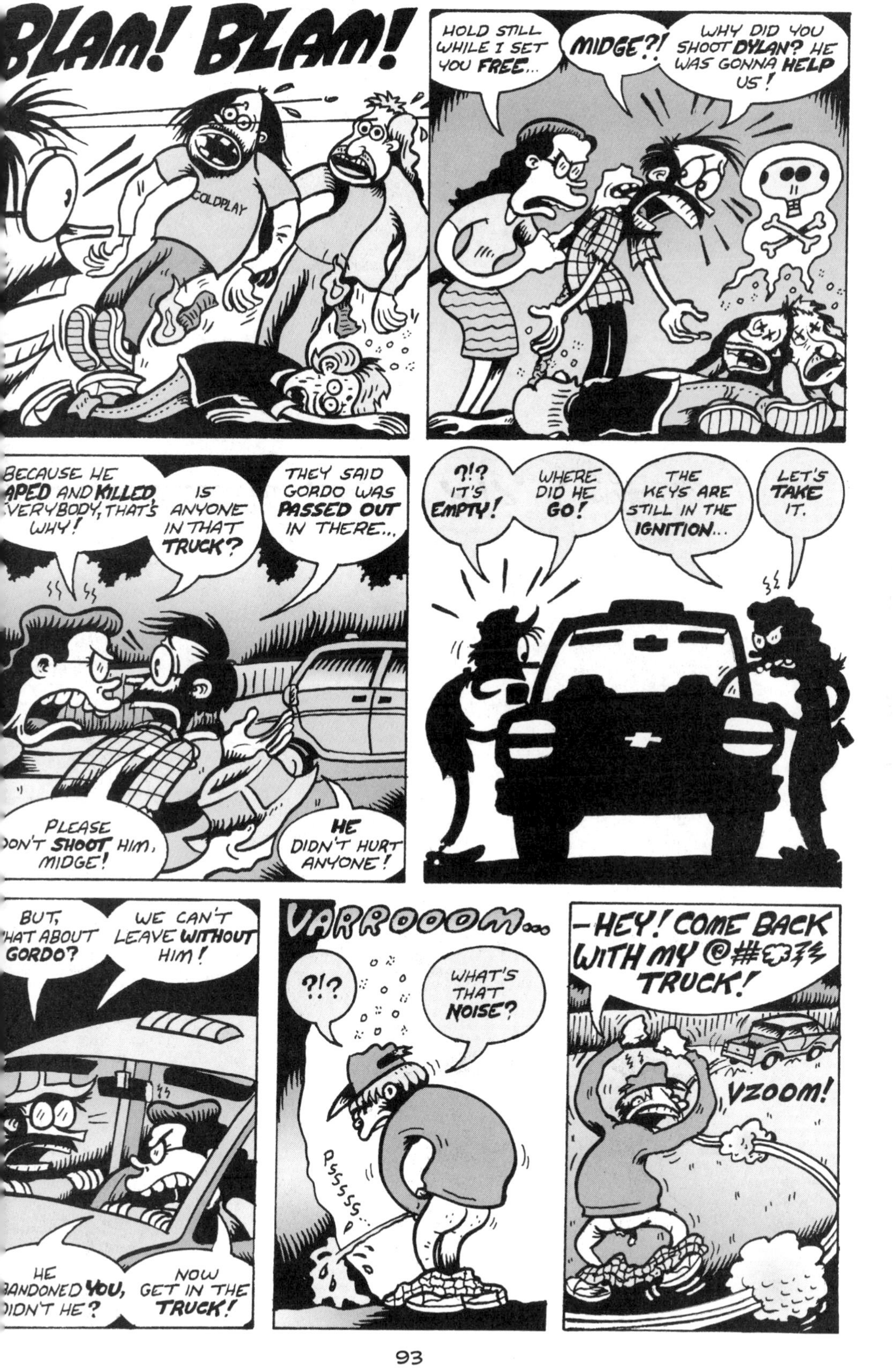
BLAM! BLAM!
COLDPLAY
HOLD STILL WHILE I SET YOU FREE...
MIDGE?!
WHY DID YOU SHOOT DYLAN? HE WAS GONNA HELP US!
BECAUSE HE APED AND KILLED VERYBODY, THAT'S WHY!
IS ANYONE IN THAT TRUCK?
THEY SAID GORDO WAS PASSED OUT IN THERE...
PLEASE ON'T SHOOT HIM, MIDGE!
HE DIDN'T HURT ANYONE!
?!? IT'S EMPTY!
WHERE DID HE GO!
THE KEYS ARE STILL IN THE IGNITION...
LET'S TAKE IT.
BUT, HAT ABOUT GORDO?
WE CAN'T LEAVE WITHOUT HIM!
HE BANDONED YOU, DIDN'T HE?
NOW GET IN THE TRUCK!
VARROOOOM...
?!?
WHAT'S THAT NOISE?
PSSSSSS...
—HEY! COME BACK WITH MY @#%$ TRUCK!
VZOOM!

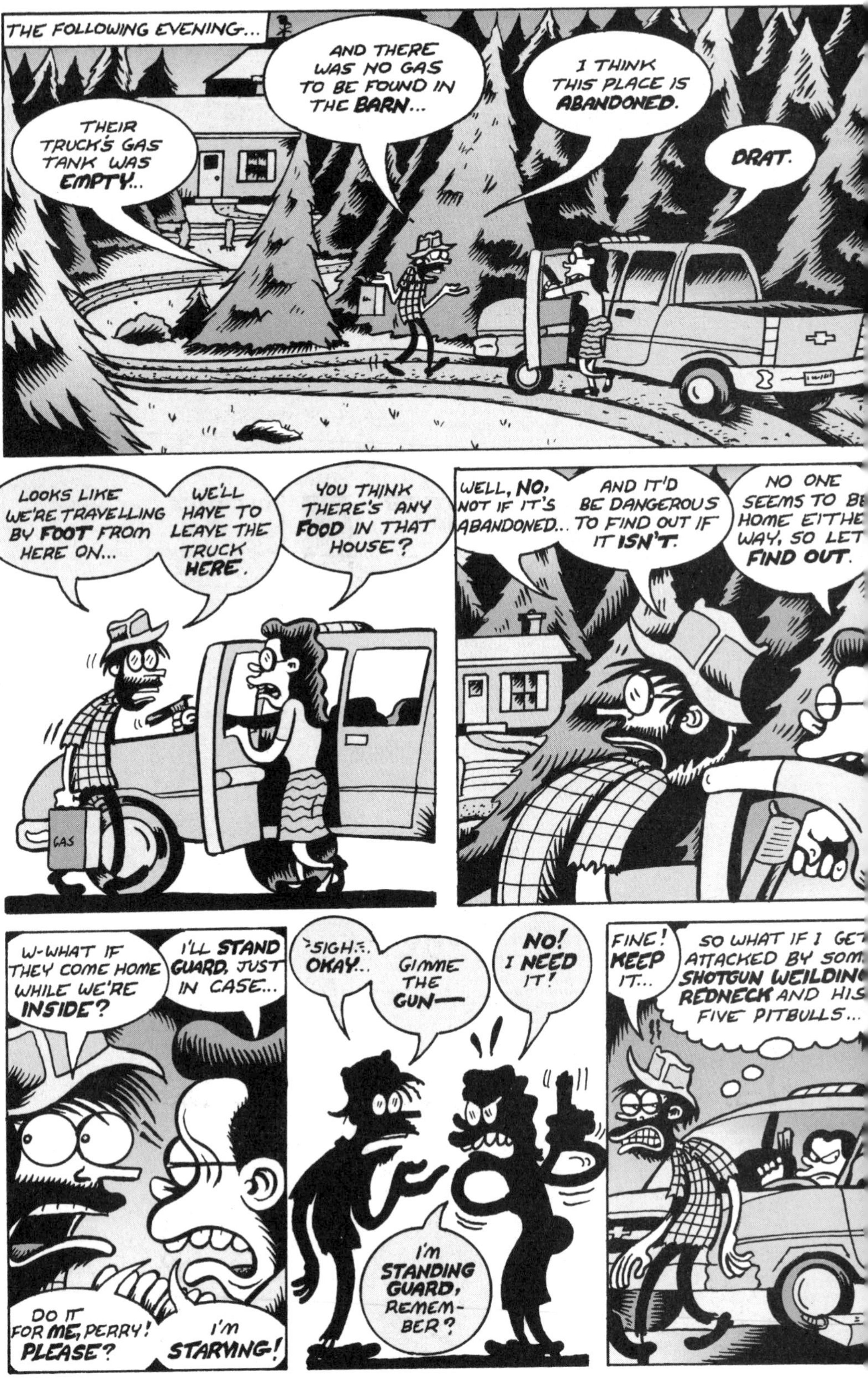
THE FOLLOWING EVENING...
THEIR TRUCK'S GAS TANK WAS EMPTY...
AND THERE WAS NO GAS TO BE FOUND IN THE BARN...
I THINK THIS PLACE IS ABANDONED.
DRAT.
LOOKS LIKE WE'RE TRAVELLING BY FOOT FROM HERE ON...
WE'LL HAVE TO LEAVE THE TRUCK HERE.
YOU THINK THERE'S ANY FOOD IN THAT HOUSE?
GAS
WELL, NO, NOT IF IT'S ABANDONED...
AND IT'D BE DANGEROUS TO FIND OUT IF IT ISN'T.
NO ONE SEEMS TO B HOME EITHE WAY, SO LET FIND OUT.
W-WHAT IF THEY COME HOME WHILE WE'RE INSIDE?
I'LL STAND GUARD, JUST IN CASE...
DO IT FOR ME, PERRY! PLEASE?
I'M STARVING!
SIGH... OKAY...
GIMME THE GUN—
NO! I NEED IT!
I'M STANDING GUARD, REMEMBER?
FINE! KEEP IT...
SO WHAT IF I GE ATTACKED BY SOM SHOTGUN WEILDIN REDNECK AND HIS FIVE PITBULLS...

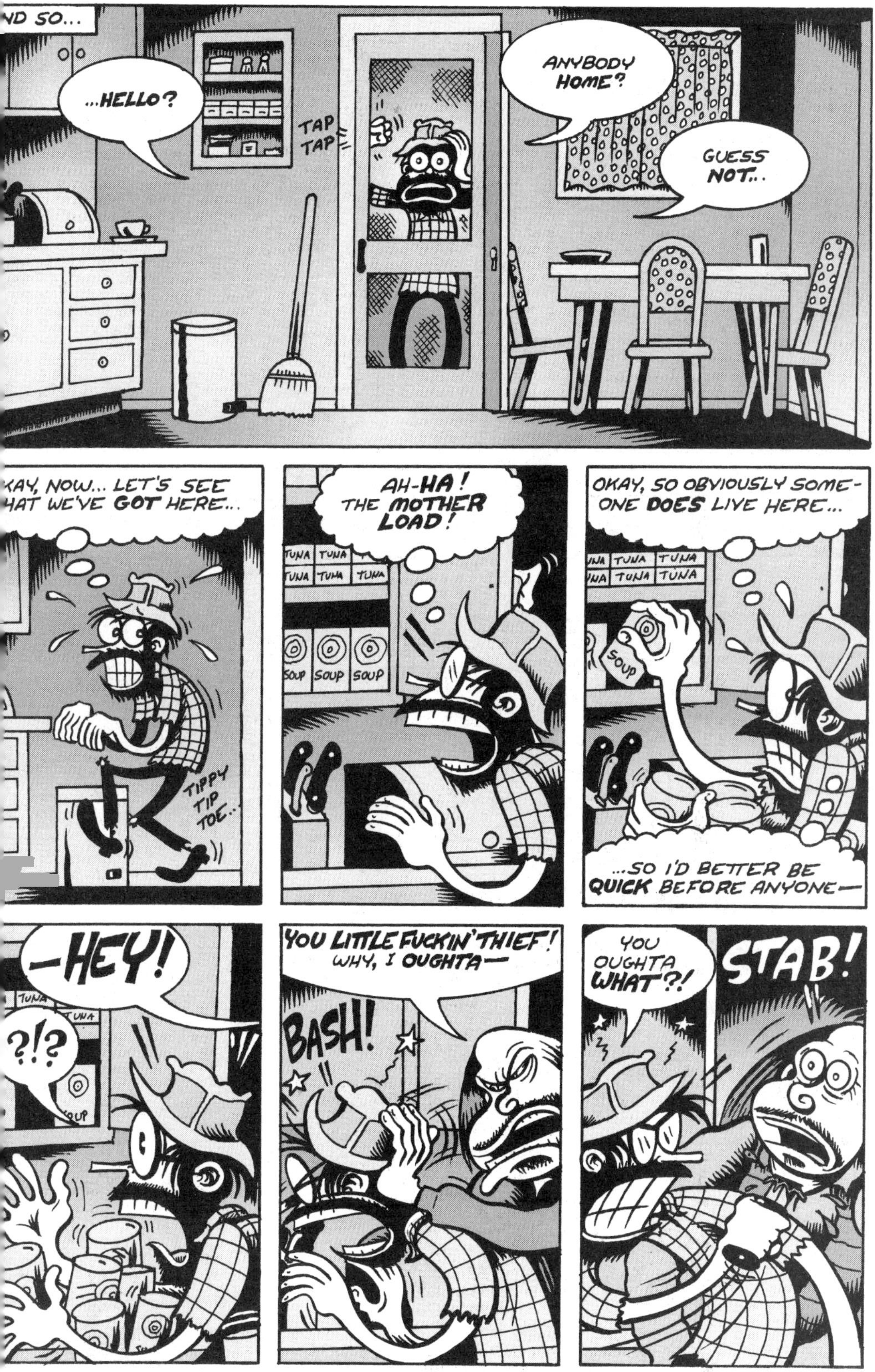
ND SO...
...HELLO?
TAP TAP
ANYBODY HOME?
GUESS NOT...
KAY, NOW... LET'S SEE HAT WE'VE GOT HERE...
TIPPY TIP TOE...
AH-HA! THE MOTHER LOAD!
TUNA TUNA
TUNA TUNA TUNA
SOUP SOUP SOUP
OKAY, SO OBVIOUSLY SOME-ONE DOES LIVE HERE...
SOUP
...SO I'D BETTER BE QUICK BEFORE ANYONE—
—HEY!
?!?
YOU LITTLE FUCKIN' THIEF! WHY, I OUGHTA—
BASH!
YOU OUGHTA WHAT?!
STAB!

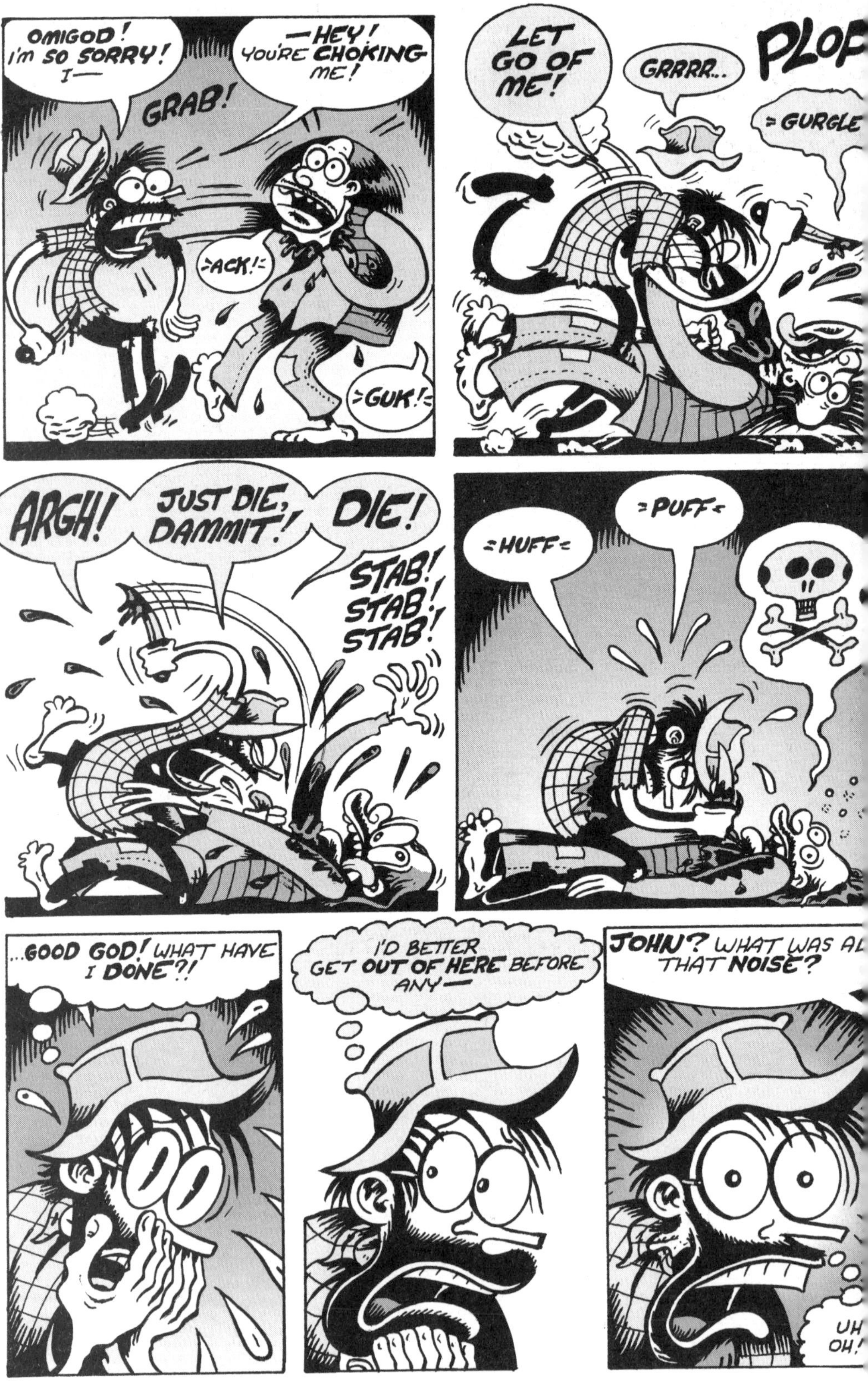
OMIGOD! I'M SO SORRY! I—
—HEY! YOU'RE CHOKING ME!
GRAB!
ACK!
GUK!
LET GO OF ME!
GRRRR...
PLOP
GURGLE
ARGH!
JUST DIE, DAMMIT!
DIE!
STAB! STAB! STAB!
HUFF
PUFF
...GOOD GOD! WHAT HAVE I DONE?!
I'D BETTER GET OUT OF HERE BEFORE ANY—
JOHN? WHAT WAS AL
THAT NOISE?
UH OH!

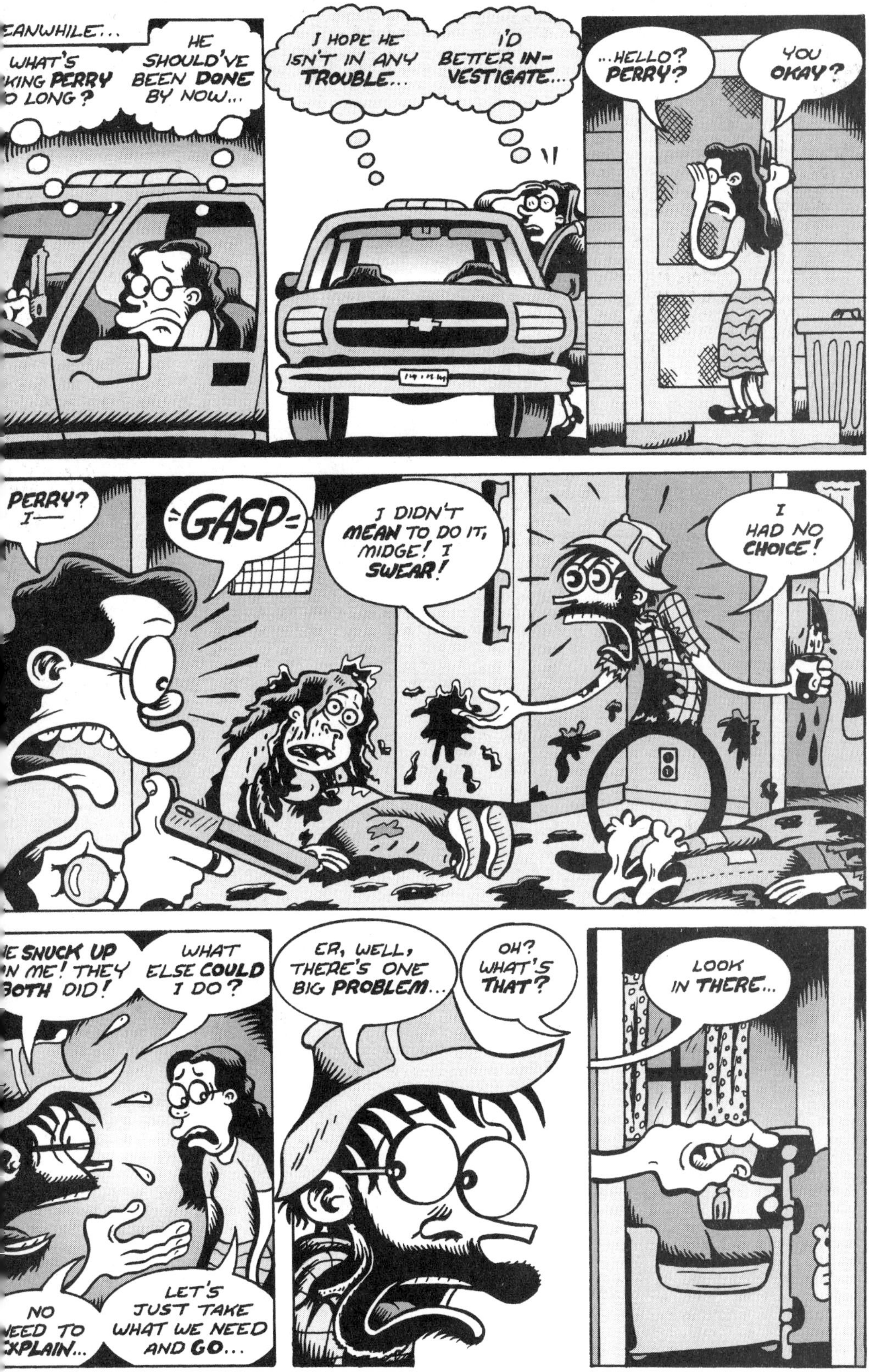

EANWHILE...
WHAT'S KING PERRY O LONG?
HE SHOULD'VE BEEN DONE BY NOW...
I HOPE HE ISN'T IN ANY TROUBLE...
I'D BETTER INVESTIGATE...
...HELLO? PERRY?
YOU OKAY?
PERRY? I—
GASP
I DIDN'T MEAN TO DO IT, MIDGE! I SWEAR!
I HAD NO CHOICE!
E SNUCK UP N ME! THEY OTH DID!
WHAT ELSE COULD I DO?
NO EED TO XPLAIN...
LET'S JUST TAKE WHAT WE NEED AND GO...
ER, WELL, THERE'S ONE BIG PROBLEM...
OH? WHAT'S THAT?
LOOK IN THERE...

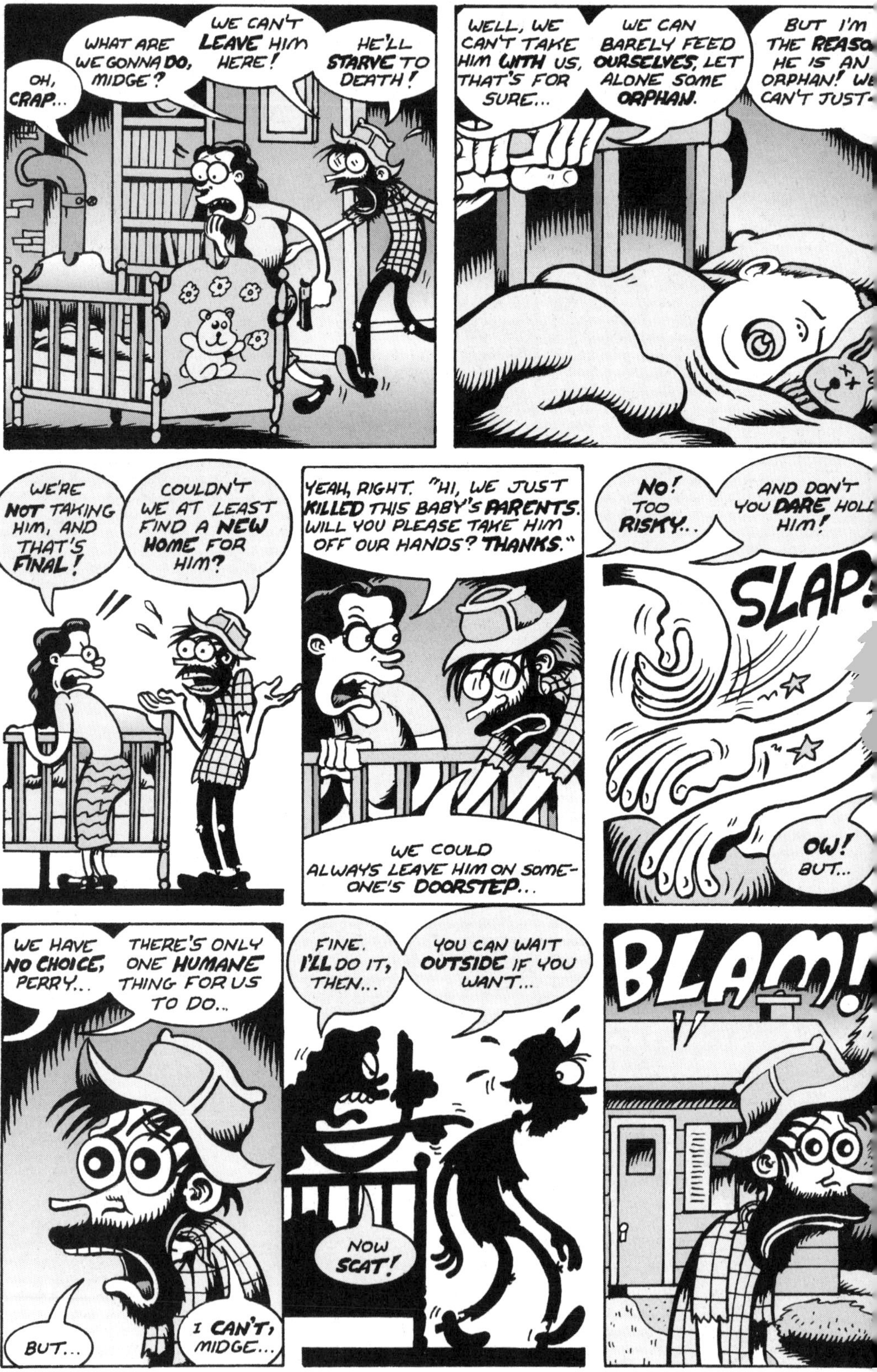
OH, CRAP...
WHAT ARE WE GONNA DO, MIDGE?
WE CAN'T LEAVE HIM HERE!
HE'LL STARVE TO DEATH!
WELL, WE CAN'T TAKE HIM WITH US, THAT'S FOR SURE...
WE CAN BARELY FEED OURSELVES, LET ALONE SOME ORPHAN.
BUT I'M THE REASO HE IS AN ORPHAN! WE CAN'T JUST-
WE'RE NOT TAKING HIM, AND THAT'S FINAL!
COULDN'T WE AT LEAST FIND A NEW HOME FOR HIM?
YEAH, RIGHT. "HI, WE JUST KILLED THIS BABY'S PARENTS. WILL YOU PLEASE TAKE HIM OFF OUR HANDS? THANKS."
WE COULD ALWAYS LEAVE HIM ON SOME-ONE'S DOORSTEP...
NO! TOO RISKY...
AND DON'T YOU DARE HOL HIM!
SLAP!
OW! BUT...
WE HAVE NO CHOICE, PERRY...
THERE'S ONLY ONE HUMANE THING FOR US TO DO...
BUT...
I CAN'T, MIDGE...
FINE. I'LL DO IT, THEN...
YOU CAN WAIT OUTSIDE IF YOU WANT...
NOW SCAT!
BLAM!

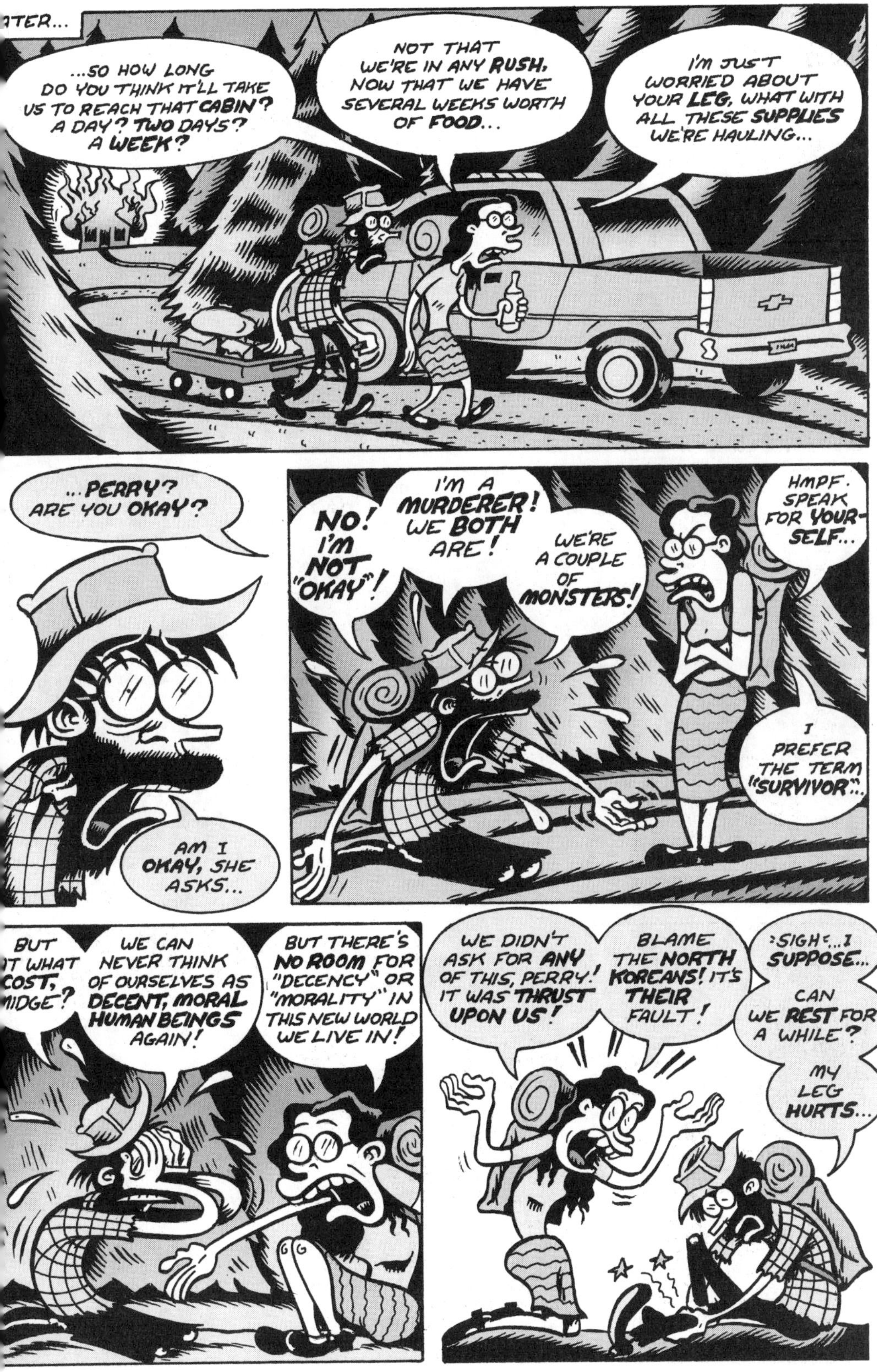
...ATER...
...SO HOW LONG DO YOU THINK IT'LL TAKE US TO REACH THAT **CABIN**? A DAY? **TWO DAYS**? A **WEEK**?
NOT THAT WE'RE IN ANY **RUSH**, NOW THAT WE HAVE SEVERAL WEEKS WORTH OF **FOOD**...
I'M JUST WORRIED ABOUT YOUR **LEG**, WHAT WITH ALL THESE **SUPPLIES** WE'RE HAULING...
...**PERRY**? ARE YOU **OKAY**?
AM I **OKAY**, SHE ASKS...
NO! I'M NOT "OKAY"!
I'M A **MURDERER**! WE **BOTH** ARE!
WE'RE A COUPLE OF **MONSTERS**!
HMPF. SPEAK FOR **YOURSELF**...
I PREFER THE TERM **"SURVIVOR"**...
BUT AT WHAT **COST**, MIDGE?
WE CAN NEVER THINK OF OURSELVES AS **DECENT, MORAL HUMAN BEINGS** AGAIN!
BUT THERE'S **NO ROOM** FOR "DECENCY" OR "MORALITY" IN THIS NEW WORLD WE LIVE IN!
WE DIDN'T ASK FOR **ANY** OF THIS, PERRY! IT WAS **THRUST UPON US**!
BLAME THE **NORTH KOREANS**! IT'S **THEIR** FAULT!
:SIGH:...I **SUPPOSE**...
CAN WE **REST** FOR A WHILE?
MY LEG **HURTS**...

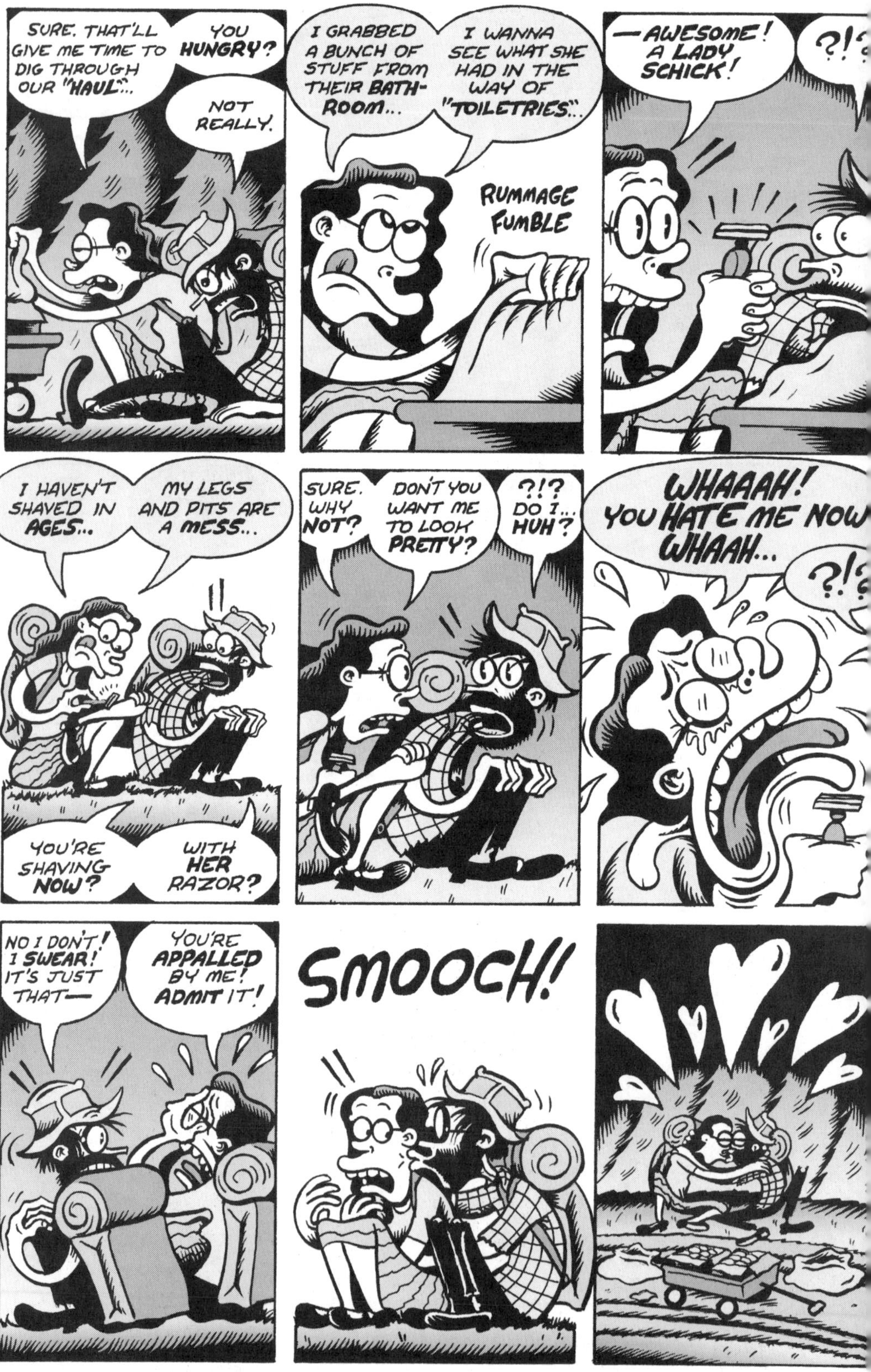
SURE. THAT'LL GIVE ME TIME TO DIG THROUGH OUR "HAUL"...
YOU HUNGRY?
NOT REALLY.
I GRABBED A BUNCH OF STUFF FROM THEIR BATH-ROOM...
I WANNA SEE WHAT SHE HAD IN THE WAY OF "TOILETRIES"...
RUMMAGE FUMBLE
—AWESOME! A LADY SCHICK!
?!?
I HAVEN'T SHAVED IN AGES...
MY LEGS AND PITS ARE A MESS...
YOU'RE SHAVING NOW?
WITH HER RAZOR?
SURE. WHY NOT?
DON'T YOU WANT ME TO LOOK PRETTY?
?!? DO I... HUH?
WHAAAH! YOU HATE ME NOW WHAAH...
?!?
NO I DON'T! I SWEAR! IT'S JUST THAT—
YOU'RE APPALLED BY ME! ADMIT IT!
SMOOCH!

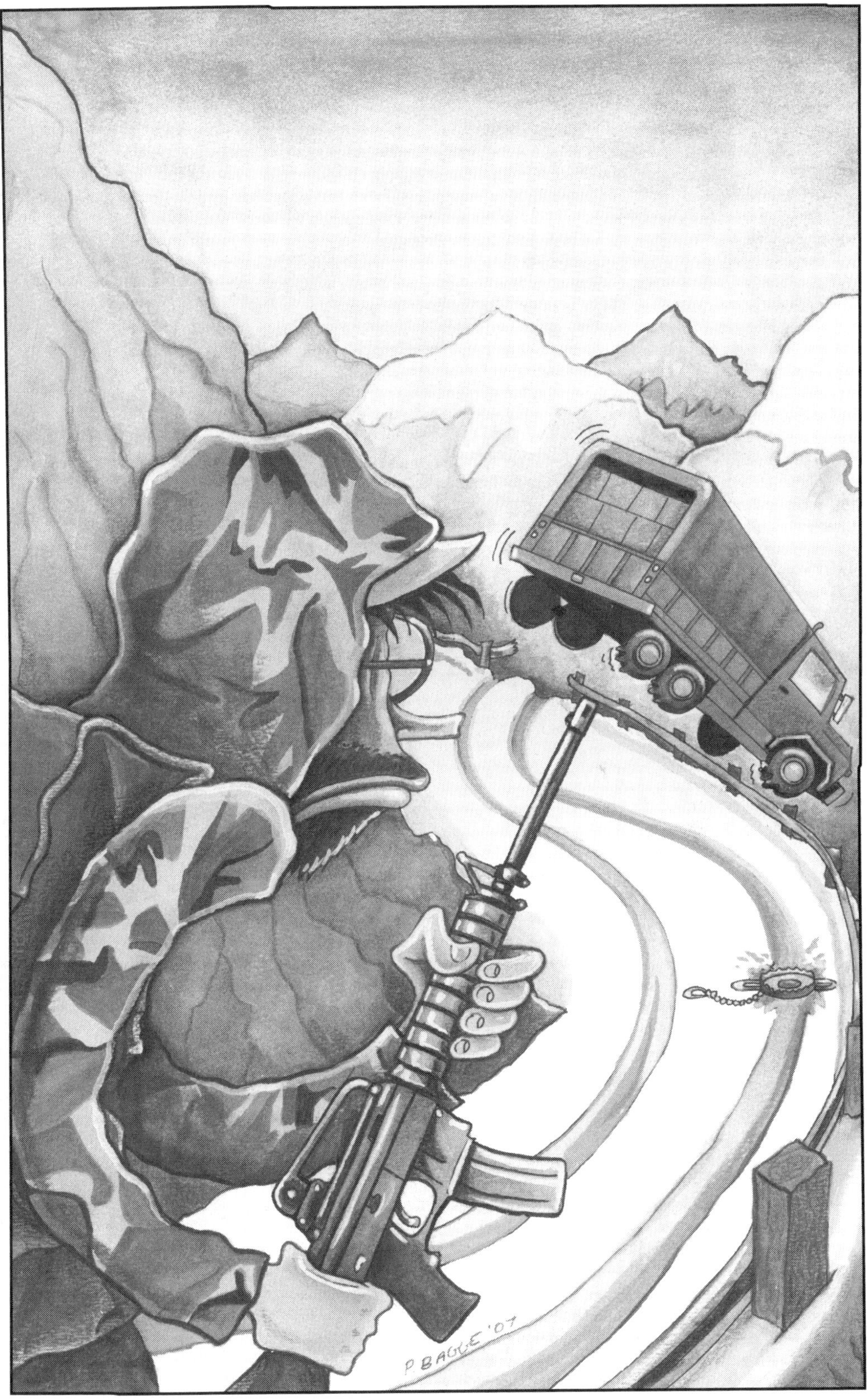
P. BAGGE '07

Chapter 6

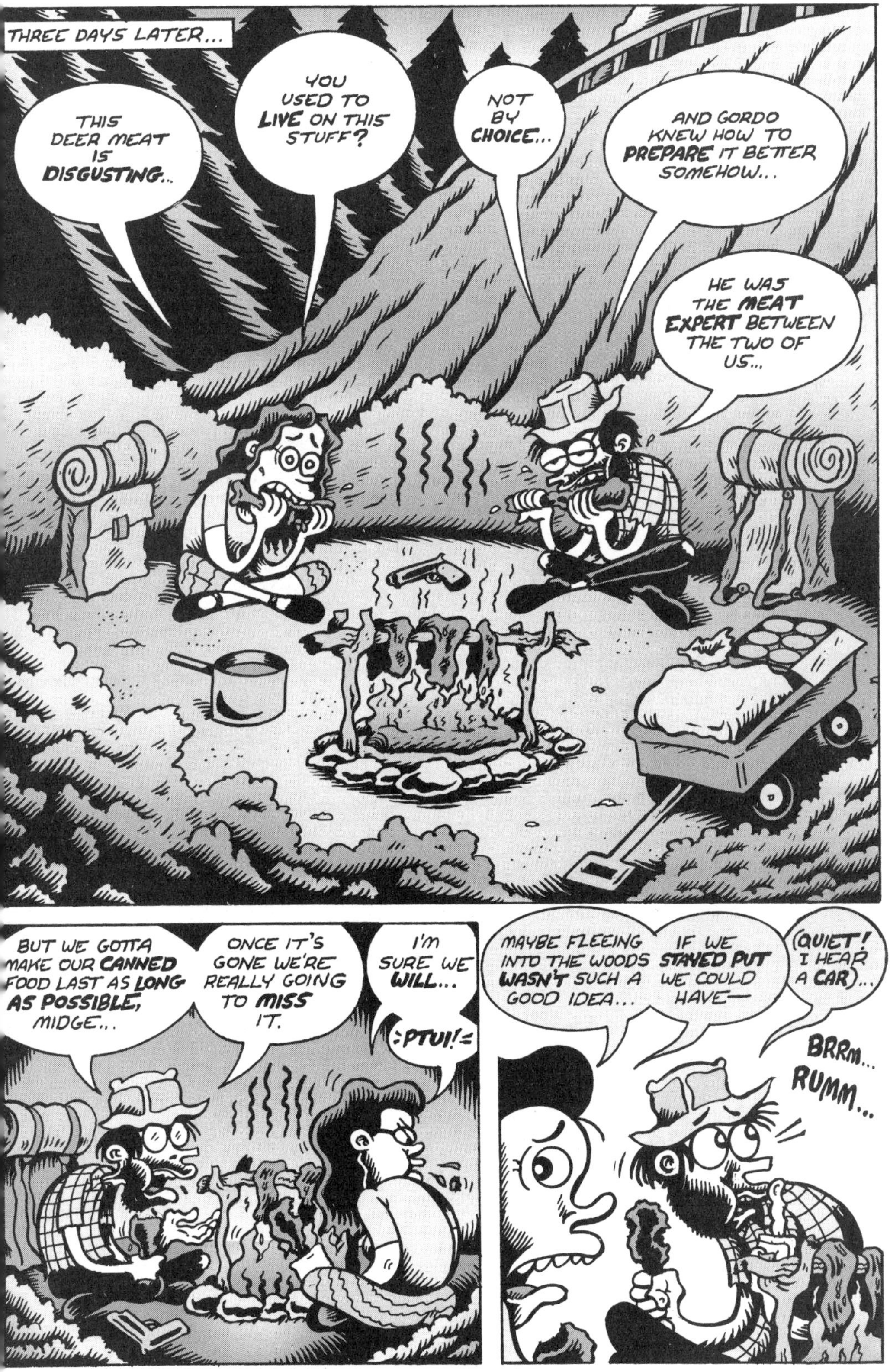
THREE DAYS LATER...
THIS DEER MEAT IS DISGUSTING...
YOU USED TO LIVE ON THIS STUFF?
NOT BY CHOICE...
AND GORDO KNEW HOW TO PREPARE IT BETTER SOMEHOW...
HE WAS THE MEAT EXPERT BETWEEN THE TWO OF US...
BUT WE GOTTA MAKE OUR CANNED FOOD LAST AS LONG AS POSSIBLE, MIDGE...
ONCE IT'S GONE WE'RE REALLY GOING TO MISS IT.
I'M SURE WE WILL...
PTUI!
MAYBE FLEEING INTO THE WOODS WASN'T SUCH A GOOD IDEA...
IF WE STAYED PUT WE COULD HAVE—
(QUIET! I HEAR A CAR)...
BRRm... RUMM...

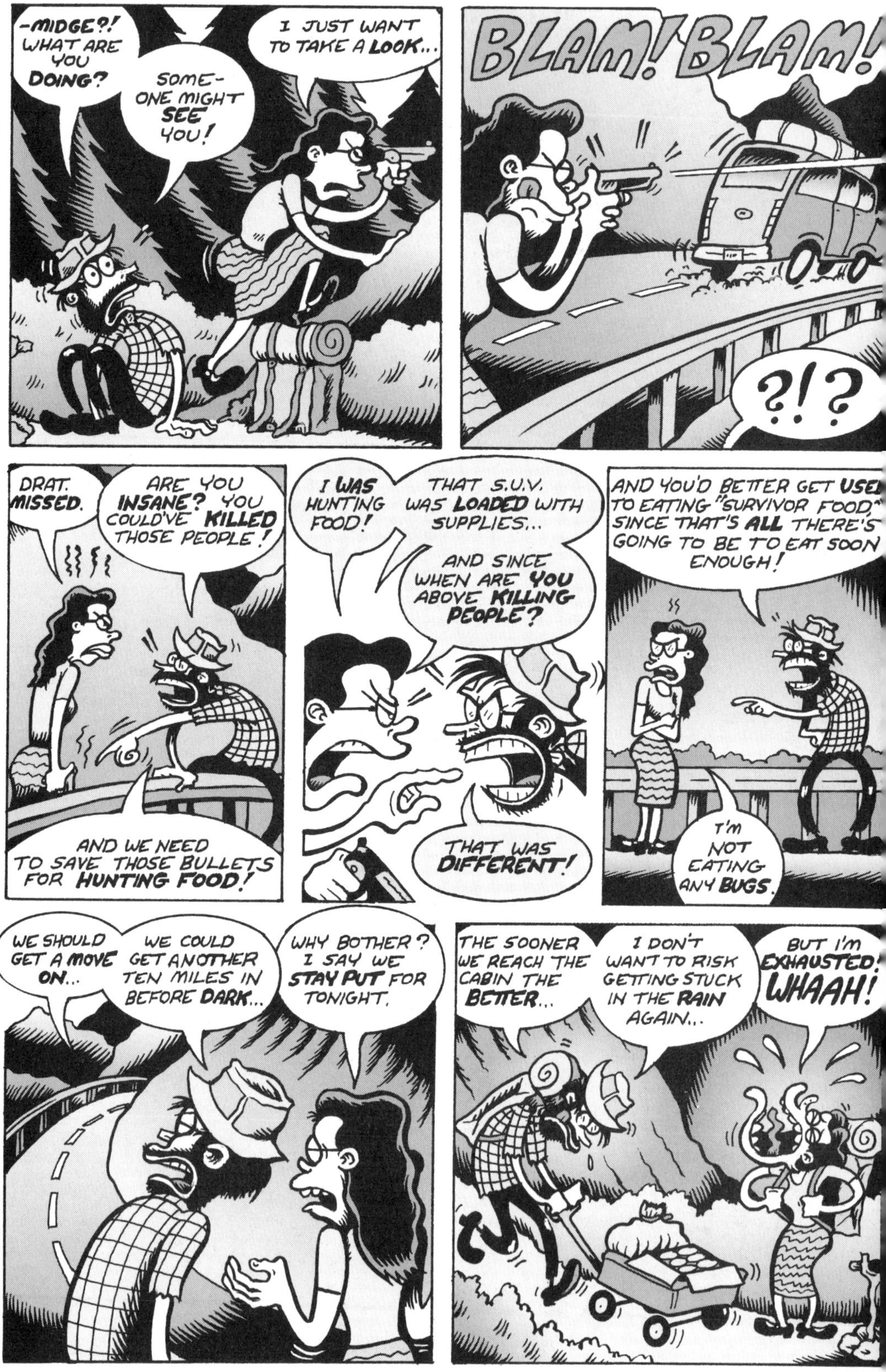

-MIDGE?! WHAT ARE YOU DOING?
SOME-ONE MIGHT SEE YOU!
I JUST WANT TO TAKE A LOOK...
BLAM! BLAM!
?!?
DRAT. MISSED.
ARE YOU INSANE? YOU COULD'VE KILLED THOSE PEOPLE!
AND WE NEED TO SAVE THOSE BULLETS FOR HUNTING FOOD!
I WAS HUNTING FOOD!
THAT S.U.V. WAS LOADED WITH SUPPLIES...
AND SINCE WHEN ARE YOU ABOVE KILLING PEOPLE?
THAT WAS DIFFERENT!
AND YOU'D BETTER GET USE TO EATING "SURVIVOR FOOD," SINCE THAT'S ALL THERE'S GOING TO BE TO EAT SOON ENOUGH!
I'M NOT EATING ANY BUGS.
WE SHOULD GET A MOVE ON...
WE COULD GET ANOTHER TEN MILES IN BEFORE DARK...
WHY BOTHER? I SAY WE STAY PUT FOR TONIGHT.
THE SOONER WE REACH THE CABIN THE BETTER...
I DON'T WANT TO RISK GETTING STUCK IN THE RAIN AGAIN...
BUT I'M EXHAUSTED! WHAAH!

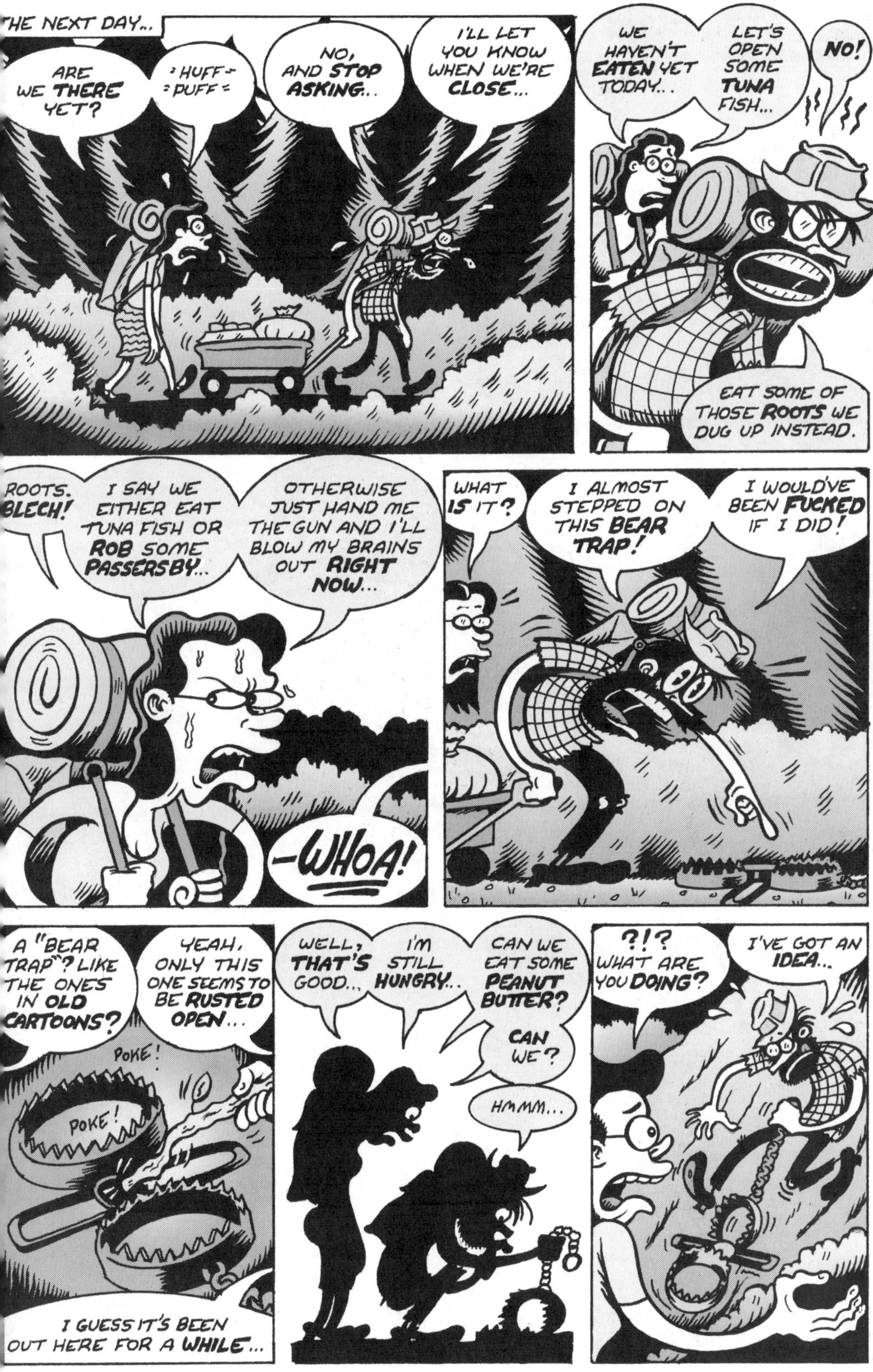
THE NEXT DAY...
ARE WE THERE YET?
HUFF-PUFF
NO, AND STOP ASKING...
I'LL LET YOU KNOW WHEN WE'RE CLOSE...
WE HAVEN'T EATEN YET TODAY...
LET'S OPEN SOME TUNA FISH...
NO!
EAT SOME OF THOSE ROOTS WE DUG UP INSTEAD.
ROOTS. BLECH!
I SAY WE EITHER EAT TUNA FISH OR ROB SOME PASSERSBY...
OTHERWISE JUST HAND ME THE GUN AND I'LL BLOW MY BRAINS OUT RIGHT NOW...
-WHOA!
WHAT IS IT?
I ALMOST STEPPED ON THIS BEAR TRAP!
I WOULD'VE BEEN FUCKED IF I DID!
A "BEAR TRAP"? LIKE THE ONES IN OLD CARTOONS?
YEAH, ONLY THIS ONE SEEMS TO BE RUSTED OPEN...
POKE!
POKE!
I GUESS IT'S BEEN OUT HERE FOR A WHILE...
WELL, THAT'S GOOD...
I'M STILL HUNGRY...
CAN WE EAT SOME PEANUT BUTTER?
CAN WE?
HMMM...
?!? WHAT ARE YOU DOING?
I'VE GOT AN IDEA...

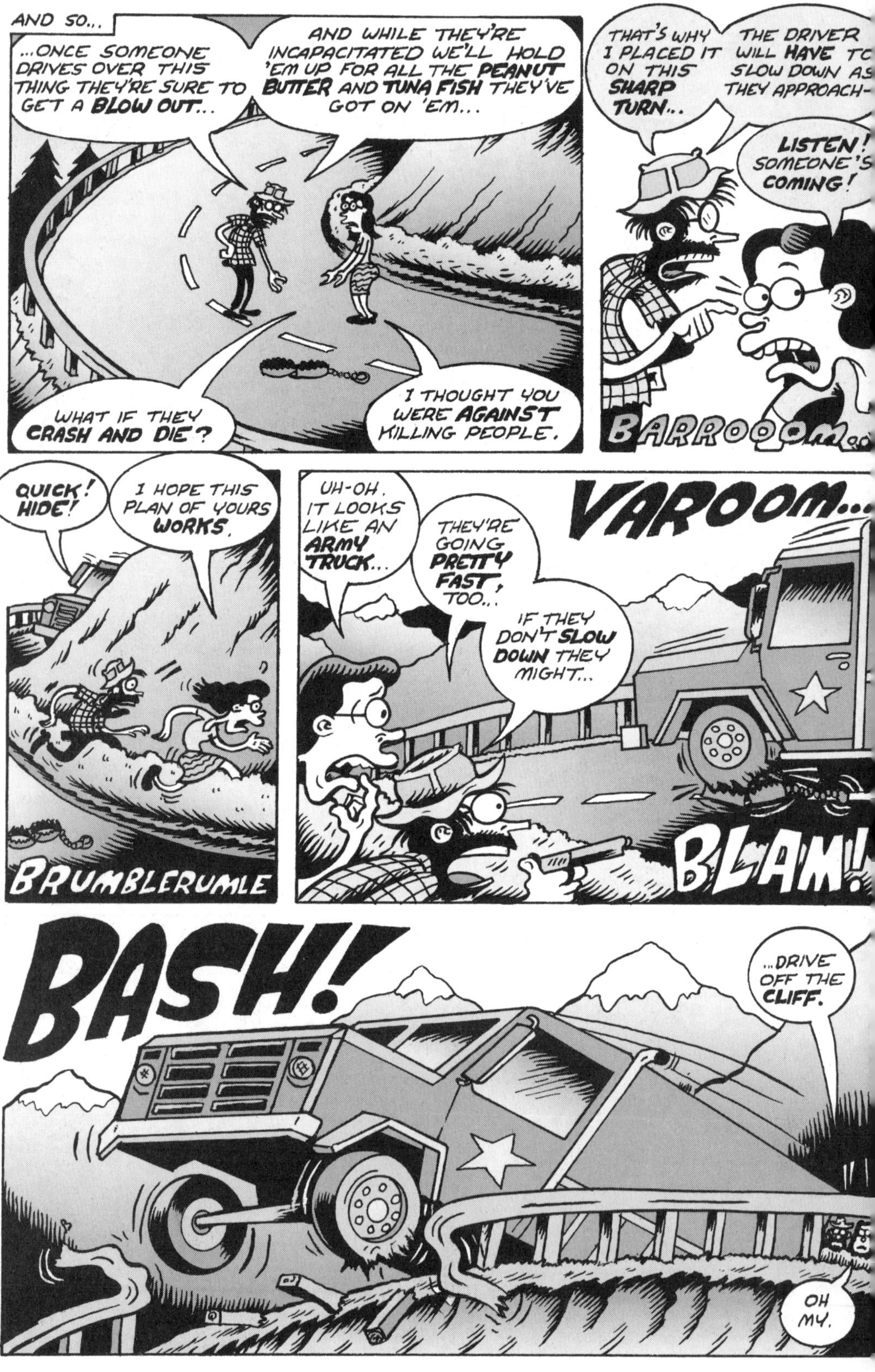
AND SO...
...ONCE SOMEONE DRIVES OVER THIS THING THEY'RE SURE TO GET A **BLOW OUT**...
AND WHILE THEY'RE INCAPACITATED WE'LL HOLD 'EM UP FOR ALL THE **PEANUT BUTTER** AND **TUNA FISH** THEY'VE GOT ON 'EM...
WHAT IF THEY **CRASH AND DIE**?
I THOUGHT YOU WERE **AGAINST** KILLING PEOPLE.
THAT'S WHY I PLACED IT ON THIS **SHARP TURN**...
THE DRIVER WILL **HAVE** TO SLOW DOWN AS THEY APPROACH—
LISTEN! SOMEONE'S **COMING!**
BARROOOM...
QUICK! HIDE!
I HOPE THIS PLAN OF YOURS **WORKS**.
BRUMBLERUMLE
UH-OH. IT LOOKS LIKE AN **ARMY TRUCK**...
THEY'RE GOING **PRETTY FAST**, TOO...
IF THEY DON'T **SLOW DOWN** THEY MIGHT...
VAROOM...
BLAM!
BASH!
...DRIVE OFF THE **CLIFF**.
OH MY.

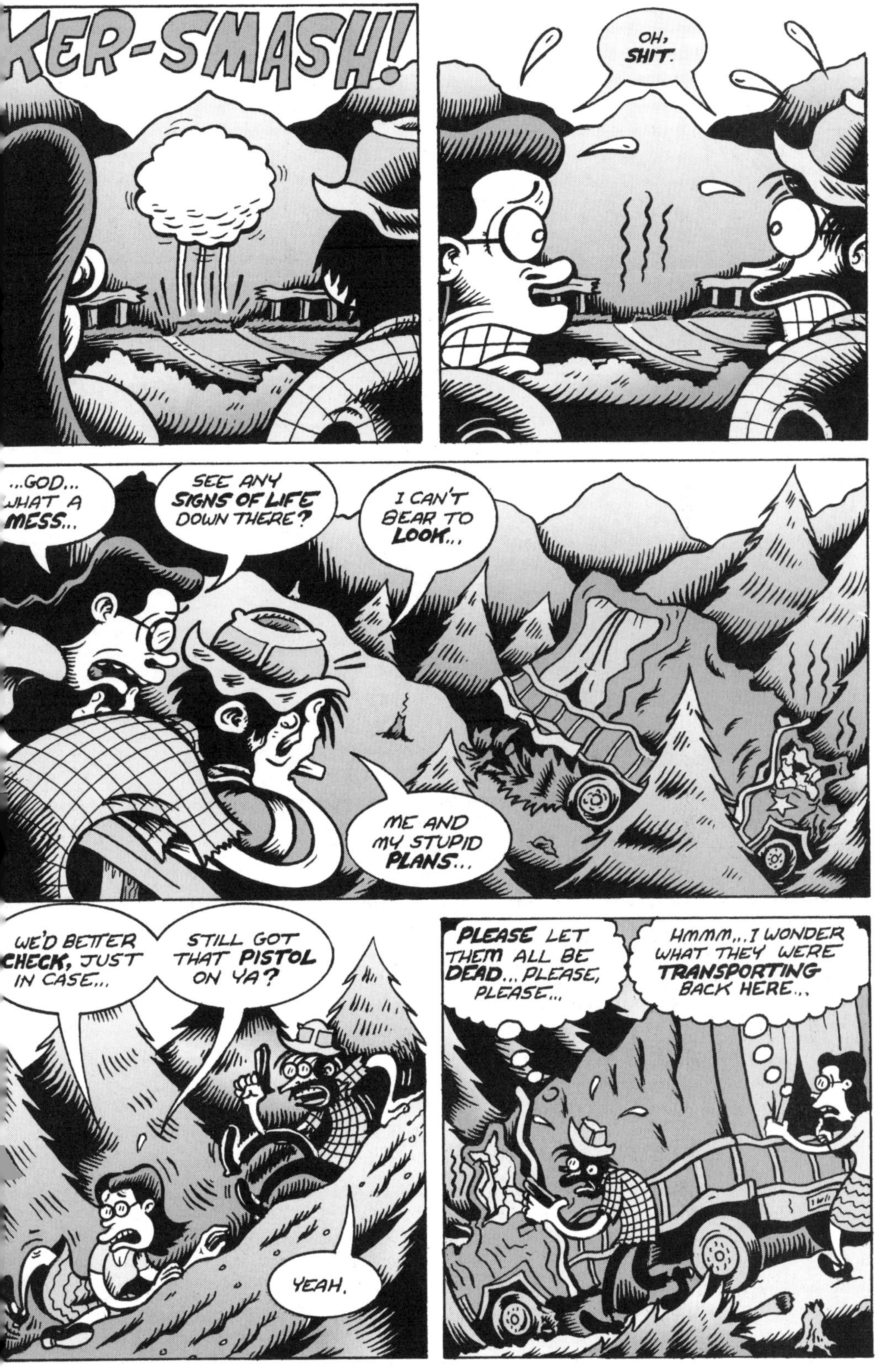

KER-SMASH!
OH, SHIT.
...GOD... WHAT A MESS...
SEE ANY SIGNS OF LIFE DOWN THERE?
I CAN'T BEAR TO LOOK...
ME AND MY STUPID PLANS...
WE'D BETTER CHECK, JUST IN CASE...
STILL GOT THAT PISTOL ON YA?
YEAH.
PLEASE LET THEM ALL BE DEAD... PLEASE, PLEASE...
HMMM... I WONDER WHAT THEY WERE TRANSPORTING BACK HERE...

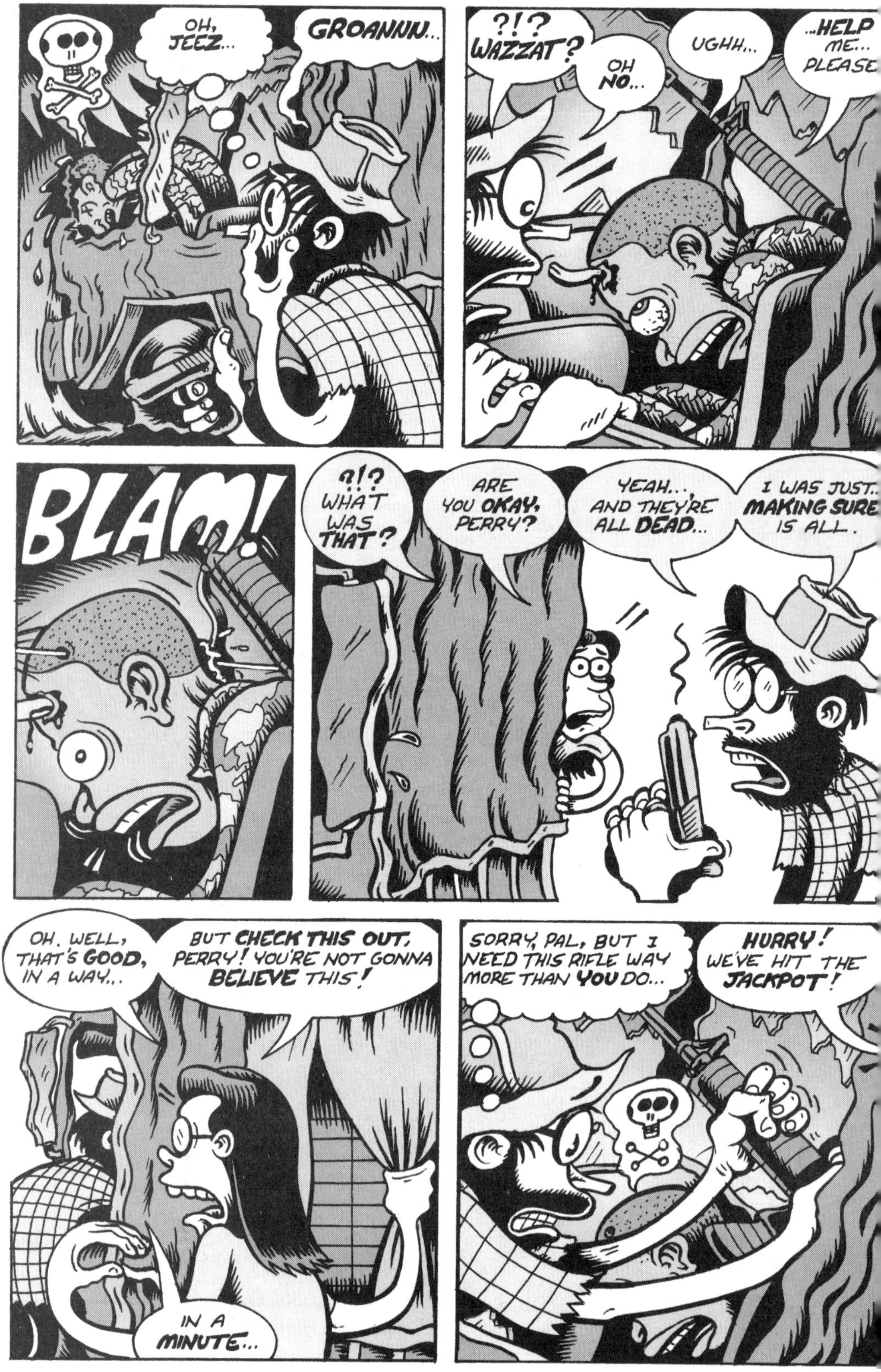
OH, JEEZ...
GROANNN...
?!? WAZZAT?
OH NO...
UGHH...
...HELP ME... PLEASE
BLAM!
?!? WHAT WAS THAT?
ARE YOU OKAY, PERRY?
YEAH..., AND THEY'RE ALL DEAD...
I WAS JUST... MAKING SURE IS ALL.
OH. WELL, THAT'S GOOD, IN A WAY...
BUT CHECK THIS OUT, PERRY! YOU'RE NOT GONNA BELIEVE THIS!
IN A MINUTE...
SORRY, PAL, BUT I NEED THIS RIFLE WAY MORE THAN YOU DO...
HURRY! WE'VE HIT THE JACKPOT!

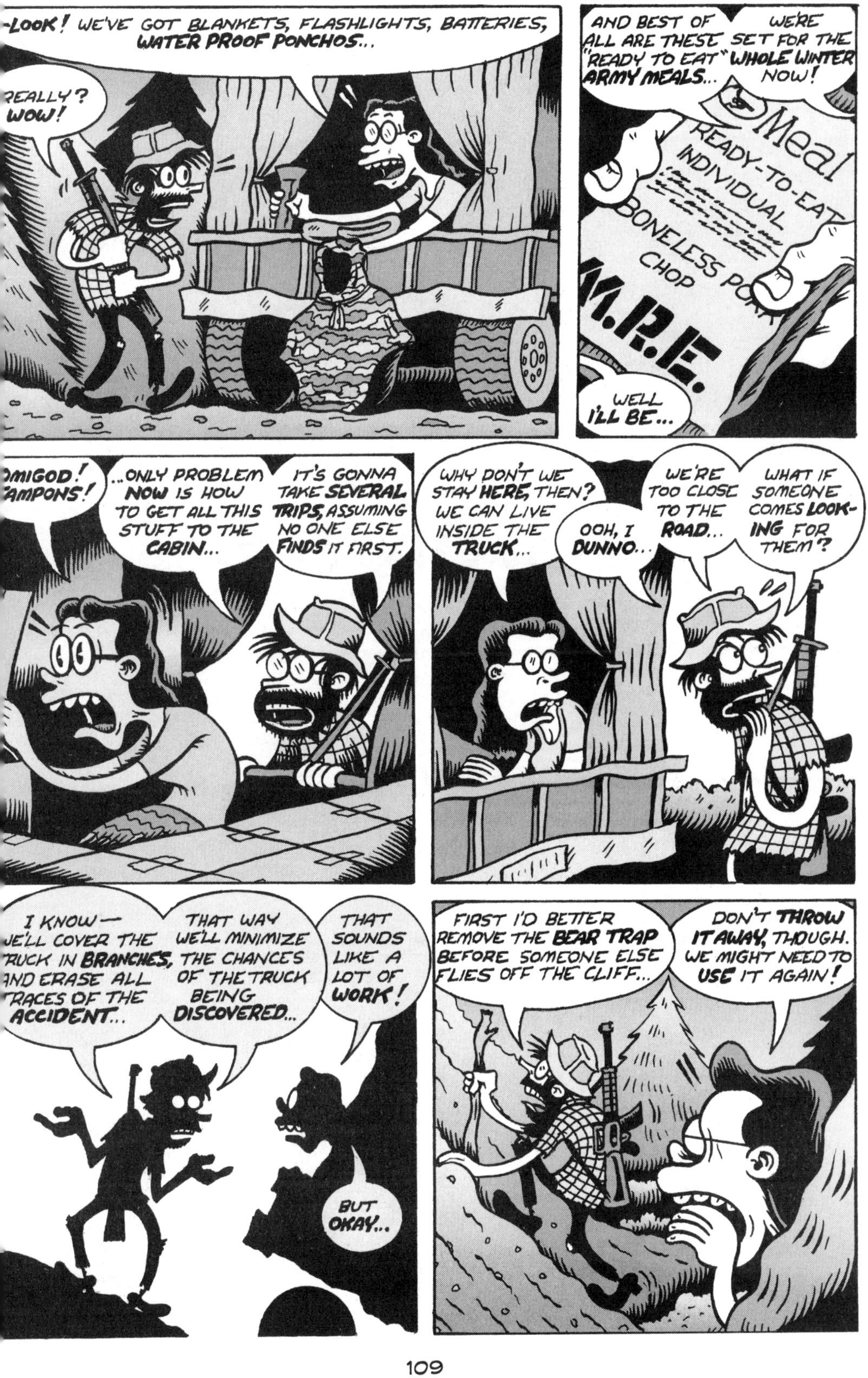
-LOOK! WE'VE GOT BLANKETS, FLASHLIGHTS, BATTERIES, WATER PROOF PONCHOS...
REALLY? WOW!
AND BEST OF ALL ARE THESE "READY TO EAT" ARMY MEALS...
WE'RE SET FOR THE WHOLE WINTER NOW!
Meal READY-TO-EAT INDIVIDUAL
BONELESS PO
CHOP
M.R.E.
WELL I'LL BE...
OMIGOD! TAMPONS!
...ONLY PROBLEM NOW IS HOW TO GET ALL THIS STUFF TO THE CABIN...
IT'S GONNA TAKE SEVERAL TRIPS, ASSUMING NO ONE ELSE FINDS IT FIRST.
WHY DON'T WE STAY HERE, THEN? WE CAN LIVE INSIDE THE TRUCK...
OOH, I DUNNO...
WE'RE TOO CLOSE TO THE ROAD...
WHAT IF SOMEONE COMES LOOKING FOR THEM?
I KNOW— WE'LL COVER THE TRUCK IN BRANCHES, AND ERASE ALL TRACES OF THE ACCIDENT...
THAT WAY WE'LL MINIMIZE THE CHANCES OF THE TRUCK BEING DISCOVERED...
THAT SOUNDS LIKE A LOT OF WORK!
BUT OKAY...
FIRST I'D BETTER REMOVE THE BEAR TRAP BEFORE SOMEONE ELSE FLIES OFF THE CLIFF...
DON'T THROW IT AWAY, THOUGH. WE MIGHT NEED TO USE IT AGAIN!

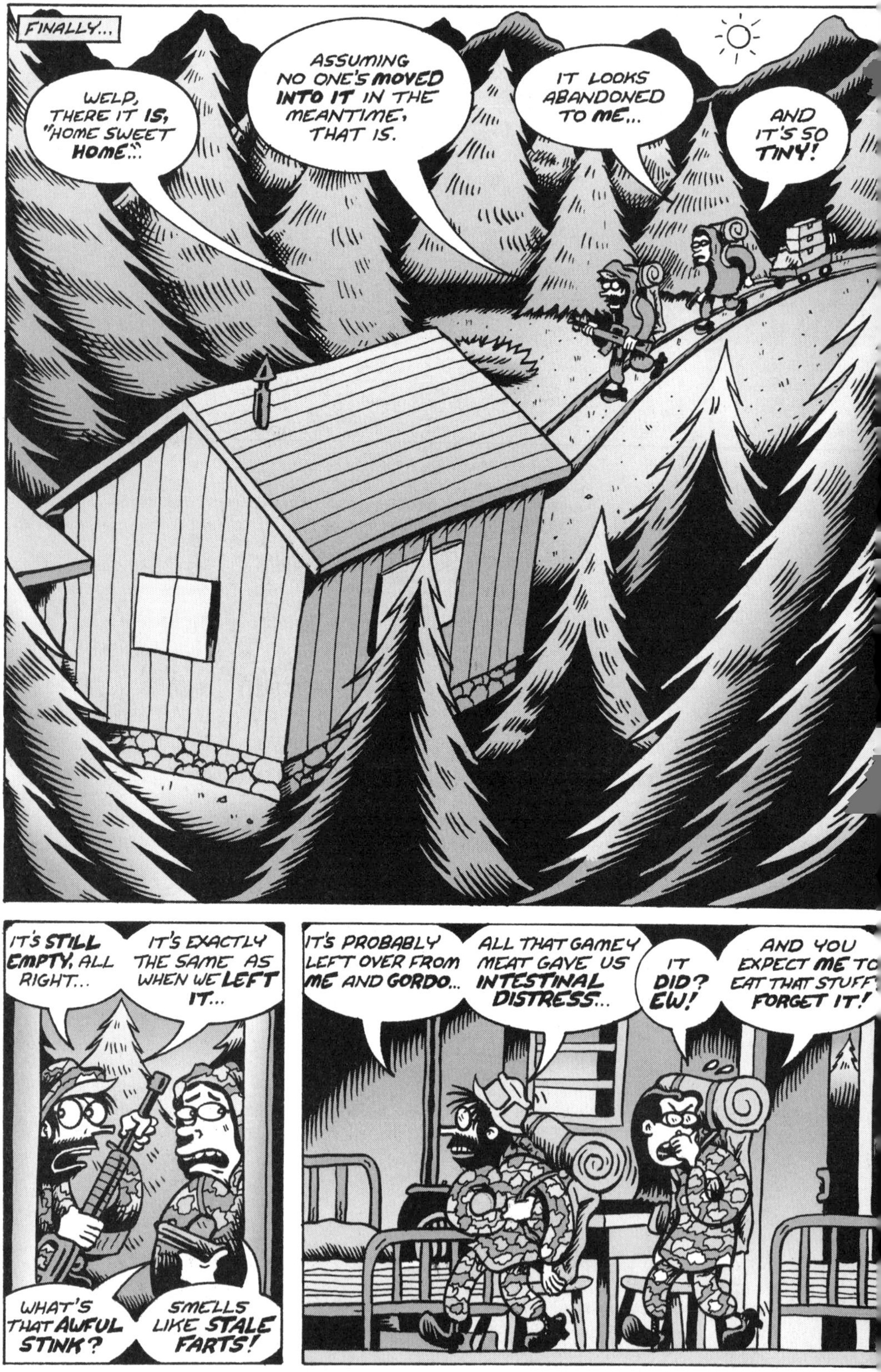
FINALLY...
WELP, THERE IT IS, "HOME SWEET HOME"...
ASSUMING NO ONE'S MOVED INTO IT IN THE MEANTIME, THAT IS.
IT LOOKS ABANDONED TO ME...
AND IT'S SO TINY!
IT'S STILL EMPTY, ALL RIGHT...
IT'S EXACTLY THE SAME AS WHEN WE LEFT IT...
WHAT'S THAT AWFUL STINK?
SMELLS LIKE STALE FARTS!
IT'S PROBABLY LEFT OVER FROM ME AND GORDO...
ALL THAT GAMEY MEAT GAVE US INTESTINAL DISTRESS...
IT DID? EW!
AND YOU EXPECT ME TO EAT THAT STUFF? FORGET IT!

THE FIRST THING WE NEED TO DO IS AIR THIS PLACE OUT...

AND WHILE I TRY TO MAKE THIS PLACE LIVABLE, YOU SHOULD GO BACK TO THE TRUCK TO RETRIEVE MORE SUPPLIES...

WHAT? NOW?

THAT'LL TAKE UP THE ENTIRE REST OF THE DAY!

CAN'T I JUST REST FOR NOW?

NO! SOMEONE ELSE MIGHT FIND IT!

YOU SAID SO YOURSELF!

SO GO NOW!

SIGH<... VERY WELL...

I SURE WAS LOOKING FORWARD TO RESTING ON THIS MATTRESS, THOUGH...

IT'S BEEN AGES...

TRY TO LOAD UP ON COATS AND BLANKETS...

IT'S STARTING TO GET COLD AT NIGHT.

SO, ARE YOU OKAY WITH THIS PLACE? I KNOW IT AIN'T THE RITZ...

IT'LL DO, ONCE IT'S CLEANED UP...

I MOSTLY LIKE THAT IT'S JUST "OURS"...

YEAH, ME TOO.

AND I'M LOOKING FORWARD TO RESTING ON A MATTRESS TONIGHT, TOO.

SMOOCH!

NOW GET GOING! BEFORE IT GETS DARK!

YES, MA'AM! I'M OFF!

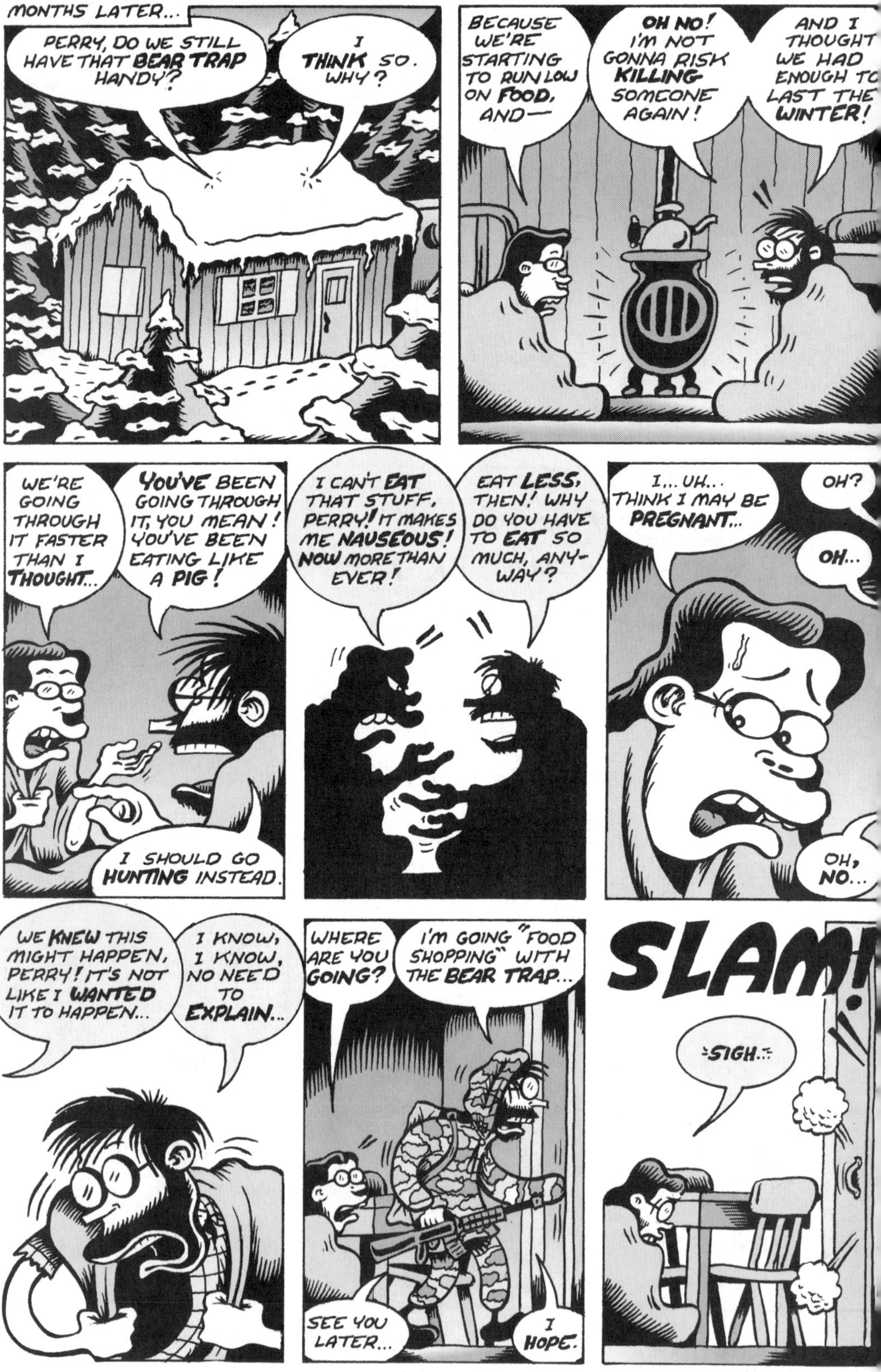
MONTHS LATER...
PERRY, DO WE STILL HAVE THAT BEAR TRAP HANDY?
I THINK SO. WHY?
BECAUSE WE'RE STARTING TO RUN LOW ON FOOD, AND—
OH NO! I'M NOT GONNA RISK KILLING SOMEONE AGAIN!
AND I THOUGHT WE HAD ENOUGH TO LAST THE WINTER!
WE'RE GOING THROUGH IT FASTER THAN I THOUGHT...
YOU'VE BEEN GOING THROUGH IT, YOU MEAN! YOU'VE BEEN EATING LIKE A PIG!
I SHOULD GO HUNTING INSTEAD.
I CAN'T EAT THAT STUFF, PERRY! IT MAKES ME NAUSEOUS! NOW MORE THAN EVER!
EAT LESS, THEN! WHY DO YOU HAVE TO EAT SO MUCH, ANYWAY?
I... UH... THINK I MAY BE PREGNANT...
OH?
OH...
OH, NO...
WE KNEW THIS MIGHT HAPPEN, PERRY! IT'S NOT LIKE I WANTED IT TO HAPPEN...
I KNOW, I KNOW, NO NEED TO EXPLAIN...
WHERE ARE YOU GOING?
I'M GOING "FOOD SHOPPING" WITH THE BEAR TRAP...
SEE YOU LATER...
I HOPE.
SLAM!
-SIGH-

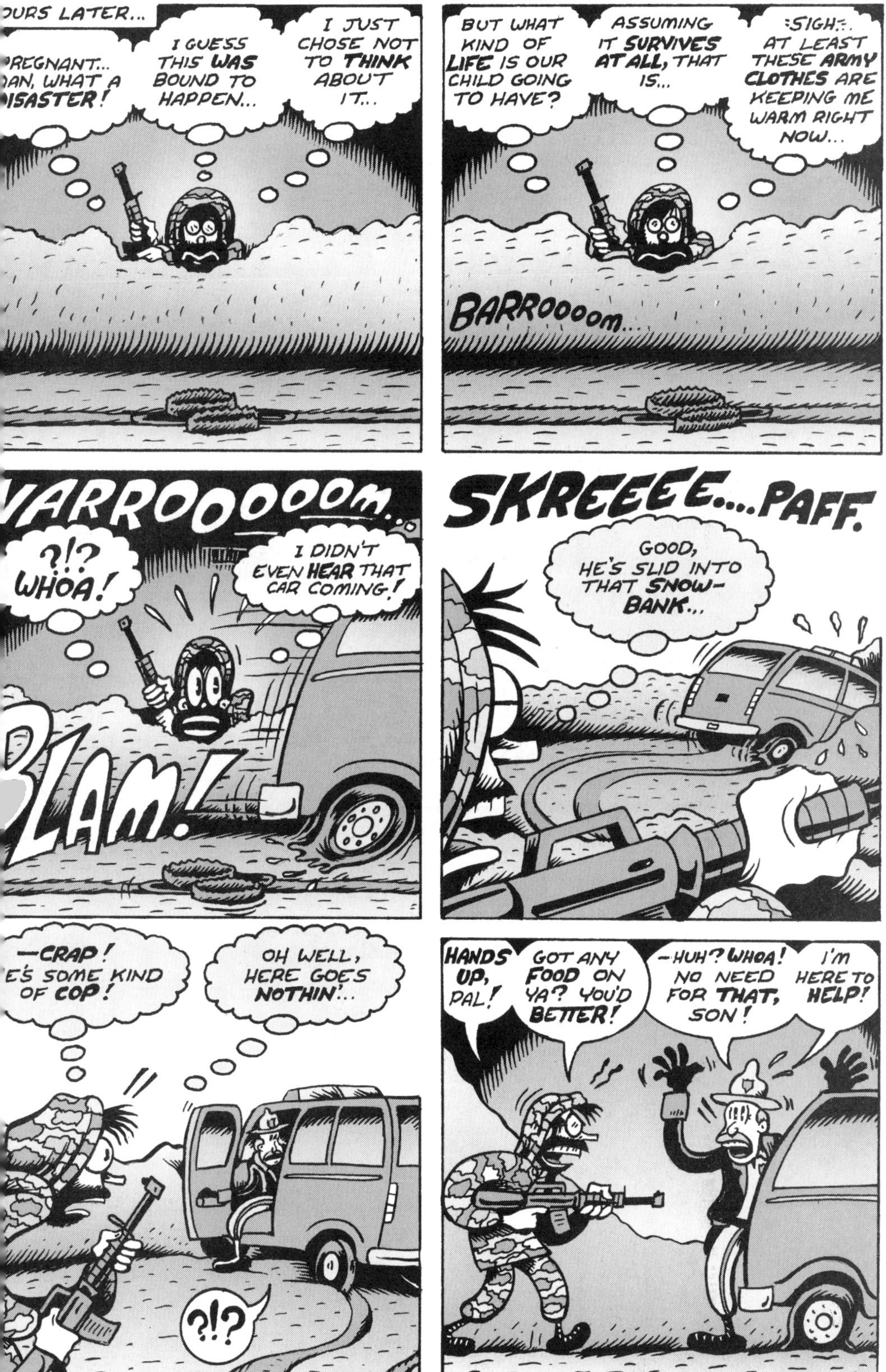
OURS LATER...
PREGNANT... DAN, WHAT A DISASTER!
I GUESS THIS WAS BOUND TO HAPPEN...
I JUST CHOSE NOT TO THINK ABOUT IT...
BUT WHAT KIND OF LIFE IS OUR CHILD GOING TO HAVE?
ASSUMING IT SURVIVES AT ALL, THAT IS...
SIGH AT LEAST THESE ARMY CLOTHES ARE KEEPING ME WARM RIGHT NOW...
BARROOOOm...
VARROOOOOOm...
?!? WHOA!
I DIDN'T EVEN HEAR THAT CAR COMING!
BLAM!
SKREEEE....PAFF.
GOOD, HE'S SLID INTO THAT SNOW-BANK...
—CRAP! E'S SOME KIND OF COP!
OH WELL, HERE GOES NOTHIN'...
?!?
HANDS UP, PAL!
GOT ANY FOOD ON YA? YOU'D BETTER!
—HUH? WHOA! NO NEED FOR THAT, SON!
I'M HERE TO HELP!

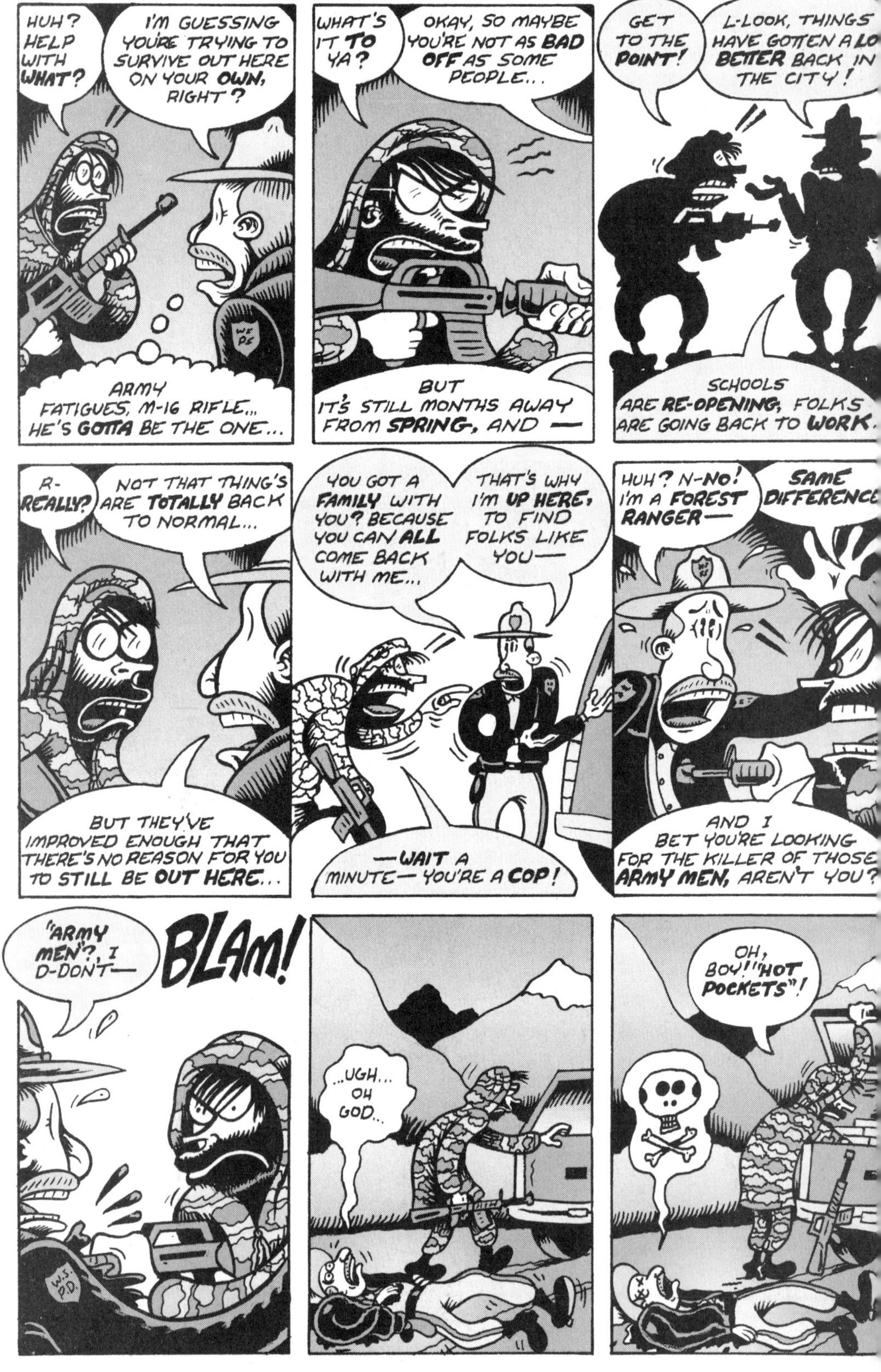
HUH? HELP WITH WHAT?
I'M GUESSING YOU'RE TRYING TO SURVIVE OUT HERE ON YOUR OWN, RIGHT?
ARMY FATIGUES, M-16 RIFLE... HE'S GOTTA BE THE ONE...
WHAT'S IT TO YA?
OKAY, SO MAYBE YOU'RE NOT AS BAD OFF AS SOME PEOPLE...
BUT IT'S STILL MONTHS AWAY FROM SPRING, AND —
GET TO THE POINT!
L-LOOK, THINGS HAVE GOTTEN A LO BETTER BACK IN THE CITY!
SCHOOLS ARE RE-OPENING, FOLKS ARE GOING BACK TO WORK.
R-REALLY?
NOT THAT THING'S ARE TOTALLY BACK TO NORMAL...
BUT THEY'VE IMPROVED ENOUGH THAT THERE'S NO REASON FOR YOU TO STILL BE OUT HERE...
YOU GOT A FAMILY WITH YOU? BECAUSE YOU CAN ALL COME BACK WITH ME...
THAT'S WHY I'M UP HERE, TO FIND FOLKS LIKE YOU—
—WAIT A MINUTE— YOU'RE A COP!
HUH? N-NO! I'M A FOREST RANGER—
SAME DIFFERENCE
AND I BET YOU'RE LOOKING FOR THE KILLER OF THOSE ARMY MEN, AREN'T YOU?
"ARMY MEN"?, I D-DON'T—
BLAM!
...UGH... OH GOD...
OH, BOY! "HOT POCKETS"!

THE FOLLOWING SPRING...

I'M GOING **FORAGING** FOR A BIT...

MAYBE DO A LITTLE **FISHING** AS WELL...

FEEL FREE TO HUNT SOME **WILD GEESE** IF YOU SEE ANY...

I **LIKE** THE WAY THOSE THINGS TASTE!

HOW YA FEELING, BY THE WAY?

FINE. BETTER THAN **YESTERDAY**, ANYWAY.

I JUST WANT THIS THING **OUT OF ME** AT THIS POINT...

WELL, TRY TO **STAY OFF YOUR FEET** TODAY, OKAY?

THAT'S EXACTLY WHAT I **INTEND** TO DO...

BYE! BE **SAFE**!

HMMM... GUESS I'LL READ MY **SURIVAL** BOOK AGAIN...

IT'S NOT LIKE THERE'S ANYTHING **ELSE** TO READ...

LATER...

...ZZZZZZ ZZ...

—HEY THERE, HILLBILLY WOMAN! WHATCHA READING?

?!

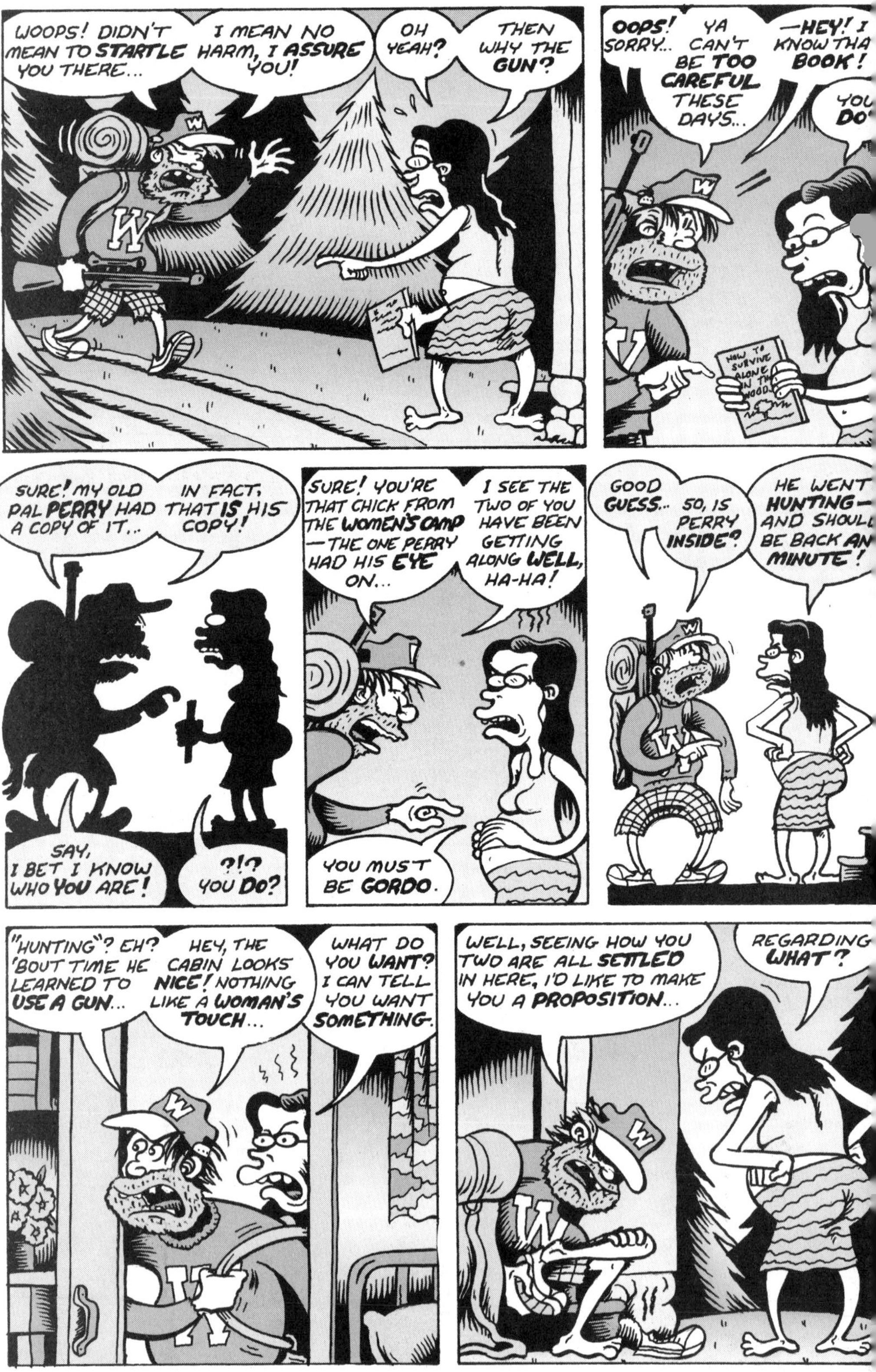
WOOPS! DIDN'T MEAN TO STARTLE YOU THERE...
I MEAN NO HARM, I ASSURE YOU!
OH YEAH?
THEN WHY THE GUN?
OOPS! SORRY...
YA CAN'T BE TOO CAREFUL THESE DAYS...
—HEY! I KNOW THA BOOK!
YOU DO
HOW TO SURVIVE ALONE IN THE WOODS
SURE! MY OLD PAL PERRY HAD A COPY OF IT...
IN FACT, THAT IS HIS COPY!
SAY, I BET I KNOW WHO YOU ARE!
?!? YOU DO?
SURE! YOU'RE THAT CHICK FROM THE WOMEN'S CAMP —THE ONE PERRY HAD HIS EYE ON...
I SEE THE TWO OF YOU HAVE BEEN GETTING ALONG WELL, HA-HA!
YOU MUST BE GORDO.
GOOD GUESS...
SO, IS PERRY INSIDE?
HE WENT HUNTING— AND SHOUL BE BACK AN MINUTE!
"HUNTING"? EH? 'BOUT TIME HE LEARNED TO USE A GUN...
HEY, THE CABIN LOOKS NICE! NOTHING LIKE A WOMAN'S TOUCH...
WHAT DO YOU WANT? I CAN TELL YOU WANT SOMETHING.
WELL, SEEING HOW YOU TWO ARE ALL SETTLED IN HERE, I'D LIKE TO MAKE YOU A PROPOSITION...
REGARDING WHAT?

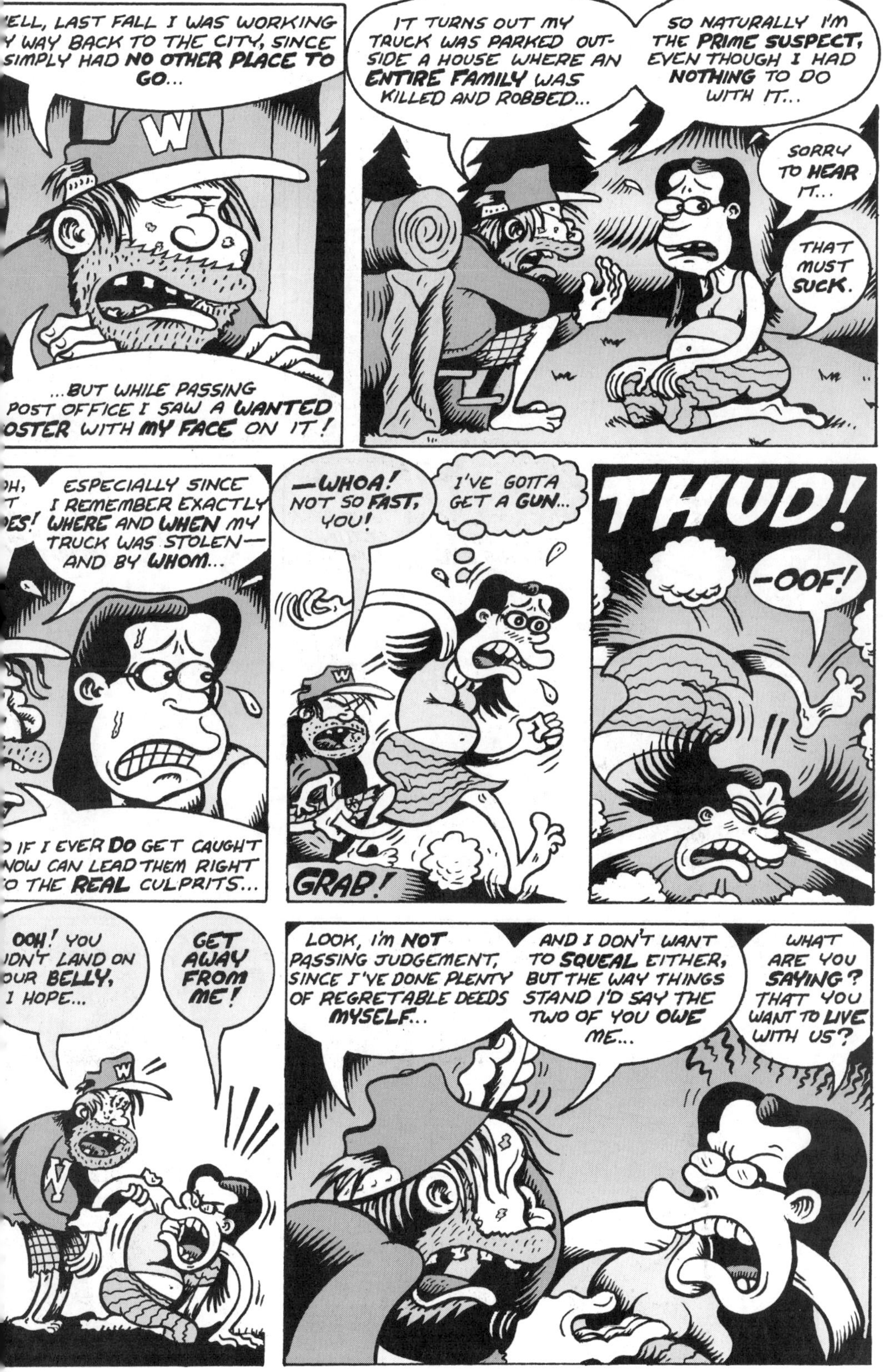
ELL, LAST FALL I WAS WORKING Y WAY BACK TO THE CITY, SINCE SIMPLY HAD NO OTHER PLACE TO GO...
...BUT WHILE PASSING POST OFFICE I SAW A WANTED OSTER WITH MY FACE ON IT!
IT TURNS OUT MY TRUCK WAS PARKED OUTSIDE A HOUSE WHERE AN ENTIRE FAMILY WAS KILLED AND ROBBED...
SO NATURALLY I'M THE PRIME SUSPECT, EVEN THOUGH I HAD NOTHING TO DO WITH IT...
SORRY TO HEAR IT...
THAT MUST SUCK.
ESPECIALLY SINCE I REMEMBER EXACTLY WHERE AND WHEN MY TRUCK WAS STOLEN— AND BY WHOM...
IF I EVER DO GET CAUGHT NOW CAN LEAD THEM RIGHT TO THE REAL CULPRITS...
—WHOA! NOT SO FAST, YOU!
I'VE GOTTA GET A GUN...
GRAB!
THUD!
-OOF!
OOH! YOU DN'T LAND ON OUR BELLY, I HOPE...
GET AWAY FROM ME!
LOOK, I'M NOT PASSING JUDGEMENT, SINCE I'VE DONE PLENTY OF REGRETABLE DEEDS MYSELF...
AND I DON'T WANT TO SQUEAL EITHER, BUT THE WAY THINGS STAND I'D SAY THE TWO OF YOU OWE ME...
WHAT ARE YOU SAYING? THAT YOU WANT TO LIVE WITH US?

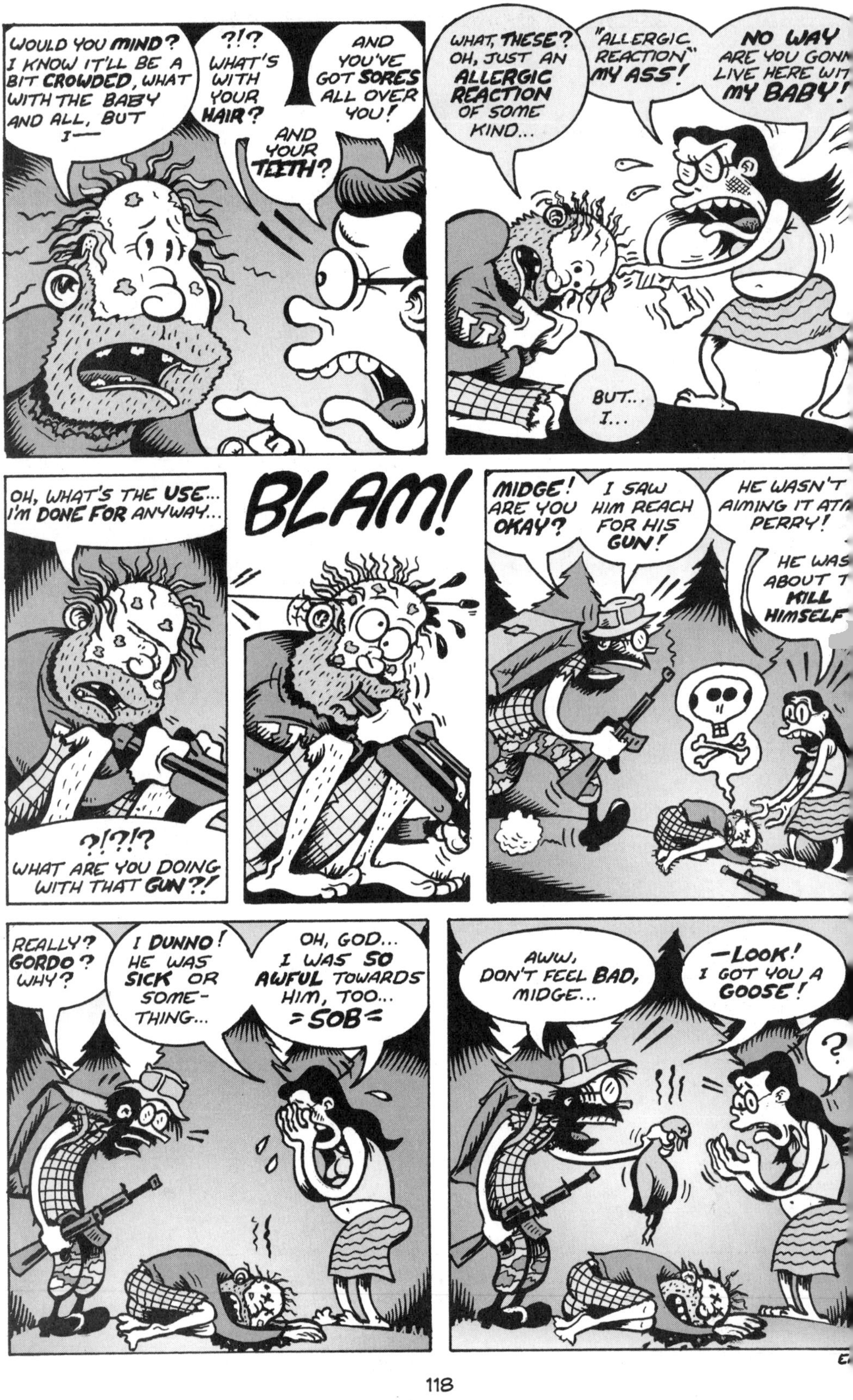
WOULD YOU MIND? I KNOW IT'LL BE A BIT CROWDED, WHAT WITH THE BABY AND ALL, BUT I—
?!? WHAT'S WITH YOUR HAIR?
AND YOU'VE GOT SORES ALL OVER YOU!
AND YOUR TEETH?
WHAT, THESE? OH, JUST AN ALLERGIC REACTION OF SOME KIND...
"ALLERGIC REACTION" MY ASS!
NO WAY ARE YOU GONN LIVE HERE WIT MY BABY!
BUT... I...
OH, WHAT'S THE USE... I'M DONE FOR ANYWAY...
?!?!? WHAT ARE YOU DOING WITH THAT GUN?!
BLAM!
MIDGE! ARE YOU OKAY?
I SAW HIM REACH FOR HIS GUN!
HE WASN'T AIMING IT AT PERRY!
HE WAS ABOUT T KILL HIMSELF
REALLY? GORDO? WHY?
I DUNNO! HE WAS SICK OR SOME-THING...
OH, GOD... I WAS SO AWFUL TOWARDS HIM, TOO... =SOB=
AWW, DON'T FEEL BAD, MIDGE...
—LOOK! I GOT YOU A GOOSE!
?